Shame

HISTORY OF EMOTIONS

Editors
Susan J. Matt
Peter N. Stearns

A list of books in this series appears at the end of this book.

SHAME

A Brief History

PETER N. STEARNS

UNIVERSITY OF
ILLINOIS PRESS
Urbana, Chicago, and Springfield

© 2017 by the Board of Trustees
of the University of Illinois
All rights reserved
1 2 3 4 5 C P 5 4 3 2 1
♾ This book is printed on acid-free paper.

Library of Congress Control Number: 2017947422
ISBN 978-0-252-04140-2 (hardcover)
ISBN 978-0-252-08292-4 (paperback)
ISBN 978-0-252-05000-8 (e-book)

Contents

	List of Illustrations	vii
	Preface	ix
	Acknowledgments	xv
1.	Exploring Shame: The Interdisciplinary Context	1
2.	Shame and Shaming in Premodern Societies	10
3.	The Impact of Modernity: Some Possibilities	49
4.	Reconsidering Shame in Western Society: The Nineteenth and Twentieth Centuries	57
5.	The Revival of Shame: Contemporary History	96
	Afterword	131
	Notes	135
	Further Reading	155
	Index	159

Illustrations

Table 1.	The abolition of public stocks	64
Figure 1.	Frequency of *shamefast*, 1500–2000	41
Figure 2.	Frequency of *shame*, U.S. English, 1800s–1980 (Google)	60
Figure 3.	Frequency of *shame*, U.S. English, 1800s–1960 (New York Times)	60
Figure 4.	Frequency of *humiliation*, U.S. English, 1800s–2000	70
Figure 5.	Frequency of *shame*, British English, 1800s–2000 (Google)	92
Figure 6.	Frequency of *shame*, U.S. English, 1980–2000 (Google)	100
Figure 7.	Frequency of *shame*, U.S. English, 1960–2010 (New York Times)	101
Figure 8.	Frequency of *shame*, British English, 1960–2000 (Google)	101
Figure 9.	Frequency of *guilt* and *embarrassment*, 1800–2000	145
Figure 10.	Frequency of *humiliation*, 1800–2000	150

Preface

Shame is a disputed emotion, which makes its history particularly interesting and unquestionably challenging. All emotions prompt debate, of course: is a society encouraging too much anger? Or unduly manipulated by appeals to fear? Are personal relations complicated by unrealistic expectations of love? But the swirl around shame reaches deeper still, involving core definitions, uncertainty about current trajectories, and outright arguments over functions and impacts.

Putting the case simply: in contemporary U.S. society a host of commentators, from several perspectives, condemn shame and urge its reduction or, were it possible, elimination; but a smaller yet vocal group, looking at various kinds of current behaviors, loudly urges more use and acceptance of shame. In a related dispute, some observers (whether hostile or favorable to shame) see the emotion in clear decline at least in modern U.S. and Western European societies, while others (mainly hostile) worry about persistently high levels and objectionable new sources for the emotion. And, finally, scholars themselves disagree about how to define the emotion itself, and particularly about whether to emphasize the individual experience of shame or the emotion's larger role in community life. Where do these disagreements come from? What impact do they, or should they, have?

There is even a recurrent cross-cultural debate. Western observers have frequently touted the advantages of a guilt-based culture—which, they over-simplistically assumed, defines their own society—over one that relies on shame: the argument is that only guilt provides a definite moral compass and adherence to standards, as opposed to simply going along with group demands. This was a crucial component of Ruth Benedict's famous but flawed analysis of Japanese emotions during World War II. It has resurfaced in comparisons between Christian and Muslim value systems, to the disadvantage of the latter in assuring civilized behavior. A history of shame that embraces some comparative dimensions inevitably encounters these issues, and might contribute to sorting out the "my shame and guilt are better than your shame and guilt" syndrome.[1]

This text frequently refers to "Western society," meaning primarily Western Europe and the United States, although Australia, New Zealand, and Canada often fit. We deal only rarely with Latin America, where a few indications suggest traditional forms of shame lasted longer than in Europe and the United States. Exploring Latin American emotions history more fully, shame included, is highly desirable in the future, and of course specialists debate whether Latin America is best termed Western or not.

Definitions of shame, and its functions and drawbacks, are inevitably complicated by several factors. Shame is not a basic emotion in the sense of being wired into human biology from infancy. Indeed, a key question involves what basic emotions it does embrace: it may prompt sadness, it certainly may express disgust, but it may also generate anger. (There's no single facial expression associated with shame, though we might consider what "shame-faced" involves; and some cultures offer specific facial definitions.) Sorting the possible combinations is no easy task, and—this is where history most clearly contributes—they have unquestionably changed over time.

Problems of language enter in strongly, as is so often the case in emotions study. As we see throughout this book, shame is defined variously in different societies and in different time periods—sometimes for example sharply distinguished from guilt, as in contemporary English, but in other cases simply merged. A perceptive article notes the difference, even in English, between shame as noting a failure to do one's duty (arguably a dominant view in the seventeenth and eighteenth centuries) and a more modern sense that shame reflects a desire to be lovable. Shifts and divergences in word use often reveal key aspects of shame, but their imprecision also complicates discussion and further reveals the challenge of core definitions.[2]

Shame also hovers between the individual—which is where most emotions analysis centers—and the social, and any full assessment must embrace both aspects. The chapters that follow address both shame and shaming—the former as the emotion the individual encounters, the latter as what groups or group standards impose. Even when shame is defined as a personal experience—the most common emphasis in many current psychological studies—it operates against some sense of audience, and various social groupings clearly play their own role in defining and using shame, regardless of individual experience. It's no accident, to take one of a host of contemporary examples, that California in its current water crisis has taken to "drought shaming" as a means of controlling water use—a clear case of perceived social need.

Further, shame is one of several "self-conscious" emotions, along with guilt and embarrassment. How can it best be distinguished from its neighbors? One analyst declared that embarrassment is simply the contemporary version of shame, which in itself has fallen into disrepute—this is doubtful, but interesting in indicating a fuzzy boundary.[3] A few psychologists, focused on the individual experience of shame, see it as essentially equivalent to guilt, and there are studies suggesting that contemporary Americans sometimes see an internally focused shame as essentially a guilt equivalent. Other research, however, particularly when directed toward societies that seem to value shame but downplay guilt, but also in judging contemporary U.S. emotional strategies, see clear distinctions between shame and guilt, to the great advantage of the latter. The pathway for shame is not clearly marked.

Finally, there are disputes about shame's impact. A social scientist offers a recent quotation by an international lobbyist: "shame is for sissies," and goes on to lament the decline of shame in political and financial circles. The Wall Street banker associated with an investment scandal pops up two months later heading another corporate board: where is shame when we need it?[4] A host of observers worried about a lack of shame in the U.S. presidential campaign of 2016. More generally, though in a more hopeful vein, some recent commentary on shame claims a host of merits: "there are times when shame can also renew, uplift and fight back;" or, from the psychiatrist and bioethicist Willard Gaylin, "shame and guilt are noble emotions essential in the maintenance of civilized society."[5] On the other hand, the dominant psychological view, focused particularly on shame's role in the treatment of prisoners or in family discipline, sees no really constructive function for shame (in contrast to guilt): the emotion simply generates resentment, even aggression, making behaviors worse. And another batch of recent commentary deplores the indiscriminate use of shame in social media.[6] There is simply no agreement about where this emotion stands and what its constructive uses are, if any.

A history of shame can hardly pretend to sort all this out. It can help on the definitional side: at various points in time, shame has embraced somewhat different elements, particularly in the balance between community reliance and individual experience. Further, while historical analysis cannot posit tidy boundaries between shame and the other self-conscious emotions, it can assist here too. Much more clearly, a history of shame, like constructive emotions history more generally, can center squarely on the question of trajectory, or change over time. It's quite certain, as we discuss, that shame in some senses declined in U.S. society between 1850 and the 1960s but has recently revived; exploring this complex track addresses the resultant confusion over dominant current trends quite directly. And a historical treatment also contributes, at least, to sorting out some of the uncertainties over shame's function. A better understanding of shame-based societies in the past, as well as in contemporary comparisons, must involve a more sensitive grasp of how and why shame can work usefully—while also incorporating and potentially embellishing the role of cultural variables. But reviewing the treatment of change over time, and particularly the tensions between the rise of individualism and the persistence of shame, also helps us explore the emotion's negative features. Shame may well be more damaging in some current contexts than it was traditionally.

Many disciplines study shame. Psychology heads the contemporary list, but sociology, anthropology, and philosophy all claim important roles. History has contributed as well, though without the consistent effort that the emotion's significance would justify. There is scattered but interesting work on the history of shame in classical East Asian culture, particularly around Confucianism, and in ancient Greece. The most elaborate historical scholarship, some quite recent, explores the history of shame in premodern Europe, from the advent of Christianity through the early modern centuries. Several important studies tackle the more modern history of shame, in Britain and on the European continent, and a major article sketches a vital turning point in the United States experience as well.[7] For all the regions and periods involved, most of this interesting scholarship has been monographic, appearing in research articles and, more rarely, in book-length treatments of individual societies.

This study seeks to sum up most of the existing historical findings, with related insights from other disciplines, while also extending historical analysis particularly around developments in the United States over the past two centuries; the need for more work on modern patterns is compelling. The result is not a global history of shame, which would be premature. Many cultures are omitted from the analysis. Even cases that can be cited, as with East Asia, are constrained by the lack of careful historical work—signaled for example by a recent claim that shame in China has existed "from time immemorial," that ignores both origins and evolution.[8] It is possible, however, to offer a status report that shows the ubiquity but also some of the variety of shame experiences in many societies while also, primarily for Western Europe and the United States, exploring some of the patterns of change over time. The goal is a work that benefits students of emotions history while providing some sense of historical contributions for scholars in other disciplines—and a work that may also encourage some of the next research steps, particularly in the comparative domain, that are so clearly desirable.

We begin, in the following chapter, with a brief summary of current psychological and sociological takes on shame, and some of the disputes and dilemmas attached: though the psychological approach raises some problems for the historical analysis of shame, it provides an empirical starting point that will help guide ensuing assessments. Chapter 2 takes up the various uses and outcroppings of shame in many premodern societies. The importance of shame and shaming rituals constitutes an obvious point here, at least with the advent of agriculture; but the chapter also allows a sense of the emotion's variety and, for Western culture, a summary of major stages in historical change before modern times. Chapter 3, a brief one, focuses on the issue of modernity, and the argument that modern conditions progressively limit shame's role, with due attention to comparative complications. Chapter 4 follows this general review with a more specific treatment of the new attacks on shame in Western society from the eighteenth century onward, with the United States as a particular case study, allowing an assessment of causes and impacts but also inevitable complexity even amid a substantial reevaluation of shame's role. Chapter 5 then deals with renewed disputes over shame, and new uses for the emotion, in the contemporary United States, where some of the earlier agreements about shame's drawbacks have come undone. A short conclusion then reviews the argument and discusses any lessons that might be drawn from historical analysis.

∴

The history of emotions, summoned in principle more than seventy years ago, has blossomed over the past two decades into a surprisingly diverse and vigorous field.[9] Its practitioners have already addressed a number of individual emotions, though there is real room for updated historical summaries in many instances. Shame has won serious attention in the process of emotions research—both in explorations of earlier uses of the emotion in several societies, including its associations with honor, and in identifying the unprecedented disengagement with shame in Western European and U.S. cultures about two centuries ago. A summary and some further historical assessment are both timely, particularly given the opportunity to link historical issues with some of the current controversy that swirls around shame and its impact. Finally, as a work of emotions history, this short book seeks to maintain conversations with relevant findings from other disciplines, even some, like psychology, that do not usually take historical change into account. Emotions history works best in an interdisciplinary context, for historians do not have to reinvent the definitional wheel, and at the same time the key historical findings contribute directly to serious social science research.

The overall goal is a grasp of key aspects of shame's history, particularly in the United States, but within a wider context that will contribute seriously to the ongoing inquiry about a crucial emotion. Shame, clearly, can have devastating effects. We see this in the past, and we suggest why its damaging potential has emerged even more strongly in recent decades. But shame also has its uses, and it seems unavoidable as well—even in societies that profess to reject it. This aspect—the extent to which shame seems to survive and even flourish amid official disapproval—will help sort out a number of current confusions. The history of shame may even suggest, very tentatively and along with recent commentary in some other emotions disciplines, how we can improve this aspect of emotions management going forward.

Acknowledgments

A number of people have been unusually helpful as I worked on this book. Colleagues June Tangney, Janine Wedel, Roger Lathbury, Robert Baker, David Wiggins, Mandy O'Neill, Helen McManus, and Brian Platt provided a variety of insights, and scholars from several other institutions have been generous with suggestions as well—duly noted in relevant sections of the book. Two of my children, Deborah Stearns and Clio Stearns, have worked on aspects of shame themselves, and contributed substantively to my thinking on various points. (My other children are not necessarily shameless, but had less to add.) Particular gratitude goes to Vyta Baselice, who assisted greatly both in research and in manuscript preparation. Laurie Mathieson and James Engelhardt, at the University of Illinois Press, and Susan Matt, coeditor of the History of Emotions series, have been most helpful, and Susan Matt also provided specific suggestions on the manuscript. Several readers of an earlier draft provided important commentary. I also must thank the staff at Fenwick Library for lots of interlibrary loan service. My wife, Donna Kidd, has put up with far more excitement about shame than she had signed on for.

Shame

CHAPTER 1

Exploring Shame
The Interdisciplinary Context

Shame, as an emotion, has a core meaning, in relating individuals to wider social groups and norms—real or imagined. Threatening and defining shame is one way many groups help establish identity and enforce or seek to enforce desired behaviors. Shame can also be used to support social hierarchies, both formal and informal. But shame, or fear of shame, is also an emotional experience or anticipation for individuals, as they consider wider relationships. Shame is thus one of the "self-conscious" emotions, along with pride, humiliation, embarrassment, and guilt, that forms or may form a significant aspect of individual emotional life, but that depends on group standards and—to some extent at least—group enforcement.[1]

An initial effort at definition hardly resolves all the shadings that shame elicits. Further meanings emerge as we explore the emotion's history, in comparative context, in ensuing chapters—and even then there is room for debate. Most obviously the gray areas, where shame overlaps with guilt or embarrassment, will continue to condition our analysis. While even a basic assessment of shame's value—whether it has any really positive features at all—must be informed by historical and comparative analysis, it is vital to begin with the dominant viewpoint in the social and behavioral sciences.

This chapter lays out current thinking on what shame means, both to the individual experiencing the emotion and to that individual's relationship to a relevant social group. There is a distinction between scholarly analysis and popular understanding, and we must explore this as well for it links to the broader historical issues we take up in chapter 2. But it is appropriate to make a clear beginning: over several decades researchers in several disciplines, though particularly psychology, have widely, though not uniformly, agreed on what shame involves. And while this must ultimately be seen as (in part) a cultural product—an expression of contemporary but not timeless standards—it does provide a vital interdisciplinary launching pad. There is no need to start from scratch.

• • •

Shame has become a central topic in psychology, with some attendant interest in sociology and particularly anthropology as well. This was not always the case. Freud, for example, was notoriously uninterested in shame, dismissing it as a "feminine characteristic." Since World War II, however, shame has generated massive psychological interest, focused mainly in its deleterious effects.[2] Indeed, shame researchers are numerous enough to gather together occasionally—as in Amsterdam in summer 2014—to discuss mutual findings.[3] Interest is both theoretical, as part of more general attention to the self-conscious emotions, and quite practical, with findings applied to child rearing, mental health, and penology.

Definitions logically begin with the whole idea of self-conscious emotions, in which shame is part of a larger family of emotions that develop during childhood.[4] These emotions are not immediately apparent—in contrast, for example, to anger or fear. And they depend on a larger cognitive component. All emotions, even the "basic" or instinctual, are filtered through cognition, as part of deciding on appropriateness and ensuing strategies.[5] But the self-conscious cluster needs some real awareness of self, on the one hand, and appropriate group norms on the other. Without this—to refer to shame explicitly—there can be no sense of failing or potentially failing to live up to audience expectations, and no sense as well as to what the consequences to self and self-image might be. The self-conscious emotions generally require the capacity to evaluate self in light of others. Many psychologists argue that this does not begin to emerge until age one or so and does not mature for several years beyond this. By age three, consciousness is advanced enough that a child will show real signs of distress when he or she has violated the relevant social standards.

There has been some effort, deriving in part from a Freudian background (despite Freud's inattention to shame, as opposed to his investment in exploring guilt), to see shame as somehow emerging inevitably, regardless of cultural context. The clearest argument here holds that shame first develops in response to failures in toilet training, most obviously in soiling or wetting oneself, which inevitably begin to teach how the self can fail in light of community expectations. But in fact this argument is not widely pursued. Among other things, it may not help resolve the basic dilemma *within* the self-conscious emotions, about what distinguishes one from the other: after all, depending on the person though also the group, while a lapse in toilet training might generate shame, it might instead generate guilt or embarrassment.[6]

The first point, then, is clear: shame is more complex than a reflex like fear, and requires more learning, though it may be an essentially inevitable product of a child's early interaction with the family community.[7]

The next serious definitional step has to center on the distinctions among the intertwined self-conscious reactions. Shame and embarrassment are fairly clearly different in principle. Embarrassment, when one has violated group norms or expectations, is simply less intense and noticeably less durable than shame, and is more quickly forgotten by the same token. A man is undoubtedly briefly embarrassed if he has to be told that his fly is open, but the problem is easily fixed and would be unlikely to linger emotionally: unless it's a repeated pattern, it does not really provoke shame. In contrast, shame often lasts longer—up to forty-eight hours—and its sensations can be revived through community pressure, again, in contrast to embarrassment. It is worth noting that some languages, like Lithuanian, do not have separate words for shame and embarrassment, which however results in a fairly harsh idea of embarrassment in contrast to cultures, as with English, where distinctions are easier to articulate. Finally, the shame-embarrassment distinction does not fully predict why one person might be merely embarrassed by a miscue that would cause others, even in the same culture and certainly between two cultures, to feel shame.[8] Definitional issues around embarrassment are not too distracting, at least in Western culture, but they deserve note.

Psychologists have paid far more attention to the shame-guilt relationship than to any other aspect, and it is here that the most specific definition of shame emerges—along with some key debates.

Guilt, in this widely accepted rendering, is an emotional reaction that highlights acknowledgment of a wrong act, an act against community standards, and a desire for reparation. Guilty people apologize and also take steps to avoid repetition.[9] Shame, in contrast, is a more global emotion, which can emerge in response to the same kind of wrong act and violation of standards. It may develop earlier in life than guilt—guilt requires more cognitive sorting capacity—but above all it emphasizes self-abasement. It is the self that is at fault, not the commission of the act.[10] This creates greater pain and intensity than guilt—a shamed person feels very bad indeed—but also makes it more difficult to escape. Apology may seem inadequate, since the whole individual is in play; reparation may seem meaningless. The shamed person tends to shrink, characteristically seeks to hide, because of the emotional dilemma involved. Often, efforts go into blaming someone or something else for the problem involved, or denying or forgetting if at all possible, or getting angry with oneself or others.[11] Diversions of this sort may be primarily directed toward an external audience, but they can be used as well to reduce internal emotional discomfort. For there is general agreement: shame is a deeply unpleasant emotional experience.

Some authorities argue further that it is possible to identify different childhood origins for shame and guilt. Shame emerges when the child feels that parental love may be threatened or withdrawn. This memory, recalled in later situations when some action seems to jeopardize community approval, creates the anguish that the emotion may entail; it is this that calls the whole self into question. Guilt, in contrast, builds on the memory of punishment for specific acts, with no threats to basic family acceptance. Obviously experiences of being a child can create both situations, which is why shame and guilt so often comingle and why so few individuals or societies specialize in just one of the two. But equally obviously, some societies may encourage parents to emphasize one or the other approaches to discipline, and this may be a vital component in comparative differences in emphasis that loom so large in some contemporary analysis.

Both shame and guilt can be privately experienced: a person can feel ashamed, with all the anguish entailed, even without an audience. But some psychologists admit that with both emotions, though particularly with shame, at least an imagined audience is probably present, even if no actual public is involved. But it's the difference in scope that really counts. Guilt can be constructive, though if not addressed it might lead to shame. Shame is more likely to paralyze, and it is difficult, given the blows to self-worth, to figure out a useful response—hence the greater effort to evade.[12] Psychologist Todd Kashdan puts it this way, reflecting the dominant view in his discipline: guilt encourages people to learn from their mistakes, but "people who feel shame suffer. Shamed people dislike themselves and want to change, hide, or get rid of their self."[13]

The formulation raises an obvious question, as mainstream psychologists also recognize. If the same act can generate shame or guilt, how can one explain why one reaction takes precedence over the other? The answer, apparently, is personality type: some people are simply more shame prone, others more open to guilt.[14]

Not surprisingly, this basic formulation has some critics. A few psychologists still contend that shame and guilt are really the same and that the distinction is moot. A more nuanced effort seeks to identify two kinds of shame, one private and one audience-based (admitting a contrast with guilt).[15] The claim is that people see private shame as equivalent to guilt in suggesting real apology for wrongdoing, in contrast to the more shallow acknowledgment of an external audience.

These ongoing definitional quarrels have not, however, prevented significant additional research that assumes the basic distinction between shame and guilt. One line seeks to distinguish between groups, rather than personalities. Socially dominant groups, more confident, are more likely to experience guilt; shame is the more likely response of submissive groups, or those held to be inferior. Here is an interesting contemporary version of the relationship between hierarchy and shame, which will be vital as well in historical analysis.

Another related extension looks at shame proneness as a function of psychological depression, perhaps particularly among individuals who were mistreated or sexually abused as children. Susceptibility is not, here, a personality accident, but explainable through powerful prior experience. Obviously, this research path confirms the self-deprecating and overwhelming quality of shame as a response to bad action, with guilt if not more rational at least deriving more clearly from some inner strength.[16]

Yet another research thrust, building fully on the shame-guilt distinction, elaborates further on the destructive aspects of shame. If guilt, as the basic definition holds, can lead to constructive remediation, then shame not only paralyzes but also can generate counterproductive anger or aggression.[17] This response has been studied particularly among convicted criminals in Germany and the United States, among other countries: guilt is more likely to convince prisoners to avoid crime in the future, whereas shame—though not always generating outright recidivism—produces a desire to lash out against unfair emotional pain and social blame. And this can lead to more bad behavior, not less. The formulations have led some sociologists to claim that shame is at the root of most family violence.[18] The same distinction has been applied to children and child rearing. Just as the criminal justice system should encourage guilt and seek to avoid any encouragement to shame, so parents and teachers should be extremely careful to foster the distinction in their children. Thus if a child cheats on an examination, emphasize the action—"don't cheat on exams"—rather than the individual as a whole—"you're a cheater."

What remains somewhat unclear, of course, is exactly what to do about the emotional distinction, if the problem rests in personality alone. If the same action can generate either guilt or shame, depending on the individual and his or her psychological background, how much emotional improvement can society expect? The scholars who have examined prisoner reactions to shame, for example, see no other wider factor involved in this aspect of emotional response: not religious affiliation, or ethnicity, or immigrant status. The prisoners are shame prone or guilt prone, and while remedial measures should seek to help the former group there is no larger explanation involved. Thus there may be some hope that greater psychological sophistication will lead penologists or parents to handle any hint of shame with particular care, but whether this can override the personality factor remains to be seen.

For several decades, psychologists have been endeavoring to show the bad effects of shame and to differentiate it from guilt as a self-conscious emotion. The emphasis follows a larger Western cultural evolution attacking shame, which is discussed in chapter 4: but this does not make it any less valid. The discipline that dominates the study of emotion clearly defines what shame is and equally clearly reproves it.

One effort even seeks to link the psychological approach to a sense of history—a sense that most psychologists, interested in the here and now, tend to downplay. Thus Stephen Pattison, in 2000, urged that shame not be seen as a unitary emotional phenomenon across all time periods. In his view, contemporary shame, the kind psychologists attack, is a "far more individual, personal and psychological" experience that contrasts with its counterpart in earlier periods, where the emphasis was on largely social enforcement and imposition on groups. Pattison posits a crucial transition in the "broad movement from 'social' shame to 'psychological' shame."[19] I pick up this important argument in the historical analysis that follows. Possibly, in other words, psychologists are correct about the huge downsides of shame in the present day, but their findings cannot fully be generalized to the past.

For the dominant psychological approach raises two problems that the discipline has tended to ignore but that inevitably complicate shame's history. In the first place, as we soon see, more societies have emphasized shame than not, either instead of guilt or alongside it. Does this mean that most societies have been emotionally stupid, as well as insensitive? Are the shame-based societies today, for example in East Asia, clearly inferior to regions where reliance on shame has measurably lessened? Possibly yes in both cases, but most historians would be really hesitant about claiming this kind of presentist and/or Western superiority.[20] And second: the psychology emphasis is on the shamed individual, without much attention to social context and what shame needs a community might have. These needs, in turn, may explain why shame remains common even today—in ways the psychological emphasis does not fully capture.

Happily, some sociological work on shame helps us out to some extent, in advance of further historical analysis—though it has not been fully reconciled with the psychological approach. Sociologists may well agree that shame is quite damaging, though they also explore some shame settings that may be less harsh than others. Sociologists have contributed studies of shame's utility in improving manners over time. They have examined social groups that are unusually shame prone, here often corroborating psychological findings about the emotion's unfairness. Above all, however, they insist on shame's social dimension, which operates well beyond the experience of the shamed individual.[21]

A final definitional issue in dealing with shame, fully recognizing the substantial concurrence in contemporary psychology and social science, involves the gap between scholarly distinctions and general understanding. We have already noted that some languages elide the difference between shame and embarrassment. More common still is a lack of linguistic and conceptual differentiation between shame and guilt—the very emotions that psychologists are usually so eager to separate. Thus ancient Greek, for example, had no separate words for the two emotions; they were lumped together, as we see in the next chapter when we turn briefly to Greek precedents for dealing with shame. And even contemporary English, while it clearly utilizes two separate words, offers a surprisingly fuzzy dictionary definition: shame is thus "a painful emotion caused by consciousness of guilt, shortcoming, or impropriety." While guilt, according to the same source, does indeed focus on action—"knowing or thinking that you have done something bad or wrong," the fact that shame is too hard to define without including guilt may suggest not just a quibbling over terms, but a real issue in trying to capture actual emotional experience.[22] Along with the need to avoid a priori condemnations of shame-based cultures, which too much insistence on contemporary psychology might generate, the importance of accommodating some blurriness will linger as well.

. . .

A certain amount of complexity is unavoidable, for there is disagreement within and among the disciplines that deal with shame. Attention to historical patterns, launched in the following chapter, may actually help sort out some of the issues involved.

There is, nevertheless, some common ground. Shame can be a very painful experience, when the individual experiences real or imagined community disapproval. The findings in psychology shine through clearly here, though it is possible that shame's pain and its counterproductive consequences may have increased in some contemporary cultures (as Pattison once argued) and that the guilt-shame distinction was not always as common as it would become in the contemporary period. The fact that shame imposes real personal hardship and a sense of rejection is central to its social disciplinary function, at all points in time. But an understanding of shame's social utility, and of the reasons communities so often insist on shaming, derives as well from anticipation and awareness, well beyond direct enforcement. This is the sociological side, which does not have to dispute psychology's emphases but must insist on a wider framework. This is the side, as well, that will most clearly shine through in exploring shame historically, while encompassing the insights from psychology both generally and in explaining contemporary sensitivities.

The chapters that follow build on the relationship between the individual and the social aspects of shame and shaming, seeking as appropriate to combine psychological and sociological insight. But they depend as well on the historian's interest in change and variety. Shame's pain is thus always real, but the emotion will also reflect specific historical contexts. Too much emphasis on distress risks dismissing societies where the emotion was praised and emphasized. We know from other examples in emotions history that undue modernism, approaching the past as emotionally inferior as well as unfamiliar, will mislead—particularly, given contemporary U.S. predilection for pleasant emotions, in dealing with a negative emotional field. We need a more open-ended assessment of shame, and the social strategies involved in shaming, particularly before modern hostility to shame emerged so clearly. And we need to register on the *anticipation* aspect that extends shaming's social utility, which has gained less attention, historically, than shame itself. Thus many Western languages developed a word designed to designate efforts to avoid shame, separate from shame itself: French has *pudeur*, as opposed to *honte*, and German offers a similar distinction. English itself long employed the word *shamefast*, to identify the emotional preparation for shame avoidance, though this was lost as a different emotional approach emerged in modern times, leaving only vaguer and slightly outdated terms like modesty in its place. Finally, still with the social aspect of shame firmly in mind, we must also look for societies that explicitly allowed for recovery from shame—what some modern social scientists call reintegrative shaming—another area where the variety of methods in handling the emotion emerges clearly.

Shame is a common emotion, and awareness of shame may be more common still. Analysis of differences in approaches to shame, and above all the exploration of major changes in handling this emotion, plus the reasons for and consequences of these shifts, fleshes out many key findings from psychology and the social sciences, and possibly even suggests new opportunities for synthesis. The goal is to add to our appreciation of emotional experiences in the past, from individual and social angles alike, to contribute to historical knowledge while also suggesting why nonhistorians, preoccupied with their own approaches to emotion, should add a greater awareness of shame as an experience over time.

CHAPTER 2

Shame and Shaming in Premodern Societies

Shame was a pervasive theme in many premodern societies. An English king picks up a lady's garter, trying to shame his courtiers into avoiding any criticism of her accident: *Honi soit qui mal y pense:* shamed be he who thinks evil of it—is one of the most famous phrases of the Middle Ages, still appearing on the British royal coat of arms. Greek philosophers and Christian theologians diversely spent a great deal of effort trying to explain the uses of shame, and in some cases the dangers as well. In China, it has been estimated that up to 10 percent of Confucius's writings center around the importance of shame.[1]

But it was not just a matter of words about emotion: actions and rituals were front and center as well. In several premodern societies, shame experiences produced striking signs of the emotion's power and social role. An impressive variety of regions, from ancient Egypt onward, displayed people who had misbehaved—from mischievous students who had not done their lessons to adults accused of adultery—in some form of public stocks, where for a few hours, even a few days, the general public could walk past and express their disgust.[2] In practices of this sort, shaming was more visible by far than it has become in modern societies—though some would argue that recent uses and abuses of social media constitute a contemporary communications equivalent of the old stocks, albeit somewhat more subtle.

Not surprisingly, given the harshness of some public practices, private pain could be intense as well. In some groups, serious shame could lead to suicide, the only remedy for dishonor to self and family. But, as suggested in chapter 1, premodern shame could display nuance as well. Precisely because of the emotion's power, some people figured out ways to avoid shame or to be restored into the community. Still others acknowledged shame by striving mightily to avoid misbehavior in the first place—illustrating one of the terms, like *shamefast*, that designated sensitivity to shame in advance. Some groups, tinged with shame in the dominant public view, even devised practices that in a way helped them take advantage of the situation, even deriving a certain amount of enjoyment from their careful self-presentation.

· · ·

This chapter explores several aspects of shame and shaming in premodern societies. The overall target is clear: demonstrating how ubiquitous shame was in agricultural societies, and how shaming was unhesitatingly viewed as justifiable in enforcing community standards. The following sections accordingly offer a number of illustrations to demonstrate this basic point, presenting as well various specific practices and evaluations, with shaming, even more than shame itself, front and center. The range clearly establishes the perceived social utility of shame as a factor in the human experience. It sets a baseline for exploring subsequent change, away from the common agricultural pattern; at the same time, it suggests reasons and precedents for maintaining or reviving a shame-based approach in social discipline. These are all themes to be taken up in subsequent chapters.

Within this basic framework, this chapter explores several other, related issues. First, the question of shame in the original types of human groupings—bands of hunters and gatherers—receives brief attention. Some anomalies here deserve inquiry, as against seeing shame as a universal, inevitable human experience. And this assessment leads to the more important point: the need to suggest the reasons that shame and shaming would become even more widespread with the advent of agricultural communities.

Second, the chapter lays out the variety of shame experiences and shaming activities in several premodern societies, including evaluations of the emotion's multiple manifestations, from punishment or defense of honor to the role of hierarchy and the incorporation of shaming into child rearing. Available evidence varies, with far more for examples on public shaming than on family practices; and historical work to date concentrates considerably on East Asia and the West. But without claiming anything like global coverage, the discussion not only highlights shame's ubiquity—the basic point overall—but the variety of practices and assumptions that might be attached, some of which survive to the present day. A few comparisons emerge that may link to the differing approaches to shame that continue to generate regional contrasts even today.

Shame was not, however, a constant in the premodern centuries. The third major section of the chapter explores the important work that has been done on debates and changes concerning shame in Christian Europe. Christianity itself had introduced some challenges to earlier Greek and Roman ideas about shame, but reliance on the emotion continued and in some ways may even have increased. But summarizing and explaining some of the main developments over time captures from another vantage point the fact that premodern shame was not an invariable emotional norm. This section leads to a final summary of the importance of shame and shaming in colonial America, which forms the most direct backdrop to the even more substantial changes, beginning in the eighteenth century, that are traced in the following chapter.

The overall goal of the chapter is to present some of the key varieties that describe shame before modern times, and some of the central issues that have emerged in historical analysis to date, but also to emphasize and explain the prominence of the emotion in social and individual experience. This serves as a baseline for the subsequent exploration of more modern departures. But the baseline itself harbors a number of complexities that must be explored, including some tentative comparative possibilities.

Use of the term *premodern* raises a number of legitimate questions. The term covers an immense amount of territory, and its generality can annoy many historical specialists who devote rich scholarly lives to exploring greater details in particular times and places. More importantly, it is vital to remember that a full global account of shame is not currently possible given the gaps in available scholarship. This chapter suggests some of the range of coverage that can be applied to premodern shame, but in no sense does it venture a systematic survey. And the initial section of the chapter raises questions about shame as a unifying emotion between hunting and gathering and agricultural societies in the first place. But even a focus on agricultural communities extends over a considerable amount of time. This is why, where possible and particularly in dealing with the Western experience, the issues of change are explored explicitly. But this chapter contains an undeniable hypothesis: that premodern conditions prompted some uses and experiences in shame that would significantly differ from the patterns in at least some modern societies. As Chapters 3 and 4 explore, some modern societies have attempted a far more thorough reevaluation of traditional patterns of shame than anything that premodern societies themselves ventured. A few scholars have gone so far as to argue that "modernization" will ultimately displace shame altogether, though in fact the claim is at least premature.[3] *Premodern* is thus not intended as some sterile uniformity across time and place, but is meant to call attention to the greater disruption that would be attempted in some places from the late eighteenth century onward—which then requires its own explanation and assessment.

Early Human Shame and the Role of Agriculture

A brief and tentative discussion of shame in the earliest forms of human society, explored through accounts of surviving contemporary groups, casts a bit of doubt on the idea of shame as an inevitable social product or a uniform outcome of relatively early stages of child rearing. Even more clearly, though still in terms of a suggestive hypothesis, the discussion certainly highlights the reasons agricultural communities, more complex than their hunter-gatherer forebears, came to place such heightened emphasis on the role of shame in social cohesion. And the discussion begins the larger consideration of the kinds of social forces that generate substantial reliance on shame, at any stage of human history—the reasons shame so often serves as a "social bond" between individual and group.

Though shame is not a basic emotion, we might expect it to emerge early and explicitly in the human historical experience. Some elements of shame may be universal, including the capacity to use stance and facial expression to admit fault and ward off anger.[4] The earliest human groupings, around hunting-and-gathering activities, surely required substantial community coordination, where shame might play a key role, and additionally may have preferred emotional enforcement over the more disruptive reliance on physical punishments, particularly given the lack of any systematic policing apparatus. On the other hand, hunting-and-gathering groups, often with only a few dozen people, may have been too small to require much formal development of shame for discipline or identity. Their sexual rules—for example, concerning marital fidelity or premarital sex—were sometimes relatively relaxed. To the extent that shame generates deep, sometimes unpredictable impacts—a point made by contemporary psychologists—early human communities might have preferred milder methods of community enforcement, such as humor.

In fact, anthropological studies of largely preagricultural peoples generate mixed results, but hardly a systematic concentration on shame. Thus the Ilongot, a headhunting people in the Philippines, rely heavily on shame (with no explicit evidence of guilt), using the emotion to spur achievement in children and also to regulate early sexuality. On the other hand, the San people in the

Kalahari desert of Botswana and Angola seem to use shame little if at all. If a certain amount of emotional enforcement is needed, for example against incipient signs of pride or boasting, teasing and humor usually do the job. Similarly, the Semai, a Malaysian hunting-and-gathering group, insist to observers that an emotion as intense as shame is simply not desirable. Conformity is achieved through milder methods, as in the comment that "there is no authority here except embarrassment." The much-studied Utku Inuit group also urges against shaming, as part of a general aversion to scolding lest people feel needlessly unhappy or frightened. Here too, adults prefer a gentler humor as an antidote against disapproved behaviors. Shyness is valued, against display of body or of personal achievement, but children are expected to learn this as part of growing up, without more formal shaming mechanisms. Shaming, in other words, may simply not be front and center in the earliest human experience. Indeed, as we see later in this chapter, a widely assumed absence of shame among Native Americans was one of many points that convinced many Western observers of their emotional inferiority, during the initial colonial encounter; and while this surely involved some willful misinterpretation it may actually have registered at least a significant difference in degree.[5]

Whatever the issues in defining shame in the most primitive—but longest-lasting—human communities, there seems little doubt that the next stage in complexity highlighted shame far more fully. Agricultural communities, though small by contemporary standards, were much larger than hunting-and-gathering groups—clustering several hundred people at minimum. While privacy was rarely valued, individual family housing units also complicated the enforcement of group norms, again arguably requiring more vigorous emotional tools. Further, the complexity of sexual regulation surely on average increased, and while sex is not the only target of shaming, it unquestionably looms large—as clearly suggested in the Adam and Eve story, where shame responds to nudity as the first punishment for human sin. Agricultural communities focused more strongly on reproductive sex than hunting-and-gathering groups did, which required some discipline to prevent too much nonmarital activity, and they also, as part of an effort to protect property inheritance, more strictly constrained female sexual behavior. Here too, explicit reliance on shame and shaming intensified, in the frameworks in which most people would live between the initial rise of agriculture until at least the eighteenth century.[6]

Not surprisingly in this context, a number of anthropological studies that focus on relatively simple herding or agricultural communities, even where formal political apparatus is absent, pick up an emphasis on shame far more consistently than is true for the more purely hunting-and-gathering cases. Thus the Masai, a herding people in Kenya, feature the emotion very prominently, particularly for men. Their creation stories involve a god who was shamed (by being injured by a goddess), and who blazed the sun so his discomfiture would not be noted. Adolescent boys are put through shaming tests, one of which is a rather painful circumcision around age fourteen or fifteen, and this is done in public, with bystanders calling out warnings like "if you kick the knife, we will disown you." Women, who also undergo circumcision, do not face a public audience. But there's no question about the shame emphasis.[7]

Similar reliance on shame, though with far different specifics, emerges from a study of residents of a fishing village in Bengkulu province, Indonesia. Shame is the second most commonly mentioned emotion in this group—in contrast to a parallel study in contemporary California, where shame gained a bare forty-ninth place in the rankings. Villagers report frequent classic shame events, where a significant social standard had been violated and where the shamed person adopts a shrinking stance in public or seeks to avoid contact altogether. Shame-based suicides may occur, for example when a young woman is pregnant out of wedlock and simply cannot endure the scrutiny of others. Subordination shame occurs as well, as when a poor man has to talk with the village head but is so overcome with his sense of inferiority that he displays all the standard posture and facial cues of shame. Revealingly, while villagers report considerable anxiety associated with this kind of shame, they see moral value in it because it demonstrates appropriate respect. Shame—linked to shyness and embarrassment, for which the local language has no separate terms—serves to motivate and display appeasement, which in turn allows activity within the accepted social hierarchy. Shame also shows up in competitive situations, for example where a young man feels shame because he is the worst drummer in the village—with drumming essentially a compulsory activity. Finally, residents of this Bengkulu fishing village readily identify individuals who do not show appropriate shame—"thick-eared" is the term they employ—and regard them as untrustworthy and unpredictable.[8]

Robert Levy's study of the Tahitians stresses considerable sensitivity to shame, though not overwhelming reliance. Children are more likely to be physically disciplined than shamed. But there is a sense of a need to present the self acceptably, where shame serves as counterpoint. And children do learn that parental affection will ultimately be withdrawn, which seems to encourage a sense that avoiding mistakes, rather than performing exceptionally well, is the best strategy to avoid punishment. This is a common finding about the conformity impulses shame cultures generate, and we see it in more complex societies as well. The emotion can deter: a Tahitian describes an impulse to steal, but then notes he would be "seen" as well as possibly imprisoned, so he refrains. There is ambivalence about where the emotion provides an internal guide: some note that if they could be sure not to be "seen" they would violate rules about property or sexual behavior; others note that the *idea* of being seen is sufficient constraint even when in fact there is no audience. Here is an important ambivalence—again, found in other shame examples—about shame as performance before a group as opposed to moral compass, and the choices vary both with the individual and with the culture.[9]

The Mehinaku, a tribe in the Mato Grosso of Brazil, provide a final example. This is another agricultural group, practicing a fairly simple economy with some social differentiation combined with a strong egalitarian strain. The Mehinaku feel acute shame in a wide array of circumstances. Girls reaching puberty, and attracting comments from men, are ashamed to appear in public. Uncertain social situations—such as entering someone's house, in a society that stresses privacy, or dealing with another tribe—rouse shame. Encounters with tribal leaders, or an unexpected need to speak in public, provoke a sense of shame. Even accusations against a thief may cause shame for observers, because the accusations will be socially disruptive—to such an extent that sometimes it seems better just to accept the loss of property. Reliance on shame, and its deep emotional impact, can induce sympathetic response, and not just accusatory frenzy—another complexity that crops up recurrently in shame-based cultures. Symptoms of shame among the Mehinaku are more familiar than the surprising array of provocations, though they too can be fairly dramatic: the shamed person "hurts to be seen" and tries to stay in hiding for a while, walking in the woods or tending a private garden, or even removes his clothes. Sometimes he lies in a fetal position in his hammock, described as "curled up" with shame. Gradually, though, shame dissipates after a few days, and the individual allows his friends to woo him back into interactions.[10]

The point is clear: the development of agricultural communities enhanced the uses of shame, to generate greater conformity in the group as a whole and typically to help enforce more complex rules of sexual behavior as well. Other methods of enforcement, including formal policing, remained out of reach, but this simply extended the need for shame, and the anticipation of shame, to help enforce community standards, beyond what some simpler societies had required. This in turn forms the effective historical backdrop from which more recent variations would emerge. Agricultural societies did not generate uniform approaches to shame, but they invariably highlighted the emotion in community and, insofar as can be ascertained, family alike. Correspondingly, the long agricultural period in human history provides the setting where the crucial initial historical questions can be addressed—about the functions of shame, the experience of those who were shamed, the effectiveness of shame, and the extent to which different agricultural societies developed different or similar shame formulations.

Historical Patterns in Premodern Societies

Several clear points emerge from the historical literature on shame in various premodern agricultural civilizations, always recognizing that comprehensive coverage is not yet available. First, shame was pervasive, often of course in some combination with guilt but commonly if not invariably as a prime means of social discipline. The emotion's importance explains the attention it gained from leading philosophers, as can be illustrated from both classical China and ancient Greece. It explains as well the widespread development of elaborate public shaming rituals, around sexual but also other forms of behavior—surely the most striking aspect of shame's premodern history. Yet the existing record also displays variety, as in shame's role in enforcing social hierarchy and, even more obviously, the complex forms generated by particular commitments to honor. Ultimately, we should hope for enough historical research to permit clear comparisons among premodern civilizations concerning this core emotion, as well as a clearer record of change over time. For now, this section indicates the tension between common features and distinctive patterns, turning in a subsequent section to more focused consideration of the Western case where a more definite opportunity emerges for tracing the issues of change within the premodern context.

PERVASIVENESS

It is truly tempting, given both the common factors and needs involved and the available data, to claim that substantial reliance on, and experience of, high levels of shame were characteristic of agricultural societies, purely and simply. But while a number of cases are available, as explored by anthropologists and others, they do not cover the whole spectrum; we cannot be sure that a few major exceptions might yet be uncovered. It is clear, however, that shame and shaming were very common, and that they responded to some common needs as well. This means also that the distinction that has become so popular in evaluating modern societies, between shame-based and guilt-based entities, probably does not work either, for the civilizations that emerged before the eighteenth century; many premodern societies simply did not distinguish among the disciplinary emotions, though tending to place primary emphasis on shame in the mixture that resulted.

Here is at least a partial list of the premodern societies (i.e., societies operating between the advent of agriculture but before the emergence of industrial economies and massive urbanization) in which shame has been identified and explored: ancient Egypt and classical Greece; China, Japan, Korea, India, Burma, Thailand, and Malaysia; various parts of the Middle East and East Africa; Mexico and Peru; premodern Western Europe and the Balkans; colonial America; and various parts of Polynesia and Micronesia.[11] Again, this is not proof of universality, and we will see that the specifics of shame may vary a lot, including different degrees of overlap with guilt. But a strong correlation between premodern societies and the prominence of shame is virtually certain, and as noted there are good reasons for this.

The pervasiveness of shame in many premodern societies indeed raises some analytical challenges. The need to differentiate among different definitions and implementations of shame is one, for traditional societies had not benefited from the precision of modern emotions scholarship. This is a standard problem in emotions history, but perhaps particularly great when the emotion is so widespread, generating in the process a great deal of linguistic variety. There is also, however, the impulse to overstress the bizarre. What some authorities call "shame-based" societies—though the term is undoubtedly oversimplistic—really did differ from many modern ones, including the contemporary United States, though not completely. In this setting it can be easy to highlight particularly strange practices, which can lead to exaggeration (a key problem for Japan, but also for colonial America), as well as to a neglect of some of the subtler but more routine forms of shame. We know a lot more about public stocks and "parades of shame" than we do about daily emotional experience and relevant family practice, and this can be a problem.

There is no question, however, that shame in premodern societies presents a rich canvass. Variety, but also different levels of data and scholarship, generate different emphases on types and purposes of shaming, but even a sampling offers compelling evidence about the role of this emotion in shaping agricultural societies—providing then a basis for extracting some of the larger analytical points.

THE FIRST CIVILIZATIONS

Early civilizations leave little emotional trace, but shame was there. The Hammurabic code, in Babylonia, highlights the need to respond to family shame: "If the finger has been pointed at the wife of a man because of another man, and she has not been taken lying with another man, for her husband's sake she should throw herself in the river." Reputation, in this case, undercut the code's usual preoccupation with testing the evidence for any actual offense. The code also displays early adoption of shaming as a supplement to the kind of policing and punishment the state could offer: several types of crimes, in addition to requiring the payment of fines, involving shaving part of the culprits' heads, so they would be temporarily branded within the community. Babylonian law also reveals the power of the public slap, as a means of inducing shame: unwarranted slaps of high-ranking men might require payment of a fine, but in certain situations—for example, by a mother whose adult son was mistreating her—public slaps could promote better behavior even when the victim was, in law, of higher standing, for they called forth public attention and possible shaming to cases of domestic unfairness.[12]

Thanks to writing, early civilizations also required schools, for a small minority of boys. The lessons were tedious, since most of the early writing systems were complex; hours of memorization were involved each day. Not surprisingly, not every student took to this routine. Early schools responded with some physical discipline. But ancient Egypt also put poor-performing students in public stocks, for the community to see and revile.[13] This is the first we know about shaming in education, but not the last.

SHAME AND PHILOSOPHY

Later classical civilizations, building on the first crop, provide even more abundant evidence. In the first place, discussions of shame figured prominently in intellectual life and foundational literature. This includes the centrality of shame in the book of Genesis—the only emotion discussed at length. After the serpent tempts Eve and through her Adam, and they learn the distinction between good and evil against God's commandments, God asks: "why are you hiding," and they respond, "because we are naked." Human curiosity, obviously, leads to knowledge, which leads to shame, with women, as first offenders, probably a bit more responsible than men.

The role of shame in Greek and Chinese philosophy has received considerable attention. The results here go beyond additional evidence for the importance of shame in premodern cultures. Greek thinking bore some relationship to practice, as in the types of public punishments discussed in a later section of this chapter, and it also set up a foundation for later dialogue with Christianity, which provides vital insights into distinctive Western issues with shame. Confucian thinking may have been more foundational still; it has certainly generated frequent comment as a historical backdrop to contemporary East Asian uses of shame—often, without much further historical nuance—and it certainly warrants some comparison with contemporary Greek formulations.

Socrates, Plato, and Aristotle discussed shame in various ways. Socrates argued that the shame that relentless questioning could generate, and the temporary emotional pain it produces, must sometimes form part of the educational process, as he tried to use the emotion to induce particularly stubborn students to let go of an untenable argument. Plato was at greater pains to insist that shame could be combined with respect, through an emphasis on what a teacher or a public figure shared with his opponents even as he sought to apply emotion to highlight why and how he disagreed with them. Socratic shame might be used, then, to force an interlocutor to admit that some pleasures must be restrained, or that doing injustice is worse than suffering it: shame in these discussions was deliberately intended to stir discomfort and perplexity (though not humiliation), but clearly in socially useful ways—ultimately (perhaps after an initial attempt to squirm or hide) by making the target of shame seek to return to a more rational, emotionally pleasant position. Plato more clearly identified shame as a reaction to a gap between some individual behavior and shared ideals, but he tried to be even more careful to emphasize some common values at the same time, so that the emotion would be kept well short of humiliation. Respectful shame does not depend on creating a hierarchy, with the "shamer" at the top, but rather can operate in a relationship of equals.[14] Plato also discussed, in another context, the extent to which shame might be avoided if a behavior can be kept secret—another common challenge in premodern societies that we have already noted in the anthropological findings. Talking about how shame can constructively promote marriage, as a means of avoiding publicly disapproved sexual practices, he notes the risky proposition that a person might do something "without any other man or woman getting to know about it"; but if there was any exposure, shame was the inevitable and desirable consequence.[15] Finally, one evaluation of classical Greek society—though going beyond intellectual constructs—contends that Greek shame ultimately rested on the ability to judge oneself, internally, against an ideal other, motivating ethical behavior and facilitating self-understanding.[16]

This was certainly the aspect of shame emphasized by Aristotle, who saw shame as fundamental to ethical behavior. Like Plato, Aristotle was aware of some potential downsides to shame, and particularly the emotion's capacity to generate harmful levels of fear. But he was greatly drawn to the kind of shame that might guide human conduct, whether a community audience was present or not—though he granted that greater intensity occurred when observers were involved: "We think it right for young people to be prone to shame, since they . . . often go astray, but are restrained by shame"—whereas older and wiser folk would presumably be held back by awareness of potential shame in advance of action.[17] Reflecting the lack of a Greek linguistic distinction between shame and guilt, the philosopher did not see shame, normally, as threatening the destruction of self, but rather responding to particular acts. He extensively discussed the applicability of shame both to individual behavior, but also to conditions not entirely under individual control—like the damage caused by unsavory companions. And he insisted extensively on the importance of the anticipation of shame in regulating behavior, along with the more familiar experience of shame in addressing a past action. The interest in anticipated shame clearly reflected the preeminently social uses for shame that Greek philosophers highlighted overall, as opposed to much concern with individual impact. Much the same social emphasis was maintained also in Stoic ethics, for Greeks and Romans alike.[18]

Confucius and early Confucian thinkers confronted shame even more frequently and directly than the Greek philosophers did—hence the claim that as much as 10 percent of Confucius's writings revolved around the importance of this emotion in regulating social relationships.[19] This in turn raises the possibility—though not, pending more actual historical work, the certainty—that shame was, early on, lodged particularly strongly in Chinese culture and in those other East Asian societies that later took cultural cues from China.

Certainly, a reliance on shame, as source of discipline and conformity, was central to Confucian thought. As the *Analects* contended: "Lead the people with administrative injunctions and put them in their place with penal law, and they will avoid punishment but be without a sense of shame. Lead them with excellence and put them in their place through rites and ritual practices, and in addition to a sense of shame, they will order themselves harmoniously." Scholars of Confucianism, stung by implications that China, as a traditional "shame" culture, somehow falls beneath hypothetical guilt cultures, work hard to show that, in Confucianism, shame was the emotion that propelled the internalization of moral codes. As with Aristotle, an external audience might or might not be involved: the point was that, either way, shame pushed a person to live up to standards. Others are less convinced, because Confucian shame was so intricately linked to social relationships, and so more contingent on perception than on absolute norms. References to frequent blushing interestingly suggest a frequent, though not necessarily invariable, access to external audience. All camps agree that physical exposure, or a sense of being naked, was not an explicit Confucian concern—perhaps in contradistinction to the kind of shame described in some of the less complex societies like the Balinese. By the same token, and against the psychoanalytic approach to shame, Confucian approaches to the emotion have little or nothing to do with sexuality one way or another. Rather, the Confucian idea of shame emphasizes some kind of boundary crossing, some violation of accepted patterns of social behavior and social relationships. Taint or impurity, not nakedness, in the eyes of others forms the dominant imagery. Illustrations of shame thus frequently involve references to inappropriate clothing, or food, or material goods more generally. Broader status concerns cluster the references that are next most frequent, while a third category embraces disparities between claims made in speech and one's actual actions. Less common examples of Confucian shame include the shame of not learning; or a ruler's shame in losing territory. A final category involves the shame that attaches to being a servant. Though in principle even such a lowly position has a place in the status hierarchy, if one operates toward the bottom of the heap one may be seen as incapable of wisdom of any sort—possibly even lacking the redeeming capacity for shame itself—another common problem for shame in traditional societies to which we will return.[20]

Overall, Confucian shame aims at maintaining the distance among different social levels, motivating those lower in status to show their deference to superiors, prompting superiors to uphold appropriate standards (the gentleman should be ashamed of not cultivating himself appropriately). In this sense shame is the quintessential human emotion, differentiating people from animals who lack appropriate awareness of hierarchy. Shame is clearly spurred by appropriate fears about what respectable people think of one's behavior, though this may also call attention to flaws in character: boundaries between external criteria and internal impurities are not clearly drawn. Material objects link to shame so often because they may provoke desires that cloud appropriate thought and lead to decisions that are inappropriate to status. It is good to take pleasure in a suitable portion but shameful to seek more. An extreme illustration, recurrently cited, involves men who dress in women's clothing, an obvious status disruption that should provoke shame in response. Shame, in essence, is the emotional discipline over the senses, and in turn vital to harmonious social hierarchy. Similarly speech that outstrips action is a shameful disruption of social boundaries. Still more obviously, failure to observe proper forms in dealing with superiors, or failure to display generosity in arranging for burial of the dead, are properly labeled shameful. All of this, to go back to the *Analects*, clearly distinguishes socially shameful actions from outright crime, where the law might appropriately be involved. Traditional Confucianism does not definitively answer the question about whether shame could depend on internal standards, and so serve as a secure moral guide. But it unquestionably demonstrates the centrality of the emotion to the maintenance of appropriate social relationships. And later Confucian thinkers, like Mencius, made it clear that shame (expressed in different specific words) could and should apply both to bad behavior in others, and to "what is not good in oneself."[21]

The prominence of shame in Greek and Chinese philosophy probably both reflects and explains the importance of the emotion in actual community life; certainly, the durability of a Confucian framework is frequently invoked in explaining Chinese emotional emphases. In both cases, and in contrast to now-outdated dismissals of the moral soundness of shame-based cultures, the philosophies strongly connect shame with ethical conduct, in discipline and anticipation alike. Correspondingly, neither tradition encourages the kind of formal distinction between shame and guilt that is standard in the kinds of psychological research summarized in chapter 1. Note, too, that neither philosophical approach lingered significantly over a relationship between shame and sexual behavior or explicit bodily exposure; Confucian concern about proper clothing might link to this to some degree, while the Greeks (among whom public nudity, for men, was widely accepted in any event) picked up some cues about shame's role in sexual discipline. But the wider uses of shame in social morality constituted the more important point. At the same time, the two philosophical traditions demonstrate intriguing differences within a shared reliance on a social emotion. Confucian concern about signs of blurring social boundaries simply is not reflected in Greek thinking to anything like the same degree. Many observers have found in Confucianism an early indication of the Chinese sensitivity to community standards, including an intense desire to preserve public face, that differs from shame concepts in other cultures.

There are clear limits to claiming widespread social importance from evidence in intellectual history pure and simple. Plato and Aristotle may correctly suggest the importance of shame in classical Greece, but their reflections were rather distant from some of the public ritual the Greeks constructed, where among other things sexual conformity played a much greater role. Confucianism is possibly more representative for China, but there are cautions here as well. Before turning to the most abundant evidence from premodern societies generally—the evidence from ceremony and punishment—it is desirable to note another domain where evidence for widespread inculcation of shame is suggestive, though not yet as substantial as might be wished.

SHAME IN FAMILY AND COMMUNITY LIFE

Contemporary scholarship would urge attention to past parental practices in exploring the real nature of shame in premodern life. Here, potentially, is a far more revealing entry point than formal intellectual discourse. There is every reason to believe that parental practices that expose children to an apparent threat of denial of affection, as part of discipline in such areas of toilet training, form a vital precondition to uses and experiences of shame in later life, and in larger social contexts. Unfortunately, while the history of childhood is an increasingly thriving enterprise, historians have not applied consistent attention to this aspect of emotional life. The result is an unfortunate gap—though not a total blank—in what is currently known about shame in the premodern past.

Perhaps predictably, premodern China provides some of the clearest linkages between child-rearing patterns and preparation for shame. Exciting recent research, though not centered on shame, certainly suggests that Chinese family relationships created ample opportunity for an emergent sense of shame—though the word itself was not often used in this context. A child's emotions revolved intensely around the mother, who had every reason, in an intensely patriarchal society, to build a tight relationship early on. Thus the Chinese saw love of parents, and particularly of mother, as the basis of all other virtues, as "affection daily develops into a sense of awe." As a phrase went under the Han dynasty, "there are no young children who do not know loving their parents."[22] Many mothers directly carried this emotional foundation into expectations for performance—like the woman during the Tang dynasty period who solemnly told her one-year-old son, "if you don't work hard, no achievement—I'd rather die now." Maternal references to their pain and suffering were common, helping to build the child's emotional attachment into a sense of shame-based obligation going forward. And, not surprisingly, Chinese schools carried on the use of shame. While physical punishments—whipping—did respond to some bad student behavior, there was also a tradition of having a misbehaving or poor-performing student "bare the right shoulder" for a while, to demonstrate inadequacy before his peers and teachers.[23]

Family relationships in Greece and Rome may have been slightly less emotionally intense; certainly, there was less emphasis on maternal affection and the possibility of its withdrawal. But Romans unquestionably assumed that shame would be part of familial discipline, urging a combination of praise and criticism (rather than overreliance on physical punishments) that would keep children "from what is disgraceful."[24] Studies of child rearing in early modern Europe are also a bit vague on the role of shame. One analysis of patterns in seventeenth-century France stresses the heavy reliance on physical discipline but notes that adult indifference to a child's effort to establish autonomy created a climate of "fear and doubt" that would color relationships both at that point, and potentially in later adulthood. Interestingly, efforts to toilet train in this society were rather unsystematic, without a strong shame element; but other interactions may have been more conducive to the emotion.[25]

Shame carried on into adult social relationships. Broadly reflecting Confucian principles, Chinese villages often developed and enforced standards of behavior through group judgments. A concept of face, or *lien*, emerged early on, stressing the importance of living up to obligations and being a decent human being—or, alternatively, to be subject to a loss of standing that would make it impossible to function adequately in the community. A wide variety of behaviors might carry this shame-based potential: living up to business arrangements and not trying to cheat; paying debts; fulfilling promises of marriage; dressing appropriately; if well-to-do, not seeming miserly; if well-educated, not getting drawn into angry arguments; not bragging. Economic behavior loomed large: one village account during the Song dynasty noted that anyone who dealt unfairly with a shopkeeper in the community would "never be able to raise his head," if indeed he dared try to return home at all.[26] The use of shame reflected status, obviously: standards were higher for those well up the social scale, though the relevant community judgments involved more than the status group. Family involvement was central: an individual who attracted community disapproval reflected on his parents and siblings, not just himself. Obviously, it is not always clear how much emotion was involved in all this, for community presence and evaluation operated regardless of individual capacity for shame; references to eyes and ears, that is, to a relevant audience, frequently accompanied descriptions of individual incidents. But at least some forms of shame, and shame avoidance, were central to the pattern, along with sensitivity to the desire of others to avoid community censure.[27] Again, evidence is thus far scattered, with Chinese materials particularly revealing prior to the early modern centuries. There is no reason to doubt extensive family and community engagement, but there are abundant opportunities for additional specific research, which might broaden as well the number of regions that can be explored to this end.

PUBLIC SHAMING

If evidence on the personal side is currently less well developed than one would like, the same is not true for the role of shame in public and legal rituals. Here is a real, if sometimes distorted, relationship to the advocacy of shame found in some of the philosophical texts, for a wide range of premodern societies created opportunities for shaming and experiences of shame that were clearly designed to punish bad behavior, promote anticipatory conformity, and drive home community norms. The practices may have reflected parental conditioning, but most of them did not depend on it: these were community impositions regardless of any personal emotional inventory.

Shaming practices abounded in many, and indeed probably most, of the more complex premodern societies. They sometimes enforced laws, but even more commonly they sought to uphold community standards regardless of their legal standing and often independent of any formal state action. The practices might substitute for violent punishments, or they might sometimes be combined with them. But the emotional experience, of shaming and resultant humiliation, was central, often regarded as more painful than any physical accompaniments.

Japan for many centuries publicly displayed women caught in the act of adultery. Public shaming for sexual offenses persisted in Latin America at least until the later nineteenth century. Classical Greece had a host of open shaming rituals, sometimes in conjunction with courts of law but often simply springing from spontaneous community action. In some cases, further, upper-class offenders could be subjected to community ridicule, a democratic element that did not always prevail. Plutarch notes that, in one city, women discovered in adultery were called "donkey-riders," because after first being stood for public view in the market place, they were paraded through the streets on a donkey. In another city, male adulterers were bound and led around the cities for three days, while adulteresses were forced to stand for eleven days in the marketplace in a transparent tunic—the link between nakedness and shaming made explicit. In the city of Gortryn, male adulterers were dressed in female costume for their public viewing, adding to the symbolic emotional burden. Shaving half the head was another way to expose to public scorn, at least until the hair grew back. Shaming, clearly, played a vital role in Greek social control. The adultery focus was itself complex: many Greek authorities emphasized that it was less the act itself that was shameful than the potential disruption of public order: shaming practices were clearly intended both to deter later offenses and to preempt private vendettas. Other violations also occasioned public display, for example mistreatment of parents or draft-dodging (five days and nights in the stocks in Athens, along with a fine). This was a matter of law: as Demosthenes put it, "the lawgiver thought that one who had done such shameful deeds ought to live in shame for the rest of his life."[28] In Sparta, it was cowardice or male celibacy that required emotional retribution, in this case the obligation to walk around the marketplace naked. Display, of course, was frequently accompanied by public jeering and even physical abuse, and here as in many other societies women participated at least as eagerly as men. It was the Greeks, apparently, who introduced the custom of "radishing" male adulterers, sticking a large vegetable up the anus while the miscreant was immobilized in the stocks—causing pain but, even more, adding to the humiliation by suggesting a female sexual role. The various shaming practices also, however, avoided permanent marking: despite Demosthenes's grim comment, it was possible at least in principle to survive the ritual without lifelong scars. In some cases, however, more durable punishments were imposed, such as disbarment from the temple or deprivation of citizenship not only for the offenders but for descendants—carrying on the mark of shame.[29]

Many Islamic cities similarly featured practices of ignominious parading, or *tashir*. As in Greece, the practice hovered somewhat ambiguously between formal legal punishment and popular outburst. The idea of "making someone public" was meant to be harder on the accused than flogging or imprisonment—because of the intense emotional discomfort involved. Punitive parades, sometimes embellished with a special bell, could draw large crowds; the victim frequently wore a demeaning hat or had the head shaved, or the face might be blackened with soot. In some cases, the accused was paraded while seated backward on a donkey. Public witnesses not only shouted, they often threw shoes or spat, to add to the insult. All sorts of offenses could warrant this approach. Sexual acts were one category, involving prostitutes or loose women (like those who drank wine in public in the company of men). But deceitful merchants could warrant shaming—in this case, sometimes with their shoddy goods tied to them; and also people who had perjured themselves in court. Rituals that turned a person backward on an animal thus responded to the fact of having turned the truth around in court, in a society that depended heavily on trustworthiness (Muhammad had declared false testimony to be as bad as polytheism). Religious offenses, including blasphemy, could also be involved. As in Greece, shaming might be intended to have durable consequences, as authorities urged the public to beware the individual who had been exposed; but it might also, in principle, have a shorter lifespan. In a society that valued privacy and discouraged public confession or insult as contrary to honor, the deliberately open nature of shaming was meant to answer offenses that had been equally open: "It is allowable to talk of someone if he does something in public; otherwise it is not."[30]

Western Europe offers a final set of examples, from the Middle Ages into the eighteenth century. Dutch miscreants might be paraded with various signs of shame—a special flute for bad musicians, a mocking crown for adulteresses. Donkeys were called into service here too. People who practiced medicine without qualifications were placed backward on the beasts and paraded.[31] Prostitutes might be marched through the city in a barrel; perjurers had to sit atop a wooden horse. A bigamist might be placed in a cage for an hour or so in the market place, with a large sign highlighting his offense. Forgers, in Britain, were placed in stocks or pillories with a piece of paper on their head, to denote their crime. As in classical Greece, shame parades might involve the high and mighty, displayed before jeering commoners—though sometimes a clear political calculation motivated this staging, as when the mistress of a deposed English king was thus shamed to highlight the power of the new incumbent.

Public shaming, clearly, highlights the emotions of the shamers—often, disgust, or anger, or even fear in some combination—not the experience of shame itself. The victims will certainly have felt deep emotional and often physical discomfort, whether or not they felt shame in the first place. At least in some cases, they must have experienced some of the emotional anguish that contemporary psychology associates with shame (or that Aristotle noted in referring to the potential for excessive fear)—and this would certainly have been consistent with the social goals involved. And shaming is relevant to shame despite the limitations of the evidence on individual reactions. In some cases, appropriate expressions of shame may have prevented the more drastic punishments in the first place, and certainly the harshness of public ritual might encourage regulation of behavior in advance, in light of anticipation of shaming—again the point suggested in Aristotle as well as by contemporary U.S. sociologists. While group shaming was dramatic, we also know that it was less common than is sometimes imagined—a point to be taken up below, for example, in dealing with colonial America. Anticipation of shame, and resultant caution, were more pervasive than shaming itself. Most obviously, group shaming reflected a widespread acceptance of the importance and validity of shame, and surely the rituals, combined with the pain of the emotion itself, served widely as a deterrent against some of the objectionable behaviors that might otherwise have been more commonly indulged.

PUBLIC SHAMING AND FORMAL PUNISHMENT

Shading off from public shaming and what was often considerable group spontaneity were the many instances in which a more formal, state-enforced punishment was meant to be enhanced by shame. Here, very clearly, is where the emotion was enlisted as part of law enforcement in societies with little formal policing and limited prison systems.

In Europe and elsewhere, this aspect of shaming took several forms. First was the use of physical branding for certain kinds of convicted criminals, to cause pain but above all to mark them as objects of shame and suspicion for the rest of their lives. Thieves might lose a hand or, in Europe, often an ear. Sexual offenders, like adulterers, might have to wear distinctive clothing, or a letter, if not permanently at least for a long time—a practice already suggested in Mesopotamian law.

Public whipping, in many places and many settings, was meant to inflict humiliation as well as pain. In Rome, whipping was normally reserved for slaves, so its open administration to members of other classes who were convicted of some crime was explicitly intended to shame. Again, many commentators argued that the emotional burden cut deeper, and more durably, than the whip. This was a point later made also by John Locke, in commenting on whippings of misbehaving schoolboys: the man so often associated with reforms in the treatment of children approvingly noted that shame, more than pain, was the real motivator in these situations.[32]

Shame applied to society's most dreadful punishments. Even criminals destined for the ax or the hangman were first paraded through the streets in a cart, bound, with the crowd encouraged to jeer and otherwise drive home the humiliation. (One English criminal, given a choice, actually preferred beheading to hanging because the latter was more shameful.) Public shame thus was intended to add to the ultimate penalty as a deterrent to crime, with the lessons driven home to the onlookers. This particular practice, of course, might backfire. Crowds might prove sympathetic to the condemned, undermining the shaming ritual though not interfering with the execution. And the accused him- or herself might prove defiant, not accepting shame but rather using the ritual to proclaim either their innocence or their defiant emotional independence. But the effort also might work as planned, with crowds suitably indignant and the individual, with head bowed, showing every indication that shame as well as fear were meeting the mark.[33]

Public shaming, overall, hovered somewhat uncertainly between humiliation and possible redemption, always intended of course as a warning in either dimension to others. Some shaming, particularly if joined to other punishments or branding, clearly expressed official or community outrage, and nothing more. But when shaming was limited in time, for defined periods of exposure without permanent marking, and when it clearly served as a social alternative to violence, it might at least in principle lead to subsequent reintegration. The disciplinary approach could be complex.[34]

Shame, Hierarchy, and Honor

Along with the roles of shame in intellectual discourse, personal life, and public ritual and law, two other aspects of shame in premodern contexts deserve attention, though they varied significantly from one region to the next. A certain degree of shame was often applied to larger social categories, thus enforcing hierarchy. Further, particularly though not exclusively within some upper-class ranks, a particular association between shame and personal or familial honor extended the meaning and impact of the emotion.

SHAME AND INEQUALITY

Contemporary studies of shame frequently mention its role in expressing and maintaining hierarchies, and the relationship comes up again in dealing with shame in the modern centuries. Thus officials or teachers express their authority by shaming prisoners or students, while more broadly racism is often expressed through actions and words that shame. In some cases, inequalities in premodern societies may have been so obvious, and well enforced, that shaming was less necessary as further discipline. Slavery or lower-caste status might be so clearly inferior that explicit shaming did not have to add to the burdens; only when practices applied to slaves were extended to others was shaming intended. It is possible that in more modern conditions, when legal defense of hierarchy weakens in favor of equality in principle, shaming becomes more essential in setting boundaries. But shaming and hierarchy were not always separate matters in premodern societies either, as witness Chinese practices of requiring the lowest social group (the "mean" people, including actors and prostitutes) to wear a distinctive green scarf to identify themselves in the public eye. The shame involved might not be the intense, contemporary type, precisely because all parties recognized and accepted hierarchy to a degree; but it could color social relationships and emotional experience alike.

It is well known that agricultural societies generated greater inequality than had prevailed in earlier human communities, which makes the relationship to shame particularly important. Compared to many industrial societies—though this comparison must be fleshed out in later chapters—inequality in the agricultural age was also relatively formal and widely recognized. The result significantly affected the framework for shame, both as a social expectation and, at least sometimes, as an individual experience.

For, despite formal legal recognition, reasonably settled hierarchies not infrequently create beliefs that some subordinate groups are slightly shameful in and of themselves—and on occasion some members of these groups may share this impression. Shame and inferiority thus interrelate and mutually reinforce. The result can be an expectation from social superiors that members of the lower groups should be particularly ready to exhibit shame, certainly for misdeeds and possibly, to a moderate degree, even as an emotional lubricant when encountering their betters. For inferiors, expressions of humility—and at times even a real sense of mild shamefulness—may provide a desirable emotional bridge to an otherwise awkward or uncharted situation.

Confucians thus wondered a bit about servants and shame. Were they so low that shame would be irrelevant? Or should their status be reflected in expressions of some shame? The Indian caste system, though keeping groups apart to some extent, may have inculcated similar beliefs about the untouchables—that shame and this lowest status went, or ought to go, hand in hand. Slavery, probably particularly when infused with racism, could have similar effects. Shame commonly attached to physical or mental disabilities, not only for the disabled but for the families that produced them, an important fact of life in many premodern contexts.

But the most general expression of the common association of inferiority and some shame proneness involved gender. Famously, women were supposed to be ashamed over some kinds of sexual transgressions that men could engage in more freely, and with far less expectation and often far less actual experience of shame. In Christianity and Islam, the belief that women were more likely than men to be sinners, despite technical spiritual equality, easily fed a tendency to associate the "lesser" gender with shame. Confucianism, interpreted carefully, might avoid this emotional conclusion: in Ban Zhao's famous manual for women, those who displayed appropriate deference and faithfully carried out their appropriate tasks might avoid any generic need for shame. But female humility and some distinctive openness to shame could emerge in traditional China as well.[35]

At least one branch of Hinduism, Oriya Hinduism, developed possibly the most interesting linkage between gender and shame, with an end result similar to that in the other world religions but with a much more imaginative plot line and an even more explicit connection to shame. In the Orissa region, where the god Siva reigns in the leading temple, Siva's wife, the goddess Kali, shamed herself in a distinctive fashion, and gave rise both to beliefs about gender and a distinctive physical expression of shame. Kali, in the legend, had killed an evil god whom no male could subdue. But she then used her weapons to go on a destructive rampage of her own, terrifying the other gods. So they sent her husband, the meditative Siva, to tame her; but Kali was so absorbed in her dance of destruction that she did not see him, and stepped on him. Realizing what she had done, she bit her tongue in shame—"what else but shame? Shame . . . because she did something unforgivable, she is feeling shame," as one contemporary Hindu noted—and became reasonable and calm. The moral? Women have in them a destructive force superior to that of men, but the anger behind it must be brought under control for the sake of social order. An openness to shame is the obvious path, and the expression of shame, in the protruding bitten tongue, becomes a public manifestation—widely recognized within the culture, not only in art but in daily experience, but of course meaningless outside it. And many in the culture not only know the story and Kali's tongue, but apply it to their own lives—the need to evince shame in response to mistakes, while invoking Kali. "All women . . . bite their tongues when they have not behaved properly." The result—particularly when sensitivity to shame curbs anger—is commonly viewed as a useful and desirable facet of shame.[36]

Shame and hierarchy in traditional societies—and in societies still influenced by their legacy—offer an inherently complex combination. The humble demeanor that upper elements may expect from lower might obviously be absent, or faked—and might in fact produce angry resentment, though probably not normally openly expressed. But the link between shame and hierarchy might also be accepted at least to some extent by "inferiors" as well, and thus form part of normal emotional experience while serving, in mild forms, as a tacitly agreed-upon emotional strategy to help negotiate relationships. Here, in contrast to the dominant contemporary formulations outlined in the previous chapter, a degree of shame need not be terribly intense or even unpleasant, but rather provides a type of social mediation that all parties accept.

HONOR AND SHAME

Many premodern societies develop a vigorous sense of honor, most obviously in military groups but at least in some cases more widely as well, particularly in settings where the hold of formal government and law is weak or nonexistent and when groups believe they must fend for themselves. Honor can serve to uphold social or gender status, expressing or reinforcing membership in a superior group. It rests in part in a quite different openness to shame from that expected from the lower rungs of the social hierarchy—for here shame is the emotion that will be felt if honor is not upheld. But while honor has inspired a considerable historical and anthropological literature, its take on shame is often somewhat tangential to the more standard manifestations of the emotion—hence justifying a somewhat abbreviated sketch. When honor-based impulse shows up in some of its most notorious behaviors, such as dueling or ritual suicide, it often carries an emotional and social load that goes beyond shame alone.[37]

During the Zhou dynasty in China, often described as the country's feudal period, in advance of more effective imperial government, a lord loudly proclaimed the basis for his effort to avenge an ancestor who had been dishonored by another family. "The shame of the present lord is the shame of the previous lords"—and he claimed that the resulting obligation could extend back for at least nine generations.[38] The relationship of this kind of shame to a real sense of emotional alienation from a valued group is at the least complex: anger and jealousy may be more prominent emotions in honor-based reactions than shame itself, though the assertion that shame should generate a long memory is interesting. In premodern Europe, jealousy was often highly praised precisely because it provided the emotional—zealous—basis for defense of honor: shame might be well down the list of emotional reactions when honor was invoked.[39]

But honor did highlight the central importance of reputation, and this could reflect emotional ties to a real or imagined community. Often, the central thrust of this kind of shame linked directly to concepts of masculinity: "a man who absorbs insults is no man at all"—and should be properly ashamed.[40] As such, the emotional relationship can show up in a variety of situations—in feudalism, of course, but also on the U.S. western frontier or in urban slums. It involves a fear of feeling unprotected, disconnected from the group, even made to seem foolish, and the result can unquestionably form a powerful emotional package.

Japanese samurai culture is often taken as a particularly vivid example of honor-based shame. For a member of this class, shame was the reverse side of the sense of pride and dignity that normally allowed an individual to feel that he was adhering to the group's approved norms. As a samurai noted in the mid-nineteenth century, "Shame is the most important word in a samurai's vocabulary. Nothing is more shameful than not understanding shame.... On one occasion someone asked me, which is more serious, crime or shame? I answered: Crime belongs to the body, but shame lies in the soul." Violence was the most obvious result of this culture—the need to lash out to defend honor if it was questioned, the need to display stoicism even in the most desperate situation: "The samurai who knows shame should not do anything untoward even though he is being beheaded." But on a day-to-day basis, shame, or rather the overwhelming desire to avoid shame, was probably more important in motivating decisions designed to uphold group standards, particularly in displays of courage and initiative. Even in a more bureaucratic setting, such as the Tokugawa shogunate, when warfare declined sharply, honor and shame continued to motivate samurai behavior, with protection of reputation held front and center. Honesty and trustworthiness, loyalty to one's superior, appropriate clothing, personal discipline—these were qualities, besides physical courage, that could sustain honor. They would carry the honor-based sense of shame well beyond a battlefield, into wider social and moral standards. And there is no question that, for the samurai, honor-based shame had many of the features associated with shame in more mundane settings, most particularly the idea of an imagined community that shared the standards on which shame might be based. This could mean, as with many of the contemporary definitions of shame, that an individual had an internal sense of shame even when there was no performance in front of an actual group. Indeed—and this point is important given Japanese concerns about facile Western blasts against "shame culture"—samurai leaders often made a special point of the importance of "self-watchfulness" as part of honor—the ability to do right "out of the sight and hearing of others."[41]

Honor-based shame had several other connotations, at least in some renderings. It normally embraced family as well as self—as the earlier Chinese example suggests. A person could or should feel shame if a family member was insulted or if a relative failed to live up to appropriate standards. Here, honor could link directly with some of the ideas of shame associated with social inferiority: for example, a man was responsible for the behaviors of his wives and daughters, and if they were mistreated or if they themselves stepped out of bounds, he was called upon to act. Whether men in this situation actually felt shame, or were simply trying to avoid group disapproval and were often acting out an anger at perceived bad behavior, is not always easy to determine: again, the violent manifestations of honor-based shame are complex.[42] But many groups—not just a warrior class—might vividly uphold a sense of family honor, with resultant shame showing either as a need to punish a wrongdoing relative or to avenge some external insult—if not violently, at least through another insult or, in some settings, legal action. In certain cases, as in classical Greece, the family base for honor also meant that shame could be inherited, passed from one generation to the next.[43]

Honor-based shame might also relate to a need to achieve, to measure up to group standards in this sense. Here is another way that this special form of shame connects to other manifestations of the emotion, both in the past and still today. Though the careful historical work has not been done, it seems possible that, in East Asia, aspects of honor-based shame were transformed over time into particular concern about student achievement and its role in upholding, or disappointing, family honor.

Most generally, honor-based shame reflects sensitivities to status and the need to respond to anything, however trivial, that seems to undermine or denigrate the individual's claimed position. Challenge can result from incompetence or lack of performance, or errors in propriety and appropriateness, or indeed from violations of moral standards. The emotion involved, like shame more generally, links the individual and a real or imagined group, and it can be immensely powerful. This is why, again in the Japanese version, the sense of shame so often involves references to feeling "crushed," or "injured," or "soiled."

Where there is deep community dependence, there is no question about the seriousness and intensity of the emotion.[44]

Patterns and Problems

Without trying to make too much with an incomplete historical record, a few conclusions do emerge from considering the role of shame in many premodern societies, at least after the advent of more complex agricultural communities. The potential for shame was widespread, certainly in public practices and concepts of honor, probably in more general family conduct as well. This reflected above all the need to use emotion to enforce community cohesion, though in some cases a role in maintaining hierarchy provided an additional spur to shame. But the very ubiquity of shame highlights as well some important distinctions from modern concepts. The overlap between shame and embarrassment can be hard to tease out, for example in some aspects of honor-based reactions or in the Confucian concern for social propriety. Even more challenging is the clear combination of shame and guilt in several formulations—whether the issue is the philosophers' quest for an emotional basis for ethics, or the underpinnings of public rituals intended to use shaming to enforce discipline.[45]

Premodern patterns can certainly suggest a devastating intensity for shame, at least in some circumstances, which is consistent with the current concerns in psychology. Public shaming might be hard to live down. Honor-based shame could, at an extreme, motivate suicide. In Japan, cases of samurai suicide, particularly by the procedure of ritual disembowelment known as seppuku, were actually fairly rare in the premodern centuries (the punishment was more commonly imposed by courts of law rather than emerging from individual choice), but they did occur.[46] The potential devastation of shame supports one other vital point about premodern societies: the importance of trying to avoid shame, which highlights the emotion's role in social and familial discipline. But premodern societies could also display some milder forms of shame, and some recognition that, even if unpleasant, the emotion had a valid and positive role. Groups that used shame to ease social relationships amid established hierarchies, or people schooled by religion to assume wider human unworthiness, might accept the emotion as natural, rather than always overwhelmingly disruptive.

This frequent tension, between shame's disorienting intensity and its potential acceptability, even normalcy, also conditioned the possibility of reintegration after shaming occurred. Shame in some cases was meant to stigmatize permanently, as in cases of physical branding. But many premodern societies also emphasized situations in which shaming, whether intense or not, was intended to induce a temporary state. An individual might be publicly exposed, but only for a specific period of time, often just a few hours, after which, so long as he or she seemed to accept the punishment, the incident could draw to a close. Reintegrative shaming would also include those many cases where an individual was allowed to confess and apologize before a community, even without more elaborate ritual; or where a potential offender could back down in the face of clear community disapproval—for example, prior to completing a questionable business transaction—allowing the matter to be soon forgotten.[47]

Premodern patterns also suggest great variety, despite the widespread link to community standards, though more explicit comparative work remains highly desirable. The issue of the acceptability of concealment was widely recognized in many shame-based cultures, but reactions varied, not only at the philosophical level but in actual community life. Shame might or might not be assumed when an offense was unseen.[48] The common association between shame and sexual behavior certainly shines through in many cases, but the importance of shame in other aspects of honor, in some societies, or in enforcing accepted business practices or even respectability in dress also warrants attention. Acceptance of honor codes might school individuals in some societies to accept the agony of intense shame, but surely other situations generated a sense, however tactically concealed, that shaming was unfair: convicted criminals, certainly, varied in their public reactions to shaming, some professing humility, others displaying angry defiance. The actual personal experience of shame, as an element in emotions history, needs further probes.

Finally, the premodern record must be explored in assessing shame's effectiveness, from the standpoint of society at large. Surely, given their persistence, shaming practices often had a positive result, against the contemporary impulse to dismiss them as emotionally damaging. Reliance on shame could promote greater social conformity. It could affect crimes rates; it could, as some historians of colonial America argue, constrain other offenses, such as child abuse, when combined with the intrusive community monitoring that shame cultures often generated.[49] Actual public shamings turn out often to have been less common than might be expected, precisely because the emotion's power had its anticipatory impact.

SHAME AS AN ISSUE IN THE WESTERN EXPERIENCE

Patterns of shame in premodern societies apply to Western European history after the fall of Rome in many ways, as the familiarity of some of the public rituals, compared to cases in other places and periods, already suggests. But historians and literary scholars have worked particularly hard on the Western experience from the Middle Ages to the early modern centuries, which allows greater precision on some key points, including the importance of dealing with change over time within a premodern context. And, again without claiming the possibility of elaborate comparisons, the advent of Christianity did introduce a few issues that warrant attention as well—though the results on the whole confirm the central role of shame in the emotional vocabulary of premodern societies. Finally, within the larger Western framework, significant historical scholarship on shame in colonial North America extends the understanding of some aspects of premodern shame, while setting an additional baseline for assessing subsequent change.

Christianity, Guilt, and Shame

Leading Christian thinkers frequently considered shame, from the patristic period in the later Roman Empire on through the Middle Ages and beyond. There was an obvious problem, which the Greeks and Romans had not faced: Christians had obligations to God, not just to society, and these two duties could clash. Augustine, accordingly, carefully distinguished between shame and guilt, contending that it was guilt that addressed sin and governed the individual's relation to God, whereas shame was merely a response to group opinion. Tertullian went further even earlier, writing when Christianity was more clearly a minority religion: Christians need a "contempt for shame," like the hermits who were defying public convention to live in devotion to God.[50] This distinction is the basis of the elaborate literature that has periodically emerged to distinguish between guilt-based societies (the West, better) and those relying on shame (most of the rest, worse).

But while the differentiation bears watching, it was not real for many Christian authorities, who quickly embraced the importance of shame and usually—in broad outline, rather similarly to the earlier Greeks or the Confucians—incorporated a sense of guilt within this. The Bible, after all, provided ample precedent for the assumption that shame should respond to sin, from the fall of Adam and Eve onward. Shame imposed suffering, but it was also the basis for redemption, a vital emotion in correcting debased humanity.[51] To be sure, shame could be distracting, even counterproductive if directed merely as social disapproval, but its core service must not be tainted: Christian leaders, from Augustine and through the Middle Ages, and indeed on to Protestants like Luther, stressed that shame was the basis for penitence including, in Catholicism, confession itself. Thus Augustine, in book 4 of *The City of God*, highlighted shame as the key response to sexual indecency, while Tertullian and others expounded on shame's role in protecting sacred virginity. As Virginia Burrus has noted, early Christianity, overall, "innovates less by replacing shame with guilt than by embracing shame shamelessly."[52]

It is not surprising, in this context, that ideas about shame cropped up early in Anglo-Saxon England, including the word for shame itself that first appears in the eighth century. The word had Germanic origins, associated with earlier terms that involved covering oneself; the probable link to nakedness and sexual concerns is intriguing. Significantly also, in early English, the term could mean either the emotion that resulted from dishonor or disgrace, *or* the anticipation of an experience that should be avoided precisely because of the emotional pain. Later English literature, like *Piers Plowman*, correspondingly emphasized pain that shame could cause—greater than any physical wound—but also its necessity and desirability in preserving social status and, particularly in the case of women, chastity.[53]

With due respect, then, for the importance in Christianity of a divine standard in defining sin, as opposed to fallible social convention, virtually all the evidence points to a Western Christian approach to shame that resembles other premodern formulations in many respects, above all in emphasizing the emotion's importance in spurring good behavior. The extent to which this embrace fudged boundaries between shame and guilt, and raised questions as well about internal emotional experience versus community imposition, further links the Christian approach to issues encountered in other regions.

CHANGE OVER TIME

Emphasis on shame in Western Europe also shifted in important ways, particularly from the later Middle Ages onward. Shame became more important, taking on additional meanings including the linkage to honor in chivalric culture. New public practices emerged that reflected greater social reliance on shame but that also generated greater popular involvement with emotion. Even word use shifted for a time, in English, to reflect the need to deal with new dimensions. The ability to explore change, within a still-premodern context, is a vital addition to historical analysis, which hopefully can ultimately be applied to other regional cases as well.[54]

Religious preoccupations with shame persisted. To be sure, Chaucer and others occasionally revived the distinction between guilt, as the response to sin, and shame, as a vital means of addressing community needs. But shame continued to win most of the religious press, including Luther, who argued that Christ had taken human sin and shame onto himself. Further, Protestant emphasis on original sin led to a larger preference, by the sixteenth and seventeenth centuries, for a certain level of melancholy as the appropriate human demeanor in the sight of God and people alike; and this in turn could make shame seem even more appropriate than before.[55] Some concern emerged about those who so reveled in shame and humiliation that they made a vice out of virtue, implying that their emotional pain somehow equated them with the Christian martyrs. But overall, the emotion continued to win approval as a guide to virtue.[56]

A somewhat separate spur to shame, at the end of the Middle Ages but again with extension even into the seventeenth century, was the rise of the chivalric code and a more articulate concern in the upper classes for honor. A sense of the almost constant threat of shame to one's name or personal or family reputation organized much of the resulting courtly literature. As with other cases where honor and shame were linked, the actual emotional result is not always clear: honor-based shame does not necessarily involve the same kind of internal wrestling that other forms of shame entail. Some honor issues had more to do with political and financial expediency, including ransoms for knights held captive, than any deep emotional experience. And honor-based shame could be transitory, causing a powerful uproar for a time but then resulting in surprisingly sweeping forgiveness.[57] On the other hand, again in common with honor cultures elsewhere, violations of family honor could have an impact extending beyond a single generation. A few scholars, working out from chivalric culture, have urged that shame must have required substantial redefinition in the transition from the Middle Ages—in which people were encouraged to think of themselves as sinful and therefore accepting of shame—to the more prideful, individualist Renaissance, where shame would become more complicated.[58] But the balance of scholarly opinion pushes for greater continuity, with the culture of honor a fairly durable spur to additional consideration for shame into the eighteenth century.[59]

Yet there is more, in the set of changes that seemed to enhance shame's role in Western culture. Greater attention to humoral medicine, by the sixteenth and seventeenth centuries, led to new interest of the physical manifestations of shame, including blushing, and new attention to the kinds of shame that should attend exposure of the body (including, particularly for women, exposure to doctors when seeking medical treatment). One of the many qualities that convinced Europeans of their superiority to Native Americans, in this context, was the apparent inability of the latter to blush, a sure sign of shamelessness, which in turn was a clear indication of an inferior nature. "How can he be trusted, who knows not how to blush?"[60]

Most strikingly of all, public shaming rituals accelerated from the late Middle Ages onward, throughout the Western world. The reasons are not entirely clear, though enhanced Christian, chivalric, and even medical emphasis may have played some role. As the Western economy became more commercial, with communities accordingly more complicated and personal motives more mixed, did a greater reliance on shaming—and often, as we see, a particularly nasty kind of shaming in many instances—seem essential to preserve social cohesion?[61]

Thus many of the patterns already explored for premodern societies more generally, particularly in the use of stocks and pillories, forced donkey rides and other demeaning practices, became more pronounced as Western society moved into the early modern centuries. The widespread interest in combining the physical punishment of criminals with parades of shame crested as well.

And there was more. At least from the later Middle Ages onward, in many parts of the West, the practice of charivari, or rough music, was particularly interesting. Common in many other cultures as a means of communal celebration—for example, calling attention to a new marriage—the practice in Western Europe was distinctively channeled toward shaming. Groups of young people (female and male alike), most commonly, would gather around some offender, or the offender's house, shouting and making noise to attract wide attention to the intended humiliation. Occasionally the crowd might also stage a mock stag hunt, with the offender chased by human "hounds." In Scotland, rough music was often accompanied by placing some kind of restraining device, or brank, on an offending individual, then following the pots-and-pans attention getting by parading the victim around the village; the ceremony would continue, or be repeated, until the person pledged to reform. All sorts of breaches of community standards might attract a group: adultery or an illegitimate birth; an older man marrying a much younger woman; or a widow marrying too soon after a husband's death, or sometimes marrying at all, or having sex without marriage; or a man who beat his wife. The idea, obviously, was to use loud and public shaming to defend a host of community standards. The procedure took deep roots: official or church efforts to stop the practice, out of a concern that innocent people might be wrongly targeted, were largely ignored at least in the countryside. The practice, finally, was exported to North America, and used punitively on occasion in Quebec and New England, though interestingly the disciplining as opposed to celebratory function was less pronounced in the transplantation.[62]

Heightened emphasis on shame and the importance of religious and social conformity even generated distinctive word use, which reflects shame's new

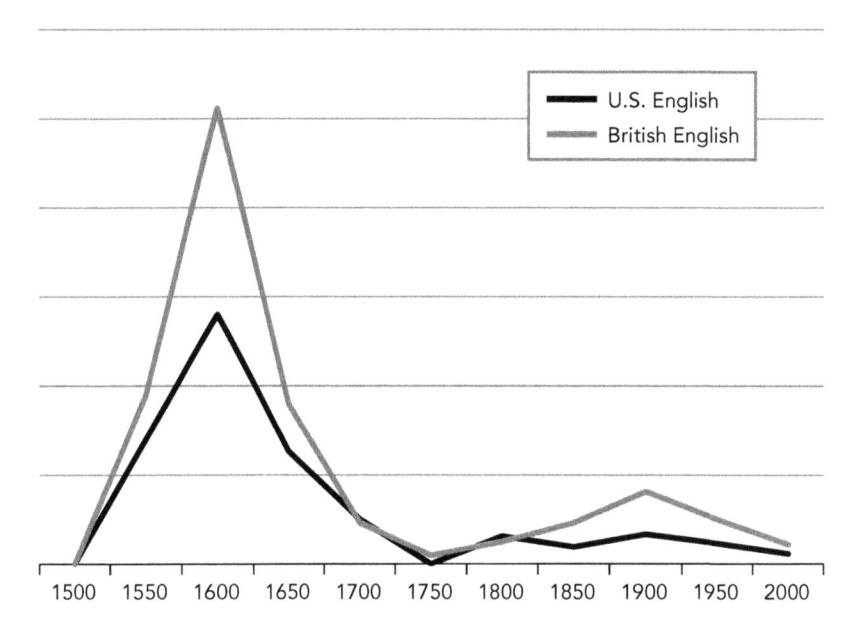

FIGURE 1. The frequency of the word *shamefast* in U.S. and British English, 1500–2000, according to Google Books Ngram Viewer. Also see *shamefast* in Angus Stevenson, ed., *Oxford Dictionary of English* (Oxford: Oxford University Press, 2010).

power and the hope of avoiding the emotional turmoil it could bring. The word *shamefast*, though not brand-new (it first appears in ninth-century English), soared remarkably, for 150 to 200 years beginning in the early sixteenth century, both in Britain and then in the British colonies. The word could mean full of shame, as a result of transgression; but more commonly it referred to the kind of anticipatory emotional discipline that would steer an individual away from bad behavior. In this sense, to use more modern words that lack the shame-related meaning, the term suggested extreme modesty or bashfulness that would serve as emotional constraint; thus, in a belated nineteenth-century reference, a person might display a "sweet and shamefast look." The term's surge responded to the punitive qualities and practices now associated with shame, and it enjoyed a remarkable peak in popularity—only to decline precipitously, on the eve of the eighteenth century, foreshadowing the new and much more cautious approach to shame that would emerge soon thereafter.

A final aspect of the evolving Western use of shame—linked perhaps in some ways to a modified chivalric approach and to the new interest in humoral medicine, but developing its own momentum—involved enforcement of an increasingly delicate sense of manners, emerging during the Renaissance. Here, a major interpretation of social relationships in early modern Europe offers another possible insight into the ways Western culture sought to heighten shame's role, at both the community and the familial level. Norbert Elias decades ago sketched what he described as a "civilizing process" by which West European elites, and gradually other social groups as well, accepted a more rigorous set of manners, particularly aimed at controlling disruptive emotions, violence, and bodily excess. It is important to note that his sketch has been contested particularly by scholars who urge that Europeans even before this were capable of considerable decorum. At least as vital for our purposes, Elias invokes a sense of shame without describing real emotional situations—leaving the emotion somewhat lifeless. But even so his claims warrant some attention in showing the range of targets to which shame can apply and in suggesting, correctly, that shame-based cultures are capable of considerable change in the ways the emotion is directed.[63]

For Elias sees shame's range expanding considerably in Western Europe, particularly by the seventeenth and eighteenth centuries. Functions that were once routine now became shameful if performed in public: urination, for example, where no less an authority than Erasmus urged "it rouses shame to show this to the eyes of others." Farting was another target, with Erasmus again noting that to avoid shame "one should make sacrifices, with the buttocks firmly pressed together." And the sense of shame in fact increased: when once men freely undressed in front of their servants, or went to an outdoor privy partially naked, they now felt ashamed at such license, and covered up. By the eighteenth century, indeed, special nightwear emerged, specifically to allow concealment without the cumbersomeness of regular dress. By this point as well, Elias argues, respectable families were relying on shame to inculcate the appropriate standards in their children, using fear of the emotion as a means of developing what he calls "automatic self-restraint."[64]

The various changes in Western formulations of shame from the later Middle Ages onward do more, obviously, than illustrate the important point that the emotion was not a constant in the premodern context—though this is an approach that should be applied to other regional cases. Increased social and personal reliance on shame ranged from the emergence of considerations of honor that were strikingly similar to those of (also feudal) Japan—as a fifteenth-century English Arthurian compilation put it, a "death with honor is preferable to a life of shame"—to a concern with respectable self-control that smacked of Confucian niceties. The surge of punitive shame is particularly interesting, suggesting a fiercer approach than was common in some other shame-based cultures. Might this have been one of the reasons that Western innovators, by the middle of the eighteenth century, were particularly persuaded that shame required major reconsideration, in the interest of human dignity? Certainly, the dramatically different take on shame that developed after 1750 contrasted strikingly with the earlier surge, and generated even greater change. The same contrast would apply to North America, where important elements of the Western enthusiasm for shame had initially been transplanted.

Colonial North America

Not surprisingly, given its growing importance in early modern Britain, shame played a large role in the emotional and community life of the colonies in British North America. The experiences involved were not, in all probability, particularly distinctive—they highlighted features already noted as common in many agricultural societies. They serve in part a role as summary. But colonial shame has also been particularly well documented in some respects, which can add to our sense of what the emotion was all about in premodern societies. And the colonial setting needs emphasis as the backdrop to subsequent change in U.S. views and practices where shame was involved. Without this baseline, we cannot evaluate the innovations of the early nineteenth century, or the reasons these innovations took shape.

Colonial reliance on shame, and the deep sadness it could entail, also further complicates many of the glib generations about Western or U.S. society as guilt-based, in contradistinction to other, perhaps inferior, shame-based regions. Guilt undoubtedly existed in colonial America, but it was usually deeply intertwined with shame and often, at least, secondary to it—as was true in Western culture more generally.

Public shaming was widely accepted. In New England, at least, it was sometimes deliberately favored as an alternative to harsh physical discipline, as many leaders sought to distance the new land from Old World practices; there was frequent identification of certain punitive practices as "barbarous and inhumane."[65] In one case an adulteress was spared the whipping administered to her lover, because of the "weakness" of her body, but she was exposed to public scrutiny and shame. It is also interesting to note that expressions of contrition—expressions and postures of shame in the public court—often led to reduction of sentences in practice. In another case, a woman in Springfield, Massachusetts, was allowed to apologize "like a woman" for insulting another person publicly, but she was also required to sit in the stocks "like a man, since she swore like one." Shaming also could be imaginatively tailored to the offense, more than with other types of discipline: thus a man who stole a pair of trousers in Virginia was required to spend some hours in the stocks with a pair of britches on his head.[66]

So the familiar apparatus of public shaming definitely had a role. Whippings were in public. Offenders might be carried around town in carts; or they might be displayed in stocks, the practice directly imported from Europe. Burglars might be branded with a *B* or have an ear cut off, those who swore might have to wear a cleft stick on their tongue. Distinctive clothing was an option, though ironically there is no definitive evidence that a scarlet letter *A* was ever required in Massachusetts; however, it was a legal option there from 1692 onward, and it was employed in Quaker Pennsylvania. Elsewhere, adulteresses might have to wear a *B*, for bawd; an adulterous couple might both have to wear *AD*. Paper signs were often used, with the offenders wearing a description of offenses for a period of time—probably a sign of the high literacy rate in the colonies that might introduce a new precision into the public shaming process. Other targets for shaming included defiling the Sabbath—in New Haven in 1650 a man had to stand on the stocks for two hours wearing a sign identifying him as "an open and obstinate condemner of God's Holy Ordinances"—overcharging for work, seditious talk, public drunkenness, or seduction through false promises of marriage. Greater crimes, like counterfeiting or forgery, warranted physical discipline and branding, but here too shaming was clearly part of the punishment. The goal, as always, was a combination of admonition to the wrongdoer himself (or herself) and of a larger public message, "that others may fear and be ashamed or breaking out in like wickedness."[67]

Several studies emphasize that the actual incidence of formal public shaming may have been low—far lower than popularizations such as the work of Nathaniel Hawthorne later suggested. Interpretation, however, is less clear: low levels of imposition may well have reflected the effectiveness of shame-based discipline, in church and home as well as in the public square. It is also possible that shaming declined as communities became more heterogeneous, forcing greater reliance on other forms of discipline. There is wide agreement, however, that in many cases the rates of crime and community offense were surprisingly limited. Towns and villages may have been able to reserve formal public shaming to cases where the offenders seemed particularly defiant or obdurate, where intense shame thus needed to be imposed. And highly cohesive communities may not have needed a frequent experience of aggressive shaming to maintain a sense of emotional identity.[68]

But infrequency did not mean resistance to the concept of public shame. Colonial courts frequently specified that punishments of various sorts, including simple display, must occur on market day, or in a public congregation, "that he (the offender) may be seen by the people."[69] And as in other cases, shame often took precedence over physical pain in the minds of those who experienced both. Thus a Massachusetts man noted that whipping was no more important than the "skip of a flea" but that the attending portion of shame counted for more. Whipping punished, according to this approach, but shame taught, for the miscreant would want to gain reentry into the community. Not uncommonly also, the physical punishment might be stipulated by the court but then suspended in return for a confession of wrongdoing and some public shaming, with the suspension designed to show the community's forgiveness.[70]

Shame played a vital role in religious life, and this aspect of community enforcement—the congregational admonition—was probably more important than formal legal impositions, particularly in New England. Thus Temperance Baldwin "was called forth in open congregation ... and solemnly admonished of her grat sin, which was spread before her in diverse particulars." The proper response was a shameful confession—to "take shame unto her face"—and apologize, often in the form of a long personal account of wickedness delivered in the most abject fashion. "With all submissive respect, prostrating himself at the feet of your clemency.... Your poor petitioner ... humbly desires to acknowledge the justice of the God who ... hath made his sin obvious for his shame." Conveying the emotion was vital, for words alone would not do the trick. And if the whole procedure fell through, the miscreant might be excommunicated from the church—pronounced a "leprous and unclean" person, cut off from God and community alike—for most people, a dire punishment indeed. Shame prone, many colonial Protestants responded readily to the fear of abandonment.[71]

Not surprisingly, in this context, privacy was neither common nor officially valued. Colonial authorities stressed the "watchfulness" both of God and his angels, and of the human neighborhood. Hiding was fruitless, for in the end the Day of Judgment would be a shaming experience writ large: "We shall every one of us stand naked before Christ's Judgement Seat ... and all, even the most secret, sins shall be laid open before the whole world." Even in the earthly plane, God might "write a sin on a forehead," allowing the surrounding community to see.[72]

Colonial shaming, particularly when religious authorities were involved, also clearly permitted reintegration, a vital point. A couple in 1689, correctly accused of premarital sex, "manifested much sorrow by words and tears," and were readmitted to their congregation. In a similar Maryland case a bit later, the couple (who had since married) showed themselves "very sorrowfull": the woman was excused from punishment altogether, the man simply banned from the county court—in essence, deprived of citizenship—for a year and a day. The record is replete with cases where public shaming and repentance did not prevent later service to the community, including even elected office.[73]

While the evidence only rarely reveals the internal emotional state of those involved in this system, the data are at least suggestive—including of course the cases of apparently sincere public performance. Admissions of weakness and humility were common, even in the private pages of a diary. Thus Thomas Shepard in his autobiography thanked the Lord for helping him "to loathe myself in some measure" and to deny a sense of self that "ruins me and blinds me." Or Isaac Pennington, who proclaimed "my nothingness, my emptiness, my weakness," and his need to feel broken in order to follow God. Shame built on this sense of desirable melancholy, but by the same token might well seem both appropriate and acceptable, even by the individuals targeted. Common imagery also stressed the importance of lowering a person's height: "Lord, I lie down in my shame, worthy to be rejected."[74] Posture, in other words, corresponded with and expressed the expected emotion.

Honor also entered into the colonial mix of shame, though it may have motivated somewhat different kinds of individuals for the most part—and possibly also reflected a less Puritan version of Protestantism. Duels to defend honor were common, even in the North; Massachusetts banned the practice only in 1784, and it continued to flourish in the South for many decades, widely supported by the public even after it was outlawed. Less extreme but possibly more characteristic in the colonial period itself were the many exchanges of insults, and lawsuits designed to protest slander and defamation. A typical suit involved two couples, one of which protested the other's claims that the wife was a base and lying woman—this kind of claim was a "deep wound" and a defamation to husband as well as wife, and to "my posterity"—a typical expression of the kind of emotion that was commonly wrapped up in the concept of personal and familial honor. Characteristically, slander, in the courts, warranted a greater fine than did physical assault. For violence could at worst kill a person, but defiling a good name "mangles" the individual in the grave and beyond.[75]

If the tightknit, usually small community was the framework for expressing and enforcing shame, it was the colonial family that birthed the emotion in the first place. A host of family historians have offered abundant evidence over the past several decades. Families varied, of course, in setting, in personalities, and in religious specifics. John Demos focused mainly on the Puritan family. Philip Greven found the evangelical family—heir in many ways to the early Puritans—the most common crucible of shame, with more moderate or "genteel" families much less involved.[76]

The apparent variety is important, but the evidence of wide use of shaming in child discipline shines through as well. Children were not to see, in the words of one Puritan divine, that they had a will of their own, but that they rested entirely in their parents' keeping. Disobedient children, by the same token, should be cast away, emotionally, until their self-abasement allowed reentry. These were emotionally intense families, with real investment of parental and especially maternal love when behaviors warranted—but an equal willingness to shut off the tap when children displayed "anything in them" that was hurtful, wild, or proud. Cotton Mather thus told a wayward son that he was "expressly forbidden for a while to come into my presence"—and the boy grown into man would continue to convey a sense of shame for the rest of his life. Mather, like many Puritan parents, and like society at large, preferred emotional means over physical discipline. And the result, as in the Mather family, was a host of people who maintained a lifelong capacity to feel shame even when their actions remained hidden from others, or who in adulthood would recall often fairly minor episodes as adolescents—like one or two bouts of drinking—with a heavy sense of shame. It is worth noting finally, even aside from deliberate emotion management, that most colonial mothers nursed their infants intensely for about a year, but then, often in preparation for the next pregnancy, rather abruptly ended the practice; whether this distancing added to a preparation for shame must be speculative.[77]

Tight communities and a deliberately emotional management of children added up to one of the classic shame cultures recorded in the premodern past, expressed and reinforced by a variety of public practices linked both to religion and to law. Two analytical asterisks must be added in. With Greven, we simply cannot know what percentage of families harbored the most intense shaming practices—some variety clearly existed, and could even serve, later on, as a component for change. More important still, given the current definitional debates, it is really impossible to tease out shame from guilt. Many colonials themselves may have experienced both emotions, including a sense of guilt in God's sight but shame in the community's. To the extent that individuals clearly developed an internal shaming mechanism, it may not have made much difference what the guilt-shame balance was, for it did not depend just on community observation—and this involves the same complexity, in other words, that some contemporary social psychologists have sought to identify.

But the colonials themselves preferred the term shame over guilt by a good measure. The image of a Last Judgment that really involved shaming before God explains the preference as well. And the colonial community structure, plus the psychological preparation developed by parents willing to offer but also to deny affection, almost certainly tilted the balance toward shame in fact.

. . .

The colonial American experience thus adds a convincing case to the varied evidence for the reliance of most if not virtually all premodern agricultural societies on some forms of shame. The interest in emotion history on the part of more than a generation of colonial historians has yielded particularly abundant evidence, which given the difficulty of exploring experiences like shame in past time is particularly welcome. The result might of course make colonial American society stand out for its shaming more than should be the case: there is no sense the American patterns were particularly unusual. Many practices and assumptions were shared with other premodern communities, many indeed directly imported from Europe and from the changing approaches to shame that had been developing across the Atlantic. This includes, of course, the interesting shared use, but then abandonment, of the anticipatory approach implied in the word *shamefast*.

Amid important variations, shame commanded a major place in the emotional arsenal of many societies on the eve of modern times. Its validity and utility were widely accepted and translated into a variety of settings and practices. The emotion caused pain, though degrees here may have varied; some recognition that shame might also ease social relationships or modify reactions to a violation of norms also applied. Pain and social acceptance also feed the common impression that *anticipations* of shame also formed a powerful element in emotional and social life, reducing though never eliminating the need for shaming outright.

CHAPTER 3

The Impact of Modernity
Some Possibilities

The pervasiveness of shame in premodern communities, but also the adaptability of the social uses of the emotion to different regional cultures and to changes over time, raise an important additional question: how would shame fare with the advent of more modern conditions and institutions?

The influence of modernity is a debated issue in emotions history. Many scholars, particularly with premodern specialties, tend to argue that emotions are such an inherent part of the human condition that it is misleading to expect a sea change just because of developments like industrialization and urbanization.[1] One approach urges that various emotional communities, that operate over extended periods of time, offer more important organizing principles than modernity itself. On the other hand, some emotions may attach so clearly to modern conditions that a divide is both accurate and useful. Envy, for example, has to be redefined for a consumer society; parents may intensify their love for individual children differently, on average, when the birth rate drops in the modern demographic transition; nostalgia may take on new meanings.[2]

The modernity thesis has directly been applied to shame, though largely by nonhistorians. This chapter briefly explores the main arguments but also notes their limitations, particularly when confronted with evidence from contemporary East Asia. A partial modernity framework remains, but as the following chapter indicates, it requires additional cultural stimulus to effect more systematic redefinitions of shame, and even then important continuities remain. A relationship between shame and modernity is real, but at the very least complex. Not surprisingly, given the deep roots of shame in premodern history, and the many social functions it served, a thorough reevaluation of the emotion would require unusual stimulus.

A study published in 2007 that compared an Indonesian fishing village with Southern California around the uses of shame predictably found that shame loomed large in the former, promoting civility among the villagers as well as a tendency to conform; Californians, however, in a large metropolitan region amid great geographical mobility tended largely to downplay shame in favor of more casual social relationships and a greater willingness to take risks. The report ends by suggesting that since the conditions in the Indonesian village are on the way out in the modern global economy—which is surely true—the basis for shame that "likely played a central role in the evolution of human cooperation in small-scale groups" is ending as well. "In today's world of globalized and hypercompetitive markets, there are intrinsic costs to relying on shame as a mechanism of social regulation"—and to preferring conformism and civility over the values needed in modern life: "the era of shame may be passing."[3]

Leaving aside the virtues of civility, why should modernity undermine shame—as many social scientists, who generalize about the decline of shame in modern life, often assume? At least three factors deserve consideration, and they may of course operate in combination.

Contention 1: Shame declines with urbanization, for the cohesive communities on which shame depends begin to disappear in this more anonymous modern environment. There is no doubt that urban environments complicate the emotion, and probably make it easier (at least until recently) for a shamed individual simply to pack up and move away rather than accept community dictates; but even in the rural world, movement had been much more frequent than we commonly recognize. The problem is that urban societies can easily form new communities—in neighborhoods, professional groups, other associations—and indeed we see this happening even in the nineteenth-century United States and certainly in the highly urban societies of East Asia, helping to explain a persistence of shame even amid new challenges.[4]

Contention 2: Increasingly, commercial societies simply cannot maintain traditional concepts of honor. Pursuit of the almighty dollar will take precedence over the often costly distraction of honor codes and their attendant shaming: heroic ideals and calculations of self-interest cannot long coexist. In the long run, this proposition may be accurate to a point—even in Japan, as I discuss later in this chapter. And it is true that, already in the eighteenth century, commentators—particularly in Britain—were citing growing passion for the "love of gain" or the "avidity of acquiring goods and possessions," noting that this narrowing of interests was incompatible with the "interest of honor."[5] Here too, however, there are problems. Even in brashly commercial contexts like the nineteenth-century United States, honor concerns did not yield quickly to business motives—and in some cases (France as well as Japan) the first century of what might be termed industrial commercialism actually spurred some groups to double down on honor rather than loosen their hold.[6] In the United States, key regions, notably the South and West, maintained a strong commitment to honor and its emotional enforcement through shame. Further, as we have seen, honor culture had only been a part of the traditional setting for shame in most places, so even when honor did decline, the utility of shame might well persist.

Contention 3: modern societies create institutions that provide alternatives to shaming, and indeed they may insist on their superior performance. Most obviously, as in Western countries during the nineteenth century, modern societies establish or expand formal policing, and develop new institutions for the treatment of offenders. Here is a key reason that, ultimately on a global basis, public shaming rituals largely disappeared—in the West by the end of the nineteenth century, elsewhere by the later twentieth century, even in societies that otherwise maintained strong reliance on shame. The emotion might well be reconsidered when discipline could be sought by other means.

Taken together, urbanization, the ultimate decline of honor, and the new approaches to social discipline unquestionably raised questions about shame that every modern society has had to grapple with. Pressures for change might be further enhanced simply by global examples—once the West began to reconsider shame and label some traditional practices as barbaric, other societies might feel a need to innovate in response. And they could be furthered as well by larger shifts in value systems—for example, in new ideas about women's rights, as against a traditional sense that the gender was slightly shameful. As modern conditions spread increasingly widely during the twentieth century, aspects of shame had to be reevaluated.

Yet the reevaluation did not have to be complete. Against too much emphasis on innovative modernity, a host of societies found reasons to maintain a strong reliance on shame, in family and community contexts, while becoming triumphantly "modern" in other respects—including massive urbanization.

East Asia, beginning with Japan, provides the prime example that complicates any easy generalizations about shame and modernity. Here were societies, after all, that had already translated shame into complex settings—far more complex than an Indonesian fishing village—and linked the emotion to a larger Confucian cultural framework. Here were societies that, according to a host of contemporary comparisons, maintain a strong reliance on shame in considerable contrast to their Western counterparts.

The key was culture, and a related capacity to maintain and adapt an older emotional tradition. Japan was the East Asian society that most clearly debated the possibility of moving more fully toward a Western-style value system, and ultimately turned away. During the heady days of school reform in the early Meiji era, during the 1870s, the nation imported a number of school officials, particularly from the United States, and widely copied Western teacher training standards. But for a host of reasons the results were not entirely palatable, and one critical response was to pull back from the dangers of excessive individualism. A new Memorandum for Elementary School Teachers, in 1881, urged the importance of group values, including of course loyalty to nation and emperor but also "faith in friends." Loyalty and obedience were stressed as central virtues, in a system that placed new emphasis on appropriate character training. Shame was not explicitly discussed in this effort, but it proved consistent with the values that were being highlighted, and it unquestionably played a lead role, in the schools and beyond, as a result.[7]

There are, admittedly, dangers in discussing only briefly the ongoing role of shame in East Asia, as part of introducing a more complex comparative context than modernity alone can provide. The assessment rests mainly on recent observations, not a careful history of continuity and adaptation—though a few additional historical elements can be introduced. It risks overgeneralizing and stereotyping about East Asian regions that in many ways, as with current political systems, are quite varied. It ignores personality variables, yet other studies of current shame reactions stress their importance. It risks falling into some of the earlier traps in discussions of "shame-based" cultures, though it is possible to avoid some of the crudest misrepresentations, beginning with the idea that shame is somehow incompatible with a rigorous and internalized sense of standards.

But the evidence for a distinctive approach to shame is both diverse and compelling. It begins with child rearing. Studies on modern Japan, China, and South Korea show a frequent pattern in which a mother responds to a child's bad behavior by openly withdrawing affection. From a Taiwanese mother: "We don't want you. You stand over there. We don't like you anyway." From examination of Japanese mothers: they rarely spank and are shocked at examples of U.S. parental behavior, but they often, responding to ill discipline, walk away from the child and pretend the child is not there. And the parents openly invoke shame: a three-year-old Chinese child asks a neighbor for candy, and her mother shouts "shame" in response, while scratching at the child's face. Not surprisingly, East Asian children learn the word and concept of shame earlier in life (at about age two and a half) than is true of their U.S. or British counterparts.[8] Further, East Asian parents respond much more affirmatively to propositions such as "a preschooler should be shamed if he or she does not follow social rules" than do U.S. parents (where, in one survey, literally no Chicago parent signed on to the idea, in contrast to the 43 percent of Taiwanese who embraced the notion).[9]

Shame continues in school and in adult life. The Chinese are held to value shame over guilt—though they are aware of and use both emotions—because shame guides in real situations and relationships, rather than focusing on more abstract standards, and in social settings where important decisions must be made. Many East Asians respond positively to shame, seeing it as an encouragement to self-scrutiny and self-improvement, rather than withdrawing as many Westerners do.[10] They also strongly associate shame with family behavior, not just individual action. Inappropriate acts by family members, the presence of disability, or prior family poverty can evoke a strong sense of shame, leading to shunning more than any effort at public humiliation. At the same time, while shame causes pain to those who experience it, the pain may be moderated by a lower level of emotional intensity overall; and as in earlier shame-based settings, the emotion is also often cushioned by a good bit of teasing and humor.[11]

Several observers note other special features. Experience of shame in childhood helps many East Asians keep the emotion in bounds when they encounter it later on; there is an expectation that people should be able to handle shame, though it unquestionably promotes feelings of inferiority and smallness. Many shaming situations carefully maintain possibilities for reintegration. Apology, or its equivalent (Koreans may prefer not to apologize directly), can respond successfully to shame. Other rituals may help. A misbehaving Chinese school student is clearly shamed, required to wear a shabby sweater for most of the day; but toward midafternoon, he is allowed to wear a shirt over the sweater, and by the day's end take it off entirely; the lesson, presumably, has been delivered, and the shaming is over. Not surprisingly, reintegration can be less than perfect, for memories are long.[12] A shamed person in Korea may be told later on, "You did a wrong thing—just keep quiet." But the emotional experience is not intended to be destructive; there is meant to be a distinction between shame and complete loss of self-esteem or discouragement. While shame can rouse defiance even in the East Asian context, as in human rights resistance to China's political manipulation of the emotion, the kind of systematic and often destructive resentment reported in the West seems largely absent. By the same token, the sensitivity to shame, and to awareness of what others are thinking, looms very large.[13]

Significant change has been possible within this overall framework, though a more focused history would be desirable. Standards have shifted. Divorce, once a reason for shame in Korea, now merits no particular response amid the younger generation. Older rituals have loosened. A longstanding shaming practice in Japanese schools—forcing children to "stand in the hall" in response to bad behavior—was largely abandoned in the 1970s in favor of less formal approaches. The lingering samurai sense of honor in Japan was thoroughly reviewed. It burned bright during the reform era and into the twentieth century: even more than in Europe, honor codes gained greater intensity in response to wider change, and the rate of honor-based suicide actually accelerated quite markedly. But this culture went down in flames in the World War II defeat and no longer serves as part of the Japanese approach to shame. Even more obviously, East Asian shame has been directed ever more strongly toward achievement, for example in schooling—in contrast, one study holds, with ongoing uses of shame in India.[14] Overall, an emphasis on considerable emotional continuity must include important adaptations as well, where aspects of the modernity argument, though suitably modified, still have merit.

But shame does count. The tearful Japanese businessman who publicly confesses to some misdeed is a product of a distinctive emotional culture. The Japanese or Korean voters who use shame in their evaluations of political behavior apply distinctive standards as well. The emotion is also readily available for new uses, as in Hong Kong campaigns that use shame to counter public littering. The effort to avoid shame continues to have great impact on public behaviors—motivating conformity in some cases, but also encouraging alternative means of saving face. And, where it causes personal desperation, shame may contribute to rates of suicide that, by international standards, remain relatively high. Impacts are both significant and diverse.

Overall, the recent observers—largely sympathetic—who have explored this aspect of East Asian society conclude that adapted shaming on the whole works well, despite problems in extreme cases. We have moved away from the days in which Asian cultures were lashed by Westerners for having lower moral standards or for promoting bizarre behaviors. Shame in East Asian societies, again according to recent evaluations, undoubtedly promotes conformity and discourages certain kinds of risk taking, and it encourages shyness as a positive quality in ways that may bemuse Westerners; but at the same time it directly supports good order and, in several cases, a surprisingly low level of crime.

Shame seems to have been successfully combined with rapid economic and political development, including of course massive urbanization.

One final comparative complication must be noted, in any assessment of shame and modernity, beyond the fact that some regions have clearly successfully adapted a cultural tradition of shame to the demands of modern conditions. Several societies developed new contexts for shame as part of their own approach to modernity, building on tradition in some respects but clearly innovating in others—without relaxing a grip on shame.

The pattern was clearest in communist societies, in Soviet Russia and then later in China. The collectivist emphasis in communist policy, though hardly traditional, made shame a logical instrument in contrast to Western individualism. The real or imagined needs of this particular brand of authoritarianism enhanced the embrace. Soviet leaders became adept at using public shaming as part of disciplining party officials and promoting conformity. The process continues in communist China. A reformer writes about his own experience of school shaming—required to confess his faults painfully before a class after a bout of absenteeism—and how this connects to the tactics the national leadership employed on adults as part of new campaigns both for greater party loyalty and against corruption. Suspect activists are pressed to admit to real or imagined faults on public television; unwanted party officials are exposed for real or imagined sexual or other offenses, in the best tradition of public shaming.[15]

・・・

Over time, and with steadily expanding global exchange, "modernity" may continue to erode shame on a wider geographical scale. And the desirability of further historical work, on the uses and modifications of shame amid the Asian or other modernizations that have already occurred, remains high. To date, however, available evidence suggests the need for real caution in generalizing about modernity's impacts in this particular emotional category. Shame had already proved adaptable in premodern societies, and it may retain this capacity even among larger structural changes.

Yet shame was more systematically reevaluated in the modern West, beginning in the later eighteenth century, as chapter 4 details. Modernity played some role in this, but the prime causes must be sought in more particular cultural shifts. New Western approaches would themselves have some global impact, but the main point is clearly the unusual innovation involved—for, as we have seen, Western society had not previously stood out for any particular aversion to shame.

The result was not, at least necessarily, an unusually successful Western path; distinctiveness has both benefits and costs. Comparativists, like the researcher cited above who studied the Indonesian fishing village, may well contend that shame-based societies generate too much pressure to conform and unduly discourage risk taking and innovation, but limitations of what became a somewhat different Western approach need consideration as well.

The central point is twofold: first, tracing the Western review of shame since about 1800 highlights several key factors that considerably contrast with reactions in many other parts of the modern world, where shame has not been so sweepingly attacked. For better or worse, new Western standards have emerged.

But second: the West's efforts against shame were never as fully successful as their advocates hoped, and this has become even clearer in recent decades when shame, against many expectations, has gained a new lease on life. The power and utility of shame, so apparent in modern East Asia, continue to play a role in the Western experience as well, despite a barrage of criticism.

The West's special path deserves explanation. But it may turn out that the modern Western approach to shame is not as clear-cut in the global context as many emotional reformers continue to hope. Here is a complexity to which we must return, after the Western effort is outlined.

CHAPTER 4

Reconsidering Shame in Western Society

The Nineteenth and Twentieth Centuries

When Nathaniel Hawthorne published *The Scarlet Letter* in 1850, he was participating in a major reevaluation of shame in the United States—as was obvious from the fact that he highlighted a colonial practice—the use of public lettering to maintain shame—that had already been largely abandoned. Quite probably, the novel furthered the reevaluation process as well, as its immediate and wide popularity might suggest.

The novel dealt with a woman, Hester Prynne, who commits adultery, though believing wrongly that her husband was dead, and has an illegitimate child. She is publicly shamed (standing on an open scaffold for three hours, in addition to having to wear the letter), while adamantly refusing to name her partner, a minister, who long resists open identification for fear of community reaction. The novel, probably like Hawthorne himself, was profoundly divided over shaming and the offense that might provoke it (in a society that, while reassessing shame, remained deeply hostile to adultery). On the one hand, shaming might seem vindicated. The community gradually restores Hester to decent standing. Hester's partner, deeply troubled, is possibly mysteriously marked by the letter *A* on his own body, and then at the end, in failing health, publicly admits his sin and shame. But Hester herself is far more complicated. She seems to repent, living a quiet life and voluntarily continuing to wear her brand. But inwardly she rebels: the community's values are not hers, she believes that her affair had a "consecration of its own," and she even embroiders the letter on her dress. This is not acceptance of shame, though it is also not open defiance.

So how might the novel have been read at the time of its publication? Careful readers, identifying with the protagonist, might well emerge thinking that shaming had gone too far, that the emotion conflicted with appropriate personal autonomy. Interestingly, several New England communities objected to the book, believing that this representation of colonial history gave them a black eye—another implicit vote for reassessing public shaming. But again, the book does not fully renounce shame, and it can also be read as a contention that the emotion serves the community well while allowing reintegration (when shame seems to be accepted, though not, as in the lover's case, when it is resisted). Whatever the hesitations of its author, the novel correctly suggests an interesting moment in the nation's history of shame.[1]

• • •

This chapter deals with the undeniable decline of shame and shaming in the United States, beginning probably in the second quarter of the nineteenth century, though with some prior preparation, as a case study in the larger Western reconsideration of shame during the same time period. Recalibrations from this point onward explain why so many people today, including social science experts, routinely argue that shame is in decline and is perhaps even a "taboo" emotion in contemporary society. Obviously the process of change needs a fuller characterization, and it also demands some careful assessment of the causation involved given the complexities in any sweeping invocation of modernity. There is no question that a significant redefinition took shape from the late eighteenth century onward, that altered the acceptability of shame and shaming alike, opening a growing gap with the standards and experiences that had prevailed before.

At the same time, the decline of shame was complicated and not always straightforward. The emotion not only did not disappear, it was recurrently revived because of social and individual needs. The second section of the chapter traces U.S. shame as a persistent if increasingly subordinate theme, into the twentieth century. Finally, U.S. patterns must be situated in the larger Western trends, where comparison on the whole suggests the common factors involved.

The chapter covers a timespan from the early nineteenth century until after the mid-twentieth. This is not exactly a familiar periodization, but this particular angle of emotions history seems to call for it. U.S. shame exhibits a clear, if again complicated, trajectory from the beginnings of reconsideration up to the 1970s. The inception date may seem unsurprising: this was a time defined by early urbanization and industrialization, and also by the Enlightenment as well as the establishment of the new republic. It may not be unexpected that, in the case of shame, patterns that began to be established then lasted for many decades: surviving world war, the Great Depression, the New Deal, and other familiar markers. But the end of the period, after such impressive durability, is in many ways quite jarring. For it was in the 1970s, surprisingly—for we don't usually assume that this was a particularly decisive decade for much of anything—that the pattern began to change yet again; elements of the prior trajectory would persist, even gaining new support, but on the whole shame would come back into fashion, requiring yet another analytical framework and unquestionably generating a major challenge to explanation—the subject of the following chapter.

Attacking Shame and Shaming: The U.S. Experience

SIGNS OF DECLINE

The historian who has worked most explicitly on U.S. shame, John Demos, pinpointed what he saw as a shift from shame to guilt by the middle of the nineteenth century—right when Hawthorne was agonizing about how to paint the emotion in his novel. Demos did not argue that the transition was sudden, or even complete; but he contends that there was a steady shift in predominance, concerning emotions designed to maintain social discipline and personal virtue. While Demos's sketch was hurried—he was more comfortable detailing the colonial backdrop than the modern replacement—his judgment was impressively correct. Shame did begin to lose social esteem, and the symptoms—all beginning to cluster prior to mid-century—were varied.[2]

There are three major signs of this important emotional change: overall reference to shame; huge reforms—if they should be termed that—in the treatment of social offenders, particularly around the rise of a prison system but also the new regulation of private and community efforts in using shame; and finally something of a revolution, at least in principle, in U.S. child rearing, with opinion shapers quietly rejecting shaming in favor of more positive methods of discipline.

USING THE TERM Both Google Books data from books published in the United States and the *New York Times* index show a marked and fairly steady reduction in use of the word *shame*, compared to all other words used, from the 1840s or 1850s onward—confirming Demos's contention that a real transition was taking shape by mid-century or a bit before (figs. 2, 3).[3]

CHAPTER 4

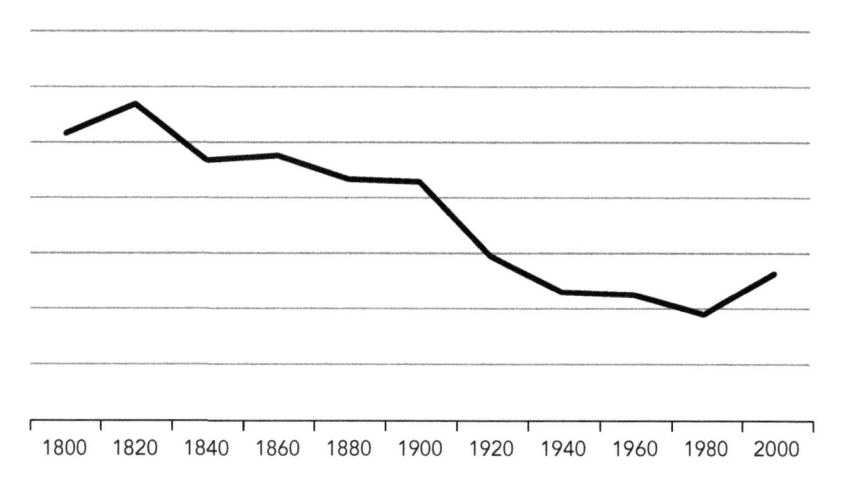

FIGURE 2. The frequency of the word *shame* in U.S. English, 1800s–1980, according to Google Books Ngram Viewer.

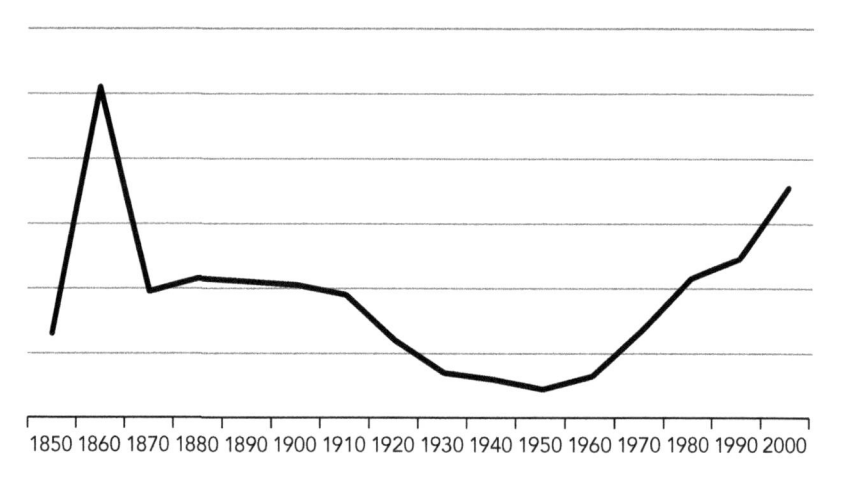

FIGURE 3. The frequency of the word *shame* in U.S. English, 1800s–1960, according to the *New York Times* Chronicle.

To be sure, evaluating the results of patterns of word use is tricky. Words may be used infrequently not because they are losing traction, but because their relevance is simply assumed. In principle, then, shame may have strongly persisted, simply falling from the kind of contested status that would provoke debate. And we see, not surprisingly, that at least for several decades shame assumptions did continue in many settings, though not requiring elaborate explanations. In this case also we do not have an eighteenth-century baseline by which to measure the extent of change involved in nineteenth- and early twentieth-century trends.

Still, the patterns suggested by the graphs are at least highly probable—and will then be bolstered by the punishment and child-rearing evidence. Debates over shame probably increased in the early to mid-nineteenth century, reflecting doubts and disagreements—as in *The Scarlet Letter*. There is a close correlation in fact with the relative frequency trends for the word *punishment*. But then greater agreement that *shame* should be replaced or reduced steadily limited the need to refer to the term, setting up a new trend that would last, essentially, for a full century. At the same time, as noted in chapter 2, both U.S. and English use of the old word *shamefast* virtually, though not entirely, disappeared, suggesting a significant reduction in the need to describe personal qualities that might resist shameful behaviors.

The few historians who have paid attention to modern U.S. shame, Demos at their head, would add further illustrations even aside from the measurable shifts in criminal justice and parental standards. Thus abolitionists, though quite capable of pointing fingers of shame at slaveholders—William Lloyd Garrison thus loudly cried "SHAME! SHAME! SHAME!" in one treatise—on the whole relied on claims of guilt more strongly—a trend that would help explain changes in word frequency even in moralistic reform movements. Evangelical campaigns in the nineteenth century, far more than their eighteenth-century predecessors, also appealed to guilt as the emotional basis for seeking conversion: guilt in the face of Christ's suffering, and guilt to preachers and family members who labored so hard for the Christian life.[4]

Quite apart from the inherent generality in relying on relative word frequencies—again if this were our only evidence for a real decline of shame, we might be in trouble—the data suggest one other issue to which we must return. If, as seems clear, *shame* as a word and concept began to diminish in acceptability, what were the results for people who continued to encounter or utilize the emotion? While the social scientists who have talked about a modern U.S. taboo on shame are going too far—the term never disappeared, and its applicability certainly did not—it is true that a gap may have begun to open, even by the later nineteenth century, between actual emotional interactions, in which *shame* may have persisted or in a few settings even gained ground, and the vocabulary needed to articulate the results. When we return a bit later to the complexities in the decline of *shame*, this problem requires more focused attention. *Shame* the word almost certainly dropped off more decisively than shame the experience.

REFORMING PUNISHMENT Penal reform was a big topic in the Western world by the late eighteenth century. Primary attention focused on physical abuse—torture and overuse of capital punishment, and also the public settings in which many traditional corporal tactics were deployed. The most famous theorist, Cesare Beccaria, did not directly address shame at all. Shaming, to some extent, was simply attached to the wider review.

But shaming drew its own new critique. Thus Benjamin Rush, one of the nation's founding fathers, in 1787: "Ignominy is universally acknowledged to be a worse punishment than death. . . . It would seem strange that ignominy should ever have been adopted as a milder punishment than death, did we not know that the human mind seldom arrives at truth upon any subject till it has first reached the extremity of error." Rush even went so far as to advocate physical punishments, though administered in private, as a preferable alternative to shaming: "All public punishments tend to make bad men worse."[5]

British intellectuals and penologists addressed the problem of shame vigorously. Some supported shame, particularly if it could be internalized; this was David Hume's position. But more advised against shame, for several reasons: shaming returned criminals to society too quickly; it was cruel and counterproductive. Jeremy Bentham judged the utility value of shame to be negative.[6]

Debate would run through the nineteenth century, with the balance steadily tipping toward the reformers. The *New York Times* in a 1867 editorial blasted Delaware's obstinate refusal to end both shaming and public whipping (the state would yield only in the twentieth century, the last to do so). "If there had previously existed in the [criminal's] bosom a spark of self-respect this exposure to public shame utterly extinguishes it. Without the hope that springs eternal in the human breast, without some desire to reform and become a good citizen, and the feeling that such a thing is possible, no criminal can ever return to honorable courses. . . . With [the criminal's] self-respect destroyed and the taunt and sneer of public disgrace [figuratively] branded on his forehead, he feels himself lost and abandoned by his fellows."[7] Obviously a fundamental reconsideration was underway, yielding gradually increasing agreement that shaming was part of a barbaric past and that it was also demonstrably ineffective, indeed counterproductive—a view that many contemporary social psychologists dealing with penology continue to maintain vigorously.

Various kinds of arguments would go into the movement away from punitive shaming. In some instances, fears about rising crime rates might combine with increasing distrust of the soundness of community reactions. It would be far better to remove criminals, so they have time to ponder the error of their ways, than to restore them quickly to a corrupt society.[8] Some debates directly expressed a new fear that shaming procedures (with or without some physical torture) might be too short and therefore limited in impact: particularly when rising crime seemed a problem, the option of a longer exposure to punishment, but privately in jail, might seem attractive.[9]

But a more positive evaluation of the miscreant might come into play as well. People, even criminals, had a legitimate claim to dignity, and punishments that stripped this away would be both unfair and counterproductive. This is where shaming, like whipping, might now be judged "barbarous"—a term tossed about when the Massachusetts legislature moved in 1804 to abolish public stocks. The same sense informed a reaction to a shaming even in 1837: a naval officer disciplined drunken seamen by making them wear black bottles around their necks, in front of their fellows. His approach was quickly termed "scandalous and cruel," and he was court-martialed.[10] In yet another temporary vagary of the reform period, in some prisons convicts were shamed for violations of discipline, forced to stand before their fellows in the jail yard while holding placards or wearing a dunce cap.[11]

Between fears of rising crime, particularly property crime, and the new belief in human dignity lay a growing realization of the growing diversity of the population. Reformers in places like Massachusetts openly worried that shaming would have little effect when the audience was largely composed of mutual strangers: "Could your Honors but be spectators of . . . the negligence and unconcernedness" with which offenders now approached the stocks or the pillory, one observer lamented. One brief response, in the later eighteenth century, was to subject a miscreant to several public exposures for the same crime, to increase the community to which he was exposed; but this probably did not help much. And shaming now seemed to many observers also to generate resentment rather than contrition: "the punishment they have received has *destroyed* the fear of shame, and produces a desire of revenge, which serves to *stimulate* their vicious inclination," one commentator noted in 1784.[12] This concern could combine with the dignity impulse: a criminal might have had a "tolerable" character going into the shaming process, but now this would be ruined, leaving no recourse but heading back to crime. Popular resentments may have factored in as well, protesting disproportionate shaming of the poor; this was the implication behind a 1726 Philadelphia riot that destroyed the stocks, temporarily forcing the use of an out-of-the-way location that, authorities lamented, defeated the whole emotional purpose.

Whatever the balance of argument, a legal movement against public shaming, in the stocks or pillories, took shape quite early, in the northern and many of the border states during the first third of the nineteenth century (table 1). This was a tangible sign of the change in public emotional standards.

Debate continued, depending on the region, through the nineteenth century and beyond, despite the early start on reform recorded by some of the northern states. Delaware clung to public whippings and related shaming until the latter half of the twentieth century, though reformers began to push for a new approach 150 years before. Opponents of change in this state—and the discussion focused more on whipping than on shaming, in a context also informed by obvious racial tensions—objected to the cost of an alternative, penitentiary system, and to the notion that criminals would be publicly supported to refrain from productive work. They questioned challenging the "wisdom of the ages." Many claimed that neighboring Pennsylvania, which early opted for a penitentiary system, suffered higher crime rates. Old ways were best: "there is at the present day . . . far too much sensibility manifested toward criminals." But conservatives placed particular emphasis on the continued importance of public humiliation. "The public character of the punishment is its chief merit. The rascals who endure it care little for the pain, but they do not like to be seen."[13] Whether this argument referred to emotional distress, or to a belief that public recognition might make later thieving more difficult, was frankly unclear. It remained intriguing that, for whatever combination of reasons, shame's effectiveness claimed such support until modern standards finally caught up even with this tiny state.

TABLE 1. The abolition of public stocks

State	Date of Abolition
Massachusetts	1804–5
Vermont	1805
Tennessee	1829
Rhode Island	1835
Delaware*	1905

* Delaware was the last state to eliminate public stocks; it retained public whipping until 1952.

Overall, though obviously gradually and amid much disagreement plus important regional disparities particularly in the South, shaming punishments were increasingly linked with torture, with both approaches seen as "instruments of despotism," incompatible with the U.S. "free and humane" society. And at least for some time, the attractiveness of the modern prison as the clear alternative, where rehabilitation could take precedence over retribution, helped seal the deal, as one Tennessee reformer put it, to any "reflecting mind." Explicit shaming was increasingly separated from mainstream penology.[14]

CHILD REARING Child-rearing advice did not generate the explicit reformist rhetoric that applied to public shaming and other traditional punishments. Some leading manualists may not have been fully aware that they were replacing an older tradition in the first place, though others conveyed some sense of change. And the genre itself continued to be highly varied, with hymns to the gentle power of mothers' love coexisting with the surprisingly frequent references to children's deaths, eternal damnation—even in some cases the fate of imprisonment for the young charges who shunned virtue. Yet amid the variety there were two consistent points, and one other that was frequent though not invariable. First, shame was never recommended, and in some cases was directly attacked, on grounds of the damage it could do to the child and to a genuine, internal sense of right and wrong. Second, well into the later nineteenth century, insistence on obedience and a host of Christian virtues remained intense—shame did not yield because advice givers were trying to be soft on discipline. And frequently, finally, assumptions of obedience and supreme parental authority were coupled with references to happiness and cheerfulness, on the part of parents and children alike—and this moved child-rearing recommendations still further from any approval of shame.

Jacob Abbott, writing in what was many ways a strikingly traditionalist vein shortly before mid-century, urged that parents make it clear to children than any disobedience was ultimately disobedience against God and would reveal itself in God's punishments. The ultimate goal, however, was not obedience in and of itself, but a strong, internal sense of conscience. And this in turn required an ability independently to evaluate community pressures, including those of peers. "Unless you are sufficiently brave not to care if others laugh at you ... you will always be in difficulty." Exposing a child to the displeasure of others teaches the wrong lesson, for the goal is the internal compass, the deep understanding that bad acts are inherently bad, not simply bad because people say so. And what if the relevant community has the wrong standards? Even worse, obviously, unless the individual has the capacity for independent judgment.[15]

A standard disciplinary story, widely read, illustrates the difference between new approaches and earlier reliance on shame. A boy—who had had a rough day at the hands of schoolmates—hurts the family cat. His father calmly orders him to his room. The boy is regularly fed and cared for, but he has no other contact with family members until he finally, and quite sincerely, apologizes and shows his determination not to repeat the behavior. This was not shaming, or a psychological preparation for it. The entire family is sorry for the boy, they pray for him, they do not cut him off emotionally; they do not try to judge him as a person. The point is that the boy has internal work to do, without reference to an audience. It's guilt, not shame that will bring him around.[16]

More widely still, the lessons of the nineteenth century emphasized the harm bad actions did to loving family members and possibly other segments of the community. But now it was not their judgments that would generate proper behavior, but a guilty realization of the damage caused by misdeeds—and a desire to repair, if not to avoid in the first place.[17]

Increasingly, the most popular family advice, stressing the power of parental and particularly maternal love, created a clear alternative to any temptation to turn to shame. The child was an innocent; he or she would learn bad habits only from adults who displayed fear or anger. Proper child rearing involved, as Catharine Beecher put it, "great gentleness and patience," and consistent displays of maternal affection. The child should never be openly criticized or embarrassed, never exposed to a raised voice. Where discipline was needed—as would occasionally be the case—it should be offered with "tender sympathy," and without niggling insistence on petty rules that could not be nearly so important as the proper emotional atmosphere in the family. Should children become the "objects of ridicule or rebuke," their "sensibilities" will be "tortured into obtuseness or misanthropy." To be sure, this common approach avoided explicit reference to shame one way or the other, and it mounted no clear attack on colonial patterns. But the message was vivid enough even so: the children in this account have natures that are different from what many colonial Americans had assumed, they will respond to very different kinds of disciplinary guidance (and will be damaged by a more traditional approach), and their sense of self must be protected.[18]

Lydia Child echoed this common wisdom, but ultimately with a more direct message about shame. Here too, children must be shielded from bad passions. They must not be scolded, even when they themselves seem unjustifiably irritable: calm remains essential, and distractions by agreeable options must be preferred over implication that parental affection is being even temporarily modified. Parental good cheer is paramount, along with an eagerness to shower with affection at the first sign of apology. Children similarly should never be laughed at, nor should children learn that it is best to try to conceal a misdeed. The goal was a child with confidence and also the capacity to reject bad behavior because it is bad. "Punishments which make the child ashamed should be avoided. A sense of degradation is not healthy for character." On no account parade a child in front of others with some badge of misbehavior: of course community standards must be respected, but "when [the child is taught] to do right *because* people will approve of it, we begin at the wrong end." "What a change would take place in the world if men were always governed by internal passions," by the "honest convictions of their own hearts." After all, the community can also be wrong: "if young people are taught to regulate their actions by a dread of the world's laughter, they will be fully as likely to be deterred from good, as from evil."[19]

Guilt over shame; the inculcation of individual conscience over sensitivity to group judgments (with the further skepticism about whether "the community" can be counted on to be right); the interesting reference to shame now as "degradation"—these were the components of the increasingly popular approach. Lydia Child was resolute in the importance of obedience, high standards, good manners—hers was not a permissive text. But shame would not help at all. Rather, in the new wisdom, it was precisely the calm inculcation of clear rules that would produce not only good behavior, but good behavior "always cheerfully enacted"—as part of a happy home.

By the 1870s, the new advice—continuing to stress obedient behavior and a strong conscience—went beyond injunctions not to humiliate the child. Felix Adler actually invoked the concept of "self-esteem," noting that this quality, too, supported moral behavior. Shortly after 1900, Alice Birney, one of the first popularizers to pick up on psychological research, similarly advised against shame, without however using the term. Parents should not reprove their children in front of others (including relatives): this "causes [the child] pain out of all proportion to the offense and lessens his self-respect." Birney and many others began much more extensively praising individuality and creativity; they did not apply this to shame directly, but the incompatibility with group standards was clear enough. Thus Edwin Kirkpatrick even advised against modesty in a child: "The more pride and ambition a child has ... the better for his future development." Obviously, shame continued to be on the prohibited list in turn-of-the-century prescriptive literature, but without a huge sense that it required detailed comment. Rather, new work built on the earlier transition.[20]

And this pattern largely continued through the twentieth century. Writing in 1932 for the Child Association of America, two widely published popularizers emphasized how "undesirable" it was for a child to develop any deep sense of failure. Parents involved in toilet training a child must protect him "from an impression that there is anything shameful or disgusting about his behavior." Ongoing psychological research by Erik Erikson and others may have made experts more aware of shame's hold on children, while certainly reminding them of its dangers to self-worth. Thus Sidonie Gruenberg noted, in 1958, "To value his own good opinion, the child has to feel that he is a worthwhile person. He has to have confidence in himself as an individual. This confidence is hard for children to develop and there are many experiences that may shake it." The child "needs real and lasting self-respect if he is to develop."[21] None of this, however, by this point required much explicit reference to shame. It could now be assumed that respectable parents knew that shame should be minimized, not only in the home but in a child's contacts with other settings such as schools. Emphasis could be placed on the positive qualities a parent should enhance, not avoidance of past mistakes. Dr. Benjamin Spock would maintain this implicit confidence that shame was under control, emphasizing parental love and friendliness and the avoidance of rigid discipline of any sort. In his first edition, he had warned against using shame in toddler training—"never make an issue or shame the baby"—but otherwise he felt no need for elaborate cautions, and this approach surfaced even more strongly in later editions. At least in principle, a transition had been completed.[22]

When Ruth Benedict made her widely publicized claim, in a 1946 essay, that in the United States "shame is an increasingly heavy burden.... We do not expect shame to do the heavy work of morality. We do not harness the acute personal chagrin which accompanies shame to our fundamental system of morality," she was largely correct—but a bit behind the actual transformation in U.S. culture.[23]

CAUSATION

There's always a danger, in exploring a relatively new historical topic like shame, to become overexcited about transitions, to claim more significance than is warranted. After all, it is clear that premodern societies had handled shame in their own way, that changes in shame had occurred within the traditional orbit as well, and that people had surely reacted differently even within a single culture—save perhaps in the very smallest agricultural communities.

With all this, the reconsideration of shame that took shape in the early nineteenth century in the United States and Western Europe was arguably really important. An emotion that—with admittedly varied specifics—had been ubiquitous at least since the advent of agriculture, as part of both social and personal experience, was now being downgraded, perhaps for the first time. Whatever the beliefs of some contemporary social scientists, arguing for the clear evidence about the downsides of shame, there was nothing automatic about the movement away from the emotion.

Chapter 3 has suggested that an invocation of modernity is probably not a very fruitful explanatory path. Reconsiderations of honor deserve some attention—for example, in the growing attacks on the practice of dueling; but they highlight regional differentiation as well, as the South moved slowly in the directions urged by emotional reformers. Some aspects of urbanization might have played a role. Certainly many Americans were quite aware, by the later eighteenth century, that the really cohesive communities that had been built in the early colonial period were becoming more complicated, less homogeneous. This was widely noted in still-small towns like Dedham, Massachusetts, well before 1900. In other words, community growth may have seemed more disruptive than it would prove to be in some other cases, simply because of earlier expectations of cohesion, or exaggerated nostalgic recollections about the good old days. Add to this, by the early nineteenth century, a good bit of immigration—with Irish, Germans, and French Canadians affecting the urban environment. Add, further, a frequent sense that in-migration from the countryside was bringing to the cities a variety of hopelessly uncivilized frontier types. Some opinion setters may have concluded that U.S. society, and particularly its urban section, was becoming too complicated for shame to work well, at least at traditional levels and in traditional formats. Elements of this may have informed, for example, the belief that rising crime rates (some of which were more imagined than real) required new forms of punishment, which as we have seen formed part of the larger transition around shame. It is also important to note that, over time, the United States would also become a uniquely geographically mobile society, not only receiving immigrants and rural-to-urban migrants, but one in which people move from region to region in city and countryside alike; here is another factor to weigh, in this particular national case, in the community cohesion argument.[24]

Even here, however, and quite apart from the fact that it is hard to connect the reevaluation of shame in parenting to the emergence of small cities, note the intriguing variable. A key reason that shaming was attacked in penal reforms was a widespread sense that many miscreants were becoming scornful of community presence, more likely to lash out or seek later retribution than to accept the sting of shame and move on. This shift was not really an automatic product of a more urban environment, though this could be a secondary factor, but rather was a change on the part of the offenders themselves: a belief that individual autonomy now trumped collective norms.[25] There is no doubt that both U.S. and European authorities were having second thoughts, amid growing and possibly unruly cities, about the salutary impact of open displays. The concern applied primarily to physical punishments—whippings and executions—that now were to be scaled back but also converted to private settings, where mob passions could not be stimulated. But the thinking spilled over into shaming as well, as authorities recognized that some targets of shaming had always used public occasions to trumpet their rage and lack of remorse, and that crowds might not always side with the forces of order. Still, the overall reconsideration of shame—particularly in the familial context—depended less on new doubts about the urban environment, and more on a set of new cultural goals for which shame and shaming seemed unsuited.

For it was the set of new goals that most obviously redefined the terminology now being connected to shame. What had previously seemed a standard set of practices might now generate the word "ignominy." Shaming in childhood was no longer shaming, but "degradation." And the term *humiliation*, though not new, hovered over the reassessment as well, generating a greater rate of word use, during the decades of particularly intense debate, than shame itself—before then trailing off.

So what was going on? Fundamentally, the reconsideration of shame reflected a prior cultural shift toward a greater valuation of individualism and

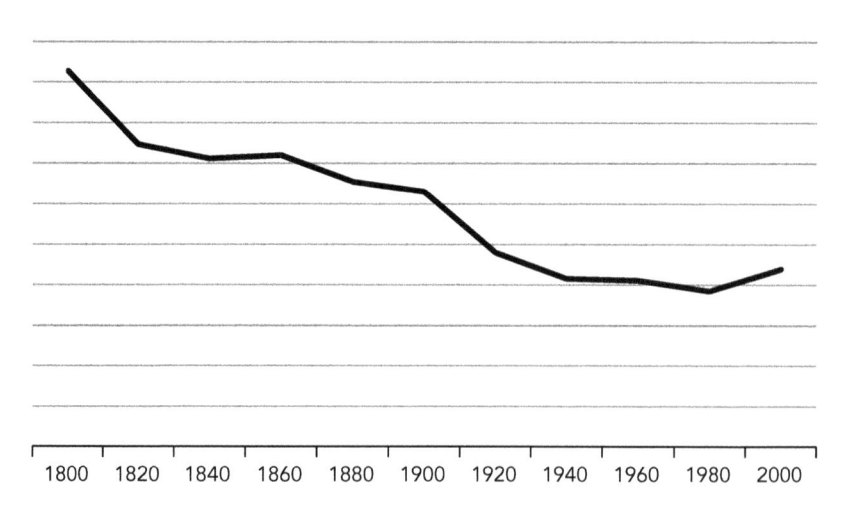

FIGURE 4. The frequency of the word *humiliation* in U.S. English, 1800s–2000, according to Google Books Ngram Viewer.

individual dignity; other developments, like urbanization or the gradual decline of honor or the emergence of new government capabilities in policing and imprisonment, contributed within this framework. Traditional levels of shame became unacceptable because the social-individual relationship was being recalibrated, in the United States as elsewhere in the Western world. The main point was the new incompatibility between beliefs about the individual and shame as a notoriously social emotional constraint.

Elements of the background for this redefinition are familiar enough. Enlightenment thought had highlighted a new view of the individual, no longer defined by individual sin, capable of improvement through rational education, deserving protection for key rights such as freedom of religion and of expression. Specific reformers like Beccaria had urged, on this basis, the sweeping reconsideration of traditional punishments, toward greater protection for personal dignity and, with this, greater effectiveness as well. His main target involved physical methods, including torture as well as capital punishment. As we have seen, however, actual debates over reform easily swept shaming into the same bucket—and indeed, given attention to the individual, shaming might now be considered a form of torture.[26]

Several historians have argued that the specifics of cultural innovation in the eighteenth century risk masking the more sweeping emergence of the new sense of individual self—what Nicole Eustace calls the "rising self," the product not only of Enlightenment rationalism but of the new early Romantic currents that gave greater visibility to individual emotion, even to new expressions such as novel kinds of consumerism designed, however inadequately, to convey personal identity to a wider audience.[27] The exploration of this new attachment to self has not, to be sure, been applied directly to shame, but the connections are fairly obvious. Self-focus would make community sanctions less tolerable, both to victims and potential enforcers; and it was often accompanied by a shift in the sense of privacy, which would further jeopardize the traditional approach.[28]

Further, while basic aspects of the cultural shift clearly were transatlantic, the American Revolution—for all its limitations—and the passions that had helped provoke it created a particular space for emotional redefinition in the new United States. Revolutionary rhetoric stressed the primary of personal liberty: "Hand down to Posterity pure and untainted the liberty . . . derived from our Ancestors." Liberty and the equally unsettling idea of the pursuit of happiness might easily translate into a review of the kinds of emotions that had previously played out in the public sphere. The establishment of the new republic created both need and opportunity to define a new kind of public life. The new constitution itself had thundered against "cruel and unusual" punishments, and this opened the door for the combined attacks on torture, on public performance, and by extension on shaming. A new idea of self might make many miscreants more defiant of community sanctions—though there is no precise evidence on this point, other than the sense of contemporaries that this aspect of shaming was encountering new resistance and that innovations in penology were essential in response.

The spur to a reconsideration of child rearing was less direct, though some child-rearing materials explicitly referred to the parental obligation to justify the new republic by instilling morality and independence in their offspring. More relevant was a growing distinction between the Evangelical religious tradition and a newly moderate mainstream Protestantism, which had direct bearing on shame.[29] Within this framework, a new type of family advice emerged in the early 1820s, Protestant in inspiration but no longer strictly denominational. At the same time, middle-class families in the United States were beginning to experience other key changes that could affect parental goals. At least in the northern states they were coming to feel a new level of obligation to provide education to their offspring, removing them from the kind of work obligations that had previously been attached to the operation of a family business, while also reducing the birth rate.[30] These classic changes could readily link with the larger emphasis on individualism. While education did not move away from drill and memorization toward some revolutionary new formula, successful students might arguably need qualities different from those instilled in children who had been destined more quickly to a life of work. Smaller family size created new opportunities for emotional ties between parent and individual child—and in fact, given paternal time in the workplace and corresponding absence at home, ties between mother and individual child became paramount. Finally, though this was nowhere yet explicitly discussed, the same developments—and particularly the decline of the child as an economic asset to the family—might prompt keen attention to that intriguing question: what, if not for work, was the function of the modern child in the family?[31]

The result, though not as openly revolutionary as the desire to create a new and U.S. response to crime, was a partial redefinition of what was sought in a child—a redefinition compatible both with greater individualism and with the need to reevaluate shame and shaming. Most obviously, without full awareness of the innovation involved, the authors of advice manuals began to argue that, in the modern family, a cheerful, emotionally responsive child should be a key parental goal. Obedience was still essential, but it too was now increasingly associated with cheerfulness. Discipline of course remained vital, but it must be reassessed, attached to ongoing assurance of familial love—it must, in fact, be moved away from shame.[32] Not surprisingly, it was also at this early nineteenth-century point that foreign observers began routinely to note the special place, including the special emotional place, that children seemed to occupy in the U.S. middle-class family. Facing new conditions, in a cultural context that increasingly stressed individualism and even happiness, many parents and most family advice givers had to turn away from reliance on shame. The emotional disruption that shame entailed, and even temporary withdrawals of parental affection, no longer made sense, and discipline had to be sought in other ways. The resultant change paralleled what was being sought in penal reform, but though less loudly trumpeted it would in fact prove far more durable and consistent.[33]

Pinning the reasons for significant emotional redefinition on cultural change is admittedly somewhat slippery. It might seem more precise to be able to point to more measurable correlations, such as urbanization or shifts in the political structure. But the cultural change was itself very real, and the effort to adapt U.S. emotion to the new, more individualistic criteria was a vital part of this larger process.

Shame's Persistence

COMPLEXITIES AND ADJUSTMENTS

Despite the very real movement away from traditional shame formulas, the emotion survived in the U.S. experience. This section notes continuities that are absolutely unsurprising, to be fully expected precisely because the basic change was so considerable. Shame had been socially useful before, and this utility did not suddenly cease, despite the more individualistic cultural context. New divisions about shame opened up, by region and social group. And new uses for shame and shaming emerged that now seemed essential—perhaps the most surprising finding. The overall result obviously adds complexity to the picture of a decline of shame. But it also raises questions about how ongoing or even novel experiences of shame might fit into a larger framework in which the emotion had less sanction, less familiar support. Is one of the reasons for the problematic aspects of shame in many contemporary societies, including the United States, the disparity that began to open up between an effort to downplay shame, in the interests of individual dignity, and its ongoing incidence? Does the history of actual shame, amid the various pressures toward its decline, call for a fuller recognition that the emotion remains inevitable?

This section does not pretend to offer a full account of shame and shaming in the United States between the mid-nineteenth and mid-twentieth centuries.

CHAPTER 4

The emotion's role in the military experience, where shame remains central even today except for growing awareness of exculpatory problems such as post-traumatic stress disorder, deserves more attention, to take one example. But the continuing interest in enlisting shame's service clearly emerges in the cases that follow.

We deal first with clear instances of continuity, in which regional and other differences also opened up amid the larger pattern of change. Concern for honor did not immediately die off, and this continued to depend on opportunities for both public and private shaming. A new idea of respectability recaptured some of the older shaming emphasis around sexual behavior and manners. In both cases, continuities would ultimately erode in favor of a fuller rejection of shame—but never to the point of complete abandonment.

School discipline forms an important category of its own. Here too, shaming displayed continuity with the past, but there were actually some novel needs to rely on the emotion as well. Ultimately, however, the newer social standards gained ground at least in principle, providing significant additional support for the implementation of emotional change—and additional evidence of its potentially confusing results.

Finally, several new, or at least partially new, shaming repertoires emerged in the nineteenth and early twentieth centuries. These were cases where new kinds of communities and community norms developed, plus at least in one instance where the federal government itself found a new reason to rally community emotional support. Larger efforts to limit shame might come into play, but they were constrained by the social needs involved.

HONOR AND RESPECTABILITY

Codes of honor, enforced by shame, declined more rapidly in parts of the United States than in many other societies, if only because, since the nation lacked a military aristocracy, such codes had been less deeply ingrained in the first place. But even so the decline was both gradual and uneven, and the result could maintain a commitment to shame and shaming well beyond the overall turning point.

Continuity has been explored particularly for the South, where among other things new penal systems took hold only slowly, amid considerable debate. Many southerners sought to rely on older community methods of discipline, and the impulse would extend well into the twentieth century. Thus in the early 1920s a young woman in the Ozarks, widely believed to be too free with her sexual favors, was greeted by a charivari—from which she could not recover and, simply left town. Many southern states long clung to the importance of public punishments, both those sanctioned by authorities and those—like lynchings and Ku Klux Klan activities—that were not, at least officially. Humiliating criminals remained a vital part of the process. Again, similar traditionalism continued to apply to many moral offenses, and here too the KKK participated after World War I, amid concerns about moral deterioration in society at large.[34]

The persistence of dueling notoriously reflected the continued hold of honor and shame. It was hard to let go of the practice, even when it began to be officially outlawed—in northern states from the late eighteenth century, in the South somewhat later. Even opponents of duels often expressed ambivalence when shame was involved. Thus a southern official, in the 1870s, noted that if avoiding a duel "would render an individual's life valueless, in his own eyes and in those of the community," it was better to go ahead and fight.[35] By the middle of the nineteenth century, challenges in the South were often directly reinforced by public shaming, through newspaper or pamphlet "postings" that advertised the cowardice of men who tried to duck a formal challenge. Dueling did begin to yield, even in the South, as public opinion gradually caught up with the law in viewing the practice as excessively violent and random, with the huge loss of life in the Civil War undoubtedly contributing to the reconsideration.

Honor and related shame did not disappear even then, of course—we discuss a newer version below, in the form of a novel boy culture and its contribution to the rise of modern sports. Even today, southern culture contains lingering vestiges of support for honor, and sensitivity to shame. It is true, however, that formal continuity in the United States was qualified by the new objections to shaming and the expansion of newer motives of self-advancement through business and profit.

Respectability—sometimes related to older ideas of family honor—offered a somewhat newer framework for shame in the nineteenth-century United States. Both sexual standards and "good" manners continued to provide both opportunity and need to keep the possibility of shame at least in active reserve.

There were however two changes in context. First, obviously, the older public shaming methods, a few regional efforts aside, were now abandoned; on the East Coast, at least, they were no longer in fact respectable. Second, community leaders now increasingly despaired of enforcing good habits in society at large—there was too much diversity and too much irresponsible behavior for this to make sense. Of course there was every reason publicly to lament the decline of public morals or the need, by the later nineteenth century, to countenance red-light districts in cities as a means of keeping the poison confined. Laws against sexual misbehavior, including adultery, remained actively on the books, as were prohibitions against "Sabbath-breaking." What was different, now, was the willingness to enforce. Increasingly, the new urban police forces tried to follow up only when the behaviors in question were "open and notorious," impossible to avoid, and above all capable of setting a visible bad example.[36]

These changes made it all the more important however to develop the capacity to define and maintain standards within one's own respectable group, and shaming—along, doubtless, with a growing preference to emphasize guilt—had an ongoing role to play.

Sexuality forms an intriguing case in point. Morals aside, middle-class Americans retained a huge stake in sexual regulation because of birth control needs. Unquestionably, more attention began to go into guilt as the key emotion in sexual self-regulation. The mid-nineteenth-century furor over masturbation involved relatively little appeal to shaming, instead applying a huge dose of guilt plus misguided health advice. The concomitant pressure on young women to feel responsible for preventing premarital sex was another area where Victorians sought self-control as an alternative to earlier community standards. But shame was alive and well in these conversations, if now a bit beneath the surface—and it also touched base with gender-specific shaming traditions from the past. Women worried about their reputations should they lose their virginity before marriage: shame anticipation strongly influenced behavior and also encouraged concealment, well into the twentieth century. A man could renounce an engagement, even divorce a wife, on evidence of premarital sex. A young woman learns that a man she knows has been accused of fathering an illegitimate child: "I fear it will injure me some. Although I never once went with him alone, I was in his company." Shaming also however extended to the efforts of many women reformers. In various U.S. towns and cities, new and eager groups might name adulterers publicly, might visit brothels and take the names of male clients, might visit employers of men who had made sexual advances to servants. Respectable middle-class America was, unquestionably, different from colonial America, but new or modified forms of shame loomed large.[37]

Respectable manners also required enforcement, as the U.S. middle class arguably imported the civilizing process Elias has described for early modern Europe. John Kasson has assessed the elaborate etiquette to which U.S. middle-class urbanites subscribed, deliberately intended to separate them from riffraff. Codes of dress, rituals of calling on friends complete with the proper personal cards, eating habits—all were subjected to detailed manners designed above all to signal restraint of appetite or excessive emotion. Children of course were trained young, at least in principle, and shaming stood in the wings for enforcement. Thus a student who was anxious about the increasingly rigorous standards for posture and sitting straight, and who expressed relief that she would sometimes be by herself was told, "You are never alone." Improper manners—for example, eating only with a knife, or smacking one's lips—were considered disgusting and, as a common phrase put it, "shameless." Etiquette books made it clear: manners were like laws, and a person could gain entry to good society—could avoid social shame—only by knowing and living up to them. How much an active sense of shame, or exposure to shaming, backed all this up is unclear. But emotional recognition of social standards was at the heart of the new regime.[38]

Rules on sex and manners, and shameful alternatives, were not confined to the middle class alone. Various working-class and immigrant groups, like the lace-curtain Irish or the Italians who carefully maintained etiquette around a cherished parlor, might develop similar standards and emotional enforcement.

Respectability shaming, like honor codes, would not fully survive into the mid-twentieth century. Here is another case of continuity that qualifies, but does not contradict, the larger process of declining reliance on or acceptance of shame. For by the interwar decades the extent of shame attached to sexual behaviors such as adultery was visibly declining—a point the Lynds noticed in comparing their Middletown of the 1930s to its counterpart just a decade before. Laxer sex was matched by what has been described as an "informalization" of manners, a reduction in rigid and elaborate codes, that arguably would reduce the potential for shame at noncompliance. Shame would not disappear—we must deal later with the revival of what is now known as "slut shaming" in the sexual sphere. But intensities did decline in some ways at least, reducing the contradiction with efforts at shame control in other areas.[39]

SHAME IN SCHOOLS

U.S. schools would ultimately participate strongly, though also incompletely, in the new moves against shame and shaming, but the relationship between the larger social trends was delayed and remains complicated even today. Shaming actually increased in the decades after 1850, even as it began to decline in the family. Some very plausible reasons explain the disparity. Ultimately, the wider standards would have an impact, but the schooling-shame interaction remained distinctive, in part perhaps because of initial hesitations, more obviously because of the tensions inherent both in peer culture and in the teacher-student hierarchy. Shaming had always been heavily directed at children as part of their socialization, and while child-rearing advisors attacked this pattern, it surfaced strongly in the expanding realm of mass education.

School shaming of course had a long history, in colonial America and in many other premodern societies, so ongoing shaming patterns in part reflected simple habit. But more was involved as, for many decades in the nineteenth century, the emotional trajectory in the schools was simply at odds with the approach to shame now being recommended in other settings. Reliance on shame went up, not down—and intriguingly, parents for a considerable time did not seem to mind. Either the parents were simply not registering the new advice, which is quite conceivable; or they were willing to create a new gap between what their offspring could expect at home and what they encountered in the classroom; or, as is quite possible in a transitional period particularly, parents were responding differentially to the new signals about emotion.[40] Parents sending children to the common schools thus might well differ from those with access to more elite educational choices.

U.S. schools would ultimately incorporate key elements of the larger emotional trend. But there was considerable lag, and a number of good reasons for the delay. This means in turn that when schools did begin to turn more systematically against shame, they might face more than a traditional residue of resistance, for example from practicing teachers. It means that many students continued to experience shaming in one part of their life, even as some of them picked up new signals, for example from parents, that shame was now a degrading experience. The complexity of the transition, and its aftereffects, deserve attention. Emotions history, a rising subfield, has yet to be applied to the educational realm, and shame is a revealing place to start.

We begin with that classic symbol of school shaming, the dunce cap, whose actual history is surprisingly obscure. We know that the idea of the cap derives from the medieval philosopher Duns Scotus, who believed that wearing a conical cap would focus intelligence. Scotus's work fell into disfavor, and by the seventeenth century *dunce* meant dullard, particularly in school settings. An early seventeenth-century reference in England cites a dunce's table, at which the less successful students were required to sit. The first explicit mention of a cap appears in Charles Dickens's 1840 novel, *The Old Curiosity Shop*. Whatever the intermediate history, it is clear that dunce caps were alive and well in many U.S. classrooms in the later nineteenth century and into the twentieth, and they intended to embrace both poor performance and misbehavior. A cited student sat facing the corner of a classroom, cap on head, for some designated period of time, sufficient though to make his (or less commonly, her) shame clear to the student as well as to the rest of the class. Only gradually, and in terms of the larger history of reproving shame surprisingly belatedly, would the dunce cap make a definitive exit.[41]

Why this prolonged, arguably increased reliance on school shame, and what is the other evidence?

Some part of the lingering relationship between shame and schooling simply involves momentum from earlier emotional standards. *McGuffey's Reader*, for example, that staple of grade school instruction from 1836 into the twentieth century, refers to shame as if children can readily be expected to know both the emotion and the warning flags it was meant to raise. The third edition of the book intones against "falsehood and deception." "Oh how dreadful must be the confusion and shame, with which the deceitful child will then be overwhelmed." Intriguingly, it went on to warn that lying would prevent a person from getting into heaven because the angels would attest to the disgrace, a nice twist on community standards: salvation could be blocked, essentially, by angelic shaming power: "Shame, shame on the child who has not magnanimity enough to tell the truth." Other references to shame, though more routine, again assumed ready recognition: "Some men are the shame of their country," for example.[42]

But more than reading matter, and more than continuity, was involved in school shame in the later decades of the nineteenth century. Laura Ingalls Wilder describes an interesting transition in one of her novels. Almanzo Wilder starts his schooling with a vivid recollection of how an older brother used to come home bruised from beatings by his teacher. But his own experience is different: light physical punishments but, when for instance he was unable to spell a word, he had to stay in at recess to learn it properly—and "was ashamed because he was kept in with the girls."[43] Similarly, Mark Twain's Tom Sawyer was shamed for his poor schoolwork by having to repeat himself over and over in front of mocking classmates.

School reports from the 1840s onward indicate a very conscious movement away from physical punishments—but a concomitant insistence that along with this, schools must be given full disciplinary authority otherwise. Parents were urged not to believe what their children told them about discipline, and schools widely dismissed complaints from parents as a function of familial overindulgence. Precisely because corporal punishment was being controlled, it seemed essential to retain all other disciplinary options—and no non-corporal punishment could really be excessive.[44] Normal schools, at the same time, were placing new emphasis on teacher authority and the need to convince students that the teacher's gaze was inescapable, her watchfulness ever-present. And there is some evidence, additionally, that many parents actually agreed, in part because they too were particularly eager to support the abandonment of physical discipline for their children, and in part perhaps because they too still saw shaming as natural. Further, many teachers, concerned about retaining control, found some combination of physical threats—little or no actual beating, but ominous reference to the possibility—with shaming a feasible approach. Additionally, common practice involved keeping "punishment books" that would facilitate identifying troublemakers—a good basis for targeting shame.[45]

Some of the most explicit reliance on shaming, including the use of dunce caps or other means of singling misbehaving children out in front of their peers, seems to have prevailed particularly in rural and frontier conditions, as in the West and Midwest both in the United States and Canada. One-room schools might for example supplement the dunce cap with a practice of drawing a dot on the chalkboard at the front of the classroom and insisting that a miscreant stand with nose on the dot for a period of time—thus combining some real physical discomfort, though not outright corporal punishment, with shaming. Practices of this sort persisted even as, on the urban East Coast, the more blatant shaming traditions were coming under serious review.[46]

Laura Ingalls Wilder, again, discusses the tension between big-city teacher idealism and actual rural conditions in her novels. In *Little House on the Prairie*, the new teacher struggles greatly with discipline, hoping that students will like her so she can rule by love, not fear.[47] But her charges do not understand, so she has to turn to shaming, requiring students who behave badly to stand in front of the class while writing apologies over and over again on the chalkboard (ultimately, even this approach fails, and the teacher has to resign). Caddie Woodlawn, a character in another pioneer novel, similarly stresses the importance of firm, noncorporal discipline, centering around trying to make classroom bullies feel bad about themselves.[48] The ideal was that moral authority, backed by shame, would be enhanced by avoiding the physical, creating even firmer control over a classroom—though in this case, too, ideal and reality clashed, and the teacher had to depend on some boys who were willing to beat the bullies up.

Not surprisingly, teachers themselves commented on the disciplinary process. Sophia Wyatt penned a diary entry in 1854, complaining that parents "sometimes chide their children too severely"—an interesting anticipation of later teacher concerns about the morale of the child. But she also worried about parental interference in discipline. "Without the aid and cooperation of parents, it will be extremely difficult for the best and most accomplished teacher, to keep a good school. Even if the rules are stringent, and the laws severe, it is no part of wisdom for the parents to object to them in front of their children.... A word of advice, or a few moments spent in helping [children] is of unspeakable benefit to them."[49] Admittedly, it is not entirely clear whether shaming was part of the regulatory package and whether in this instance parents are beginning to object. But the disciplinary concern certainly established a context in which shaming might seem valid, even essential.

For shaming of various sorts persisted or even increased into the later nineteenth century and beyond for several reasons—including, of course, established custom plus the inherent temptations of exploiting classroom hierarchy with its obvious privileging of the teacher as authority. The battle over physical discipline was very real, and only gradually successful, which meant that many teachers might actually take pride in relying on shame instead—but also feel that shaming was absolutely essential as the other traditional disciplinary prop was being challenged. The rise of women teachers created real fears about maintaining authority, particularly in more isolated settings. Women worried about their lack of physical strength compared with some of the older boys, which could heighten their dependence on shaming. The larger effort to boost the authority of the teacher, and to downplay the use of students as classroom monitors, heightened claims to moral as well as academic superiority.

Signs of change began to emerge in the later nineteenth century, though the movement was long somewhat tentative. Some new approaches have a strikingly modern ring, despite differences in language. Growing numbers of teachers and teacher-educators began to stress the responsibility of making classes interesting and engaging, within a cheerful classroom context and without making impossible demands on students themselves. This did not attack shaming directly but clearly sought an alternative.

A Missouri school journal thus in 1898 told the story of a Latin teacher whose class was visited by a local journalist, unfortunately on a day the students were not performing very well. The journalist, shocked, tried to embarrass the students for their ignorance. But the teacher, praised for his vision, responded that "it seems to me that the wise thing to do would be to do everything in our power to . . . help the boys and girls."[50] Step back and ask a bit less; provide more guidance; do not try to shame. Again, emphasis was on the positive, not a critique of some past shaming regime. Learning should be fun, and teachers should be seen as encouraging, not censorious. Classrooms should be places of laughter, not fear.

A Connecticut school official urged against expecting or even desiring servile students. In a successful classroom there is "no oppressive silence reminding of the tomb . . . but life, energy, enthusiasm are manifested in every movement." Intellect and emotion should be trained together, but if choice were needed the heart should come before the head: "the great ruling power in a school, the essential power, should be Love"—and this meant that the arbitrary disciplinary authority of the teacher must be stripped away, replaced by a resolutely positive approach.[51]

Shifts of this sort corresponded to more formal thinking by progressives like F. W. Parker and ultimately John Dewey himself. Parker talked about education freeing the human spirit, moving away from any sense of oppression. Students should learn self-motivation, self-discipline, rather than be subjected early on to control by external sources. Dewey would add his deep concern about reintegrating and rehabilitating those who had faltered, another strike against substantial reliance on shame.[52]

But while the change in tone moved school thinking closer to the kinds of advice middle-class parents had been getting about shame and shaming, it did not actually generate a systematic attack on residual practices. Teachers in many schools continued to stand students in front of the class, as a disciplinary measure, or put them in a corner with dunce caps, at least through the first decade of the twentieth century, without eliciting any clear outcry either from parents or colleagues.[53]

Routine reliance on shaming was then given an additional boost by the shifts in classroom composition in many public schools during the first third of the new century. Teachers, worried about discipline in any event and conscious of the ways their authority might be utilized, now confronted an increasingly diverse student body due to the unprecedented volume of immigration into the United States. Dealing with students with different cultural habits, sometimes with imperfect English language skills, in a climate shaped more generally by widespread assumptions about "racial" superiorities and inferiorities, many teachers undoubtedly found shaming a logical response—another case where shaming and hierarchy went hand in hand. And some immigrant groups may have implicitly agreed, given the emotional practices in their own cultures. Some Jewish parents for example urged their children to avoid anything that would elicit shame, lest the results reflect not only on the students but on the Jewish population more generally.[54]

Further, the emotion could also now be applied beyond conventional discipline and acceptable academic performance. After World War I shaming was also extended to hygiene, as a variety of forces converged to make schools a center for dealing with real or imagined deficiencies in the immigrant population. The American Cleanliness Institute, founded in 1927 and backed by leading soap manufacturers, saw school students as a prime audience for the standards they were preaching. As the institute advised, "the objective of all cleanliness teaching is the establishment of lifelong cleanliness habits." Shockingly, as it turned out, most schools did not require children to wash their hands before meals or after using the toilet. And the goals had to go beyond deficient schools themselves: students should make their homes and families responsible for good hygiene as well. This was a setting ripe for shaming. The institute conveniently provided uplifting stories and posters, but there was nothing better than public display before one's teacher and classmates. So students were told to "report on days they take baths at home." Children were enrolled in classroom "health towns," and expelled for a time if they fell down on one of the hand-washing requirements—"removed . . . until he had again proved himself worthy to have a residence there." Officially, the promoters of these campaigns urged positive rather than negative reinforcement. "Be careful not to hurt the feelings of the child with the skin trouble." Standards should not be too high, a morning inspection should stress the kids who were really clean rather than highlighting those who were not. Still, shaming was a fundamental aspect of this new campaign, and directed not just at individual children but at their home environments. Practices such as periodic lice checks, with unavoidably public results, clearly linked emotional responses with social hierarchies within the school itself.[55]

Tradition, teachers' concerns including the movement away from corporal punishment, and apparent new needs given changes in the student mix and the temptations of hierarchy all supported a wide use of shame into the mid-twentieth century, in marked contrast to the more decisive earlier shifts concerning child rearing and penology. Only after World War II was the disjuncture finally, and more systematically, addressed. Leaders in teacher education began to emphasize the importance of maintaining each child's self-respect. Formal shaming had no place in this new environment, at least to the extent that teacher initiatives were involved. At the same time, less overt uses of the emotion persisted, seemingly an essential part of classroom management for many teachers.

Change did occur, as earlier emphases in child-rearing advice began to be somewhat more systematically incorporated into teacher norms. Parents themselves, increasingly eager to protect their offspring, became more sensitive to real or imagined slights in the classroom. New expertise, particularly from authorities like Erik Erikson, though pessimistic about the possibility of eliminating shame altogether, called growing attention the emotion's devastating effects, its potential for undermining a child's self-image. In this vision, adults must avoid any additional burdens to the adjustment process. It was also at this point, in the 1950s, that more systematic attention began to be paid to classroom management in general; teachers might now be rated on their ability to stress positive behaviors and to avoid classroom disruptions (not necessarily fully compatible goals), while the whole effort to bureaucratize the teaching framework might in itself discourage idiosyncrasies in shaming.[56]

The results show clearly in teacher training films produced as early as the 1950s, which specifically characterized and reproved shaming methods. In one a hapless math teacher, "Mr. Grimes," berates his class: "the poorest class I've had in a long time"; "you don't know what study means"; "lazy."[57] The shaming atmosphere first convinces many students that there is no point trying; second, it leads to mocking defiance; and finally, it effectively eliminates any constructive interactions. The class is lost because of this outdated emotional framework. The film makes it clear that teachers must take a friendly approach to their students and never embarrass them—though a residual role for shaming persists in the idea that, properly guided, students may usefully shame each other into better academic work.

This new wisdom led to a clear termination of the various practices that had been used to shame students before their peers, but there was more besides. Alternatives were now provided: instead of shaming, a miscreant student was now "sent to the principal's office"—a move to privatize punishment intriguingly similar to the earlier shift, in penology, from public shaming to private imprisonment (with the principal's office presumably a much milder experience). Principals by this point were being separated from regular teachers more clearly, and acquisition of a role as chief disciplinarian was one of the key results.[58]

A host of other moves shifted attention away from shaming. From the 1960s onward, and beginning in California, growing investment was directed toward student self-esteem. A greater variety of learning and other activities aimed to give students more chances for a positive experience. Grade inflation and other practices, such as multiple class valedictorians, also eased shame potential, and then in the 1970s, though only at the higher education level, new laws prohibited traditional options such as the public posting of grades—again, designed to limit exposure to classmates' scorn.[59] Even critiques of self-esteem maintained the commitment to downplay shame: "There is no shame in failing; there is only shame in failing to try."[60]

In this context, the most overt shaming practices really did decline. And when a teacher might seek to revive them with appropriate new twists—as in the case of an Idaho teacher in 2012 who allowed her fourth-grade charges to apply colored markers to the faces of classmates who had not measured up to reading standards—the administrative and public outcry was immediate, with the teacher forced to stop the practice. Or in Ohio, a teacher who required a bully to listen to complaints from his classmates without opportunity for response was accused of shaming and quickly dismissed.[61]

Yet, while education leaders clearly wanted to see schools not only abandon shame but develop clear and positive alternatives, or at least avoid complaints from a now-sensitive school community, a full merger with the kinds of standards still being recommended for parents simply did not take place. Schools did not in fact ban shaming, as experts continued to urge parents to do. School and home situations differed. Parents—who in practice did not fully renounce shame either—were dealing with small numbers of children; indeed, in the post–Baby Boom household averaging no more than two kids, at a physical distance from their suburban neighbors, it was in any event actually difficult to find a familial or community audience for shaming. Not so with schools, where teachers continued to highlight how difficult classroom management proved to be in practice. Not just numbers of children, but new pressures to improve academic performance and test results, while guarding against drug use and other social ills, put a premium on effective discipline. And when positive measures did not suffice, when challenging students did not respond to appeals to self-esteem, quiet forms of shaming might seem the only recourse—all in addition to the obvious fact that, in many school settings, student peer groups eagerly engaged in shaming as part of establishing hierarchies and boundaries.[62]

Several common practices, by the later twentieth century, reflected what was in essence a modified approach to shame. Many teachers sought to avoid the ploy of sending problem children to the principal, because this would disrupt the class and signal to administrators a management failure. But this further enhanced the need to use moderate shaming as an alternative. Instead of chastising a disruptive student directly, teachers were urged to say his or her name aloud repeatedly, by asking questions—implicitly exposing the miscreant to classroom scorn. Another protocol was to distribute green, yellow, and red cards to students, with individual names attached, moving student names to different colors to indicate openly how they are behaving on a given day. Yet another was to chart student progress—in reading levels or arithmetic—as in the "data wall" fad, where grades on classroom exercises were prominently posted in the classroom as a motivational device that, some claimed, more clearly shamed rather than inspired the lower achievers.[63] A host of widely available classroom management products sought to facilitate approaches of this sort. And it continued to be tempting to identify minority students as particularly likely to warrant shaming discipline—the relationship between the emotion and hierarchy continued in many quiet ways.

Change had occurred. Classic practices had disappeared. Teachers, their supervisors, and community audiences were more sensitive to shame than had been the case before, and they were certainly more eager in principle to adopt as alternatives positive inducements that built on students' self-respect. Yet the transition was incomplete and possibly had to remain incomplete. New practices were supported by new arguments, the shaming component ignored, in part because the emotion was no longer widely discussed. A surprisingly checkered history, over the past century and a half, helps explain as well as illustrate the ongoing ambiguities. The history of modern school shaming is a vital window into actual U.S. emotional life, and the complexities form a prime example, as well, of the larger barriers that the modern movement away from shame might encounter from established groups and institutions. Most important, the ongoing encounter with shame in the schools continued to contribute to the emotional experience of many young people. Some might learn, in the classic pattern, how to anticipate the unpleasant emotion and avoid its application. Others might find its unpleasantness now compounded by its contrast with the dominant rhetoric about individuality and personal esteem.

New Paths for Shame

Several of the most decisive contraindications on shame may have resulted from much newer venues, though of quite different sorts. This section takes up, first, the somewhat unexpected emergence of shame, from the late nineteenth century onward, in the culture of boys and the related environment of organized sports; and second, a much different exposure to shame given new attitudes and possibilities around poverty and business failure; and finally, more briefly, an intriguing venture by the U.S. government to seek support from shame as it dealt with distinctive problems in military recruitment. Many of these patterns continue to feed into shame cultures, helping to explain the greater complexity that would emerge after the 1960s.

BOYS, MEN, AND SPORTS

The experience of U.S. boys changed in the nineteenth century in many ways. Particularly important was the rise of schooling and the increasing importance of social contacts based on age-graded cohorts, often seeking greater independence from parental supervision. In this context, many groups of boys spontaneously produced a set of standards that in turn used the prospect of shame as the key to acceptability. Vocabulary reflected the pattern. The word *sissy*, introduced in the 1840s as an affectionate term for sister, had by the 1880s migrated to become one of the great shaming terms in modern U.S. history, along with other terms such as *crybaby*. The boy who could not control his fears, who could not accept a variety of "dares" to prove his courage, was a shamed outcast. A variety of new games tested boys in the group, with shame the enforcer. Boys challenged each other to jump into deep water, walk across lake ice, run long distances, endure being hit with a hard ball in an odd game called "soak-about." And of course the proper boy should be able to stand up to a bully on his own, with shame a response to caving in.[64]

What was occurring, clearly, was a seemingly spontaneous creation of a kind of honor culture, as a means of establishing boyhood identities in a new setting. Worried about the results, adults did gradually intervene with more organized and supervised activities, such as scouting, and by extensions of school supervision. But of course the shaming culture continued to some extent and could be adapted by groups of boys, for example in key urban immigrant settings.

Ultimately, however, the most durable instantiation of boy shaming emerged in the organized sports gained ground from the late nineteenth century onward. U.S. sports were deliberately touted as a maker of men, in a period when worries about women's roles and feminization established obvious opportunities for shaming. References to an athlete "throwing like a girl" and to the members of a poorly performing team as "ladies" probably emerged quite early. Epithets involving homosexuality reflected a period in which increased public shame attached to this phenomenon as well.[65]

The results surrounded sports performances with the potential for shame in many ways. Athletes taunted each other. Parents would, at least later in the twentieth century, join in shaming references to other teams, sometimes to their own disappointing offspring.

But the most coherent focus for sports shaming emerged in the practices of many coaches. Initially focused simply on teaching youngsters the rules and physical skills of unfamiliar games such as football, coaches began in the 1900s to turn to a wider motivational role—as in turn they gained increasing attention and encountered increasing pressure to churn out winning teams. Thus Andy Smith, a highly successful coach at the University of California Berkeley in the 1910s and 1920s, routinely assailed players in front of their teammates if they seemed to be "quitters." In one case he berated a running back for not charging his tacklers headfirst: "Why are you hitting the line with your ass?" He then chased the unhappy back off the field, kicking at him all the way. Bill Reid, at Harvard University, used shame abundantly, not only in public settings but in notes to key players. A letter to one athlete before the 1905 season sought to spur through shame: "With your big body and splendid physique you have enormous possibilities, if you will only command your body"; and "The attitude at present seems to be one of lordly indifference, a sort of well 'I'd like to make the team if it's convenient' attitude." And when the athlete had the temerity, right before the Yale game, to say that a good grade in calculus was more important to him, Reid replied openly: "I don't see how a man can help feeling that hardly anything is more important than to beat Yale."

Shaming, often enforced by screaming voices as well as insults, built into many coaches' styles. The formula would gain ground, reaching perhaps a peak with the performances of people like Alabama's Bear Bryant in the 1950s or, in basketball, Bobby Knight. Despite skepticism that the tactics would work on grown men, the practices were exported into professional sports by football legends such as Vince Lombardi, who used shame not only against poor performance but against showing up for a season overweight, or, in baseball, by Tommy Lasorda. The rise of hard-nosed U.S. sports clearly institutionalized shame in a host of new ways. And the U.S. public, if dimly aware of the actual experiences, celebrated many practitioners not only for their victories but their redeeming toughness.[66]

Conventional wisdom suggests that sports shaming would recede from the 1960s onward, partly because African American athletes, newly inspired by the civil rights movement, would simply not stand for that kind of imposition. And certainly, many coaches, perhaps a growing number, consciously resisted shaming, and a large movement grew up around pointing out the hideous effects of the shaming style: the erosion of self-respect, and the foolhardy insistence on competing despite injury.

But the practice continued, spreading to additional sports, affecting high school as well as college levels and, intriguingly, increasingly involving women as their own athletic commitment expanded. Thus a woman's swim coach in the early twenty-first century, dressing down one of her charges in front of the whole team after a subpar performance: "You are not committed to this team. Your effort was unacceptable today. You have disappointed me and let your teammates down. . . . Now I want you to apologize to your teammates for letting everyone down and doing so badly." College athletes across a range of sports continue to express astonishment when their coach does *not* seek to shame them—a testimony to an interesting ability to accept and manage the emotion, but also to the durability of what otherwise might seem an outdated, as well as reprehensible, emotional style.[67]

FAILURE SHAME

The attachment of shaming to poverty and business failure was quite different from sports shaming, for it did not involve a clear audience—the enforcers of shame instead lay inside many a victim's head, imagining a community that was ill-defined at best. A concept of honor was involved in a way, but not the same as that driving boys and athletes. In both cases, however, new or largely new standards set the stage for important changes in potential emotional experience.

Two developments framed a new anxiety, and shame potential, around economic failure in the nineteenth century, and though neither was brand-new in Western culture there is no doubt that a dramatic intensification occurred. The potential for business failure went up: about half the enterprises formed during the nineteenth century would go under, providing widely visible marks of the businessman's inadequacy. Supplementing this was the growing system of commercial credit ratings; though confidential in principle, these could heighten the sense that the community was watching, that new reputational penalties attached to lack of success. And the credit reports themselves, whether well concealed or not, dished out plenty of shame: phrases like "worthless and always will be" were common. It was widely realized, as one historian has put it, that there was no greater failure than "the failure to keep up to par."[68]

The shamefulness of poverty was more diffuse. The reigning middle-class work ethic made it clear that men were authors of their own fortune, and he who did not climb the ladder had only himself to blame. As British author Samuel Smiles put it, "poverty is the portion of those not strong enough to provide for themselves." Particularly in U.S. culture, the opportunity to blame bad luck, or society, or position at birth was limited at best. And there is little doubt that many workers, at least, internalized some of the resultant shame, not only in the nineteenth but in the twentieth century as well: "If I had been a better person, like if I had made something of myself, then people couldn't push me around." Or as a garbage man put it, quite simply, "nobody's fault but mine."[69] Ironically, workers afflicted with the shame of failure might tighten the emotional strings for others, as in the widespread twentieth-century scorn for welfare recipients—who felt shame aplenty even without the additional stigma.

Shame at failure could be hard to shake off—like shame as an emotion more generally, for unlike guilt it could not easily be repaired.[70] It is admittedly difficult to judge the pervasiveness of the emotion, despite the identifiable cultural context. Scholars who have worked on the issue, like Richard Sennett, tend to combine persuasive generalizations with relatively few specific examples. But we know that shame can bite, and not only through scattered quotations. The phenomenon of suicide in response to business failure was already being noted in the United States as early as 1819.[71]

Obviously, different sources of modern shame could reinforce each other. Teachers who identified poor performance in school, and sometimes shamed it, could set up a sense of alienation that would then carry over into the student's later economic life, enhancing the potential for real or imagined failure and for

CHAPTER 4

possible resentment as well. Success in a masculine subculture might help a bit, most obviously through athletic talent and grit, but the combinations were complicated and it was not easy to assure success.[72]

WAR AND SHAME

War, not surprisingly, brought out new or renewed opportunities to experience or deploy shame. During the Civil War, the Union military used cloth letters to brand some soldiers drunks, deserters or rogues. Shame of a different sort visited many Confederate soldiers who could not prevent Union troops from disrupting their homes and families, particularly during Sherman's march. Both in the Civil War and again during World War I, shame at the possibility of being labeled a coward almost certainly motivated more acts of bravery than courage did. And while newer ideas, such as the growing recognition of battlefield stress, modified the military role of shame somewhat, particularly from World War II and beyond, the connections remain vivid still.

A less expected, but revealing and related, use of shaming awaited U.S. entry into World War I, which is where the more innovative use of shame materialized. The issue was raising an army, and fast. Civil War drafts had not worked well, and the subject had been much disputed since that time; indeed, many new Americans had immigrated in part to escape military conscription back home. But dependence on volunteering alone did not suffice, so registration was quickly required. And recruiters draped this effort in shame. Public parades and honors identified by name those who had obeyed the new law and signed up, with offenders shamed at least by omission. More important, the government threatened to publish the names of violators, openly branding them as "slackers." And the tactic could work: one recruit, who had hoped to avoid the military, ruefully noted that were he not to comply "at best I could never hold my head up again." Once signed up, of course, shaming could continue, as drill sergeants openly humiliated recruits as part of teaching blind obedience.[73]

• • •

Continuities and adaptations of honor and respectability; the clearly and ambivalent decisions about shaming in school; and the new paths for shame yield a few, admittedly fairly obvious, overall conclusions. Shame did decline, but unevenly and inconsistently. The change, though complicated, was important in itself, and part of a wider U.S. turn away from interest in openly accepting "unpleasant" or negative emotions. At the same time, the growing unwillingness to continue to discuss shame, at least by name, may have rendered responses to the emotion's continued importance much more difficult, harder to label and evaluate. The checkered evolution, between the mid-nineteenth and the mid-twentieth centuries, is consistent with the idea that some degree of shame is part of an innate emotional arsenal. It is even more consistent, however, with an emphasis on the apparent social (and sometimes political) need for attempting to enforce shame in complex societies, to discipline but also to set examples by encouraging emotional anticipation. Even as the emotion declined, shame continued to help some groups and institutions establish identity. It continued to express hierarchy, marking new criteria as demonstrating inferiority and—without normally using the term—shamefulness. If no longer as directly employed in supporting morality—Ruth Benedict's claim here may have been correct—shame certainly continued to enforce a number of important value systems. Clearly, the emotion proved to be extremely resilient.

Did the shame that did persist now raise more problems than it had in more traditional societies, because the emotion was less prepared and sanctioned, less carefully framed? Some people—successful athletes, for example, raised in homes that sought to minimize shame—surely learned how to juggle different emotional communities, depending on context; contradictory signals did not always create a problem. But it could, and this issue would take on even greater urgency in the later twentieth century, after the decline of shame came to an end. Even by mid-century, it is safe to conclude that a potentially troubling gap had opened between continued experiences of shame and the declining availability of larger social guidelines for the emotion and for its social role. The experience of shame, for example in the schools, might seem even more unpleasant than had traditionally been the case, because of the availability of conflicting signals about individual worth. However unsurprising, there is no question that, in a number of settings, change was complicated by a variety of contradictory patterns, both old and new.

Attacking Shame: Larger Western Patterns

While developments in the United States suggested a few distinctive features—like the reform enthusiasm that built in the northern states around the creation of a new republic, free from "old-world" abuses—the main factors that pressed for reconsideration of shame were shared with Western Europe. Here is a final context requiring brief comment, as part of the wider understanding of the unprecedented, if complicated, modern attack on shame and shaming.

European developments have not been explored along all the lines suggested in the preceding discussion of the U.S. case—for example, concerning complexities in the use of shame in schools.[74] Here is another opportunity for

CHAPTER 4

more comparative historical analysis. In broad outline, however, efforts to limit shame in nineteenth-century Europe confirm many of the causes that operated on the other side of the Atlantic, while also reflecting some of the hesitations that any review of this sort would generate. There was a Western, not just U.S., interest in reconsidering shame that contrasted in many ways with the more modest East Asian adaptations during essentially the same period.

Above all, Enlightenment cultural values stimulated extensive debates in Europe, as in the United States, over many of the traditional public uses of shame. Thus there was considerable overlap between U.S. reconsideration of shame, and innovations in European law and culture. Overall comparative differences were nuanced, at best. British shame references show essentially the same chronological pattern as those across the Atlantic: a strong peak early in the nineteenth century, when shame was under serious discussion particularly in penology, and then a fairly steady decline into the mid-twentieth century—and in the British case, even beyond. There is every reason to assume that similar factors were at work: many traditional forms of shaming seemed increasingly old-fashioned or positively undesirable. While Britons continued to apply shame to blatant cases of blasphemy and lewdness, and definitely participated in an effort to use the emotion to bolster respectability, community support for shame clearly began to decline.[75]

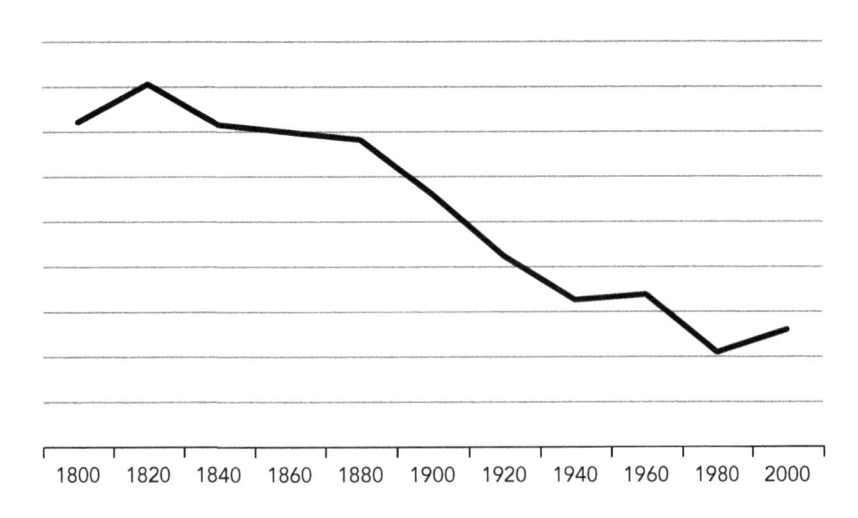

FIGURE 5. The frequency of the word *shame* in British English, 1800s–2000, according to Google Books Ngram Viewer.

As in the United States, spurred by new ideas and the revolutionary climate, France moved fairly quickly against shaming punishments. The pillory was abolished in 1789 and replaced by a milder, less physically painful exposure for offenders called "exposition," and then this was abolished in turn after another revolution, in 1832. British discussion was strongly influenced by the same kind of turn toward individualism that had occurred in the American colonies, which could lead both to a desire to protect miscreants from "barbarous" treatment and to a concern about the fickleness of crowd reactions.[76] The United Kingdom limited use of the pillory to perjury and subornation, in 1816, and then banned it in outright 1837 (two years before the U.S. Congress did the same). Reformers argued against the unfairness of exposure to the crowd, while also noting unpredictability: sometimes, given mob passions, a man might be intended for disgrace only for the event to "[turn] out [as] a sort of triumph." No less a figure than Edmund Burke spoke against the pillory in the late eighteenth century, mainly because it could incite public violence against an exposed miscreant well out of proportion to even particularly repulsive offenses, such as sodomy. Opponents did point to the importance of tradition and the probability that public exposure—even in front of a fickle mob—would still be a deterrent to others. A few added that certain crimes were so "shocking to human nature" that they deserved the uncertainties attached to public shaming. But ultimately reform won out.[77]

British movement against milder public shaming, through use of the stocks, was a bit slower than in the more reform-minded United States. Reformist zeal converged more tentatively on alternatives such as penitentiaries, and of course the availability of convict transport to places like Australia may also have complicated more systematic change. Use of stocks declined but persisted into the later nineteenth century. In 1860 one John Gambles was publicly exposed in Pudsey, for the crime of gambling on the Sabbath—though the experience was now so rare that the passing crowd was more bemused than shaming. The last known case occurred in 1865, for drunkenness. British analysis has interestingly added to the standard explanations for the decline of public shaming, in citing a special concern for making city centers places of refinement rather than coarse justice, at a time when urban leaders were eager to polish local reputations.[78]

The duel survived in many European countries far longer than was true even in the U.S. South. Debates over the duel, and its senselessness, paralleled those in the United States, but impacts might be considerably delayed. And shame played a great role. French duelists, defying laws that banned the practice, thus noted that a loss of honor, through failing to take up a challenge, was "a kind of civil death." Prussia, with its large quotas of military officers and civil servants, fed by dueling societies in the universities, yielded very slowly. By the late nineteenth century, ardent defenders had retreated a bit across Germany, arguing that dueling remained valid only for the most serious insults—and "of course" in cases of adultery. As in other settings, reformer blasts were opposed by a sense that rising commercial values were petty and demeaning—reliance on concepts of honor might actually intensify by way of contrast. Feminism and growing roles for women, including women students, fed the fires as well. Great sensitivity remained against accusations of cowardice. World War I dampened German enthusiasms a bit, because of sheer loss of life, but officers and student groups defiantly retained the practice during the next two decades. Only defeat in World War II, and a much more substantial recasting of German culture, really did away with the older ideas of honor and shame.[79]

Attachment to honor, and resultant reactions to shame, persisted strongly in other areas as well, again in partial contrast to U.S. trends in the nineteenth century, in part because of a social structure that reflected a more complex mixture between old and new elements. William Reddy has analyzed the persistence of a commitment to honor among French bureaucrats and professionals during the nineteenth century. Emphasis rested on living up to the code, even in a time of growing commercialism, rather than dwelling on the shameful effects of failure; but the connection was present. Indeed, as to some extent in the U.S. South, many French professionals found modern times themselves in some vague way shameful, because of undue emphasis on self-interest. Dueling could be part of this code, and the culture certainly embraced a large dose of misogyny.[80] Reddy sees a disappearance of this persistent pattern only in the upheavals of World War I and the subsequent inability to maintain older standards, including gender standards. A 2014 work on France highlights the intricate involvement of shame with credit and debt assessments in the nineteenth century, where the emotion could be pressed into service as a means of disciplining business behavior. We have seen comparable issues in credit reports in the United States, but the French references to shame may have been somewhat more explicit.[81]

We know less, at this point, about other changes in the European context, for example in recommended approaches to child rearing, but given the movement away from public shaming it is plausible to expect some similarities with U.S. trends. As in the United States, however, shaming remained available depending on the issues of the day. In Britain at the end of the nineteenth century, Oscar Wilde was publicly shamed, through court trials but also a new journalistic zeal in the rising mass press, for his open homosexuality and sodomy. Some have argued that this was the first case of persecution by paparazzi, eager to titillate the public with stories of "gross indecency." War could elicit shame as well: the French response to women accused of consorting with Nazis, after World War II, by shaving their heads, was a classic emotional ploy, another sign of how special crises can generate a fierce return to shame despite cultural change.[82] Shame's decline in Western Europe, perhaps a bit more gradual than in the United States, was certainly open to its own set of complications and complexities.

Seeing the U.S. movement against shame and shaming as part of a larger Western pattern reemphasizes the cultural factors involved, as both sides of the Atlantic sought to work through the implications of the Enlightenment for emotional life—in obvious contrast to many of the East Asian adjustments to modernity. Not surprisingly the result has been ongoing overlap in psychological research on shame, where a transatlantic community builds on the disapproval of the emotion that has emerged so strongly over the past two centuries, and also widely shared individual reactions, for example in resentful and aggressive responses to the shaming of prisoners. In addition to a standard plea for more precise comparative work, the Western context will however raise one final set of question. During the later twentieth century, as we see in the following chapter, the modern U.S. response to shame has been revisited in several respects, creating new divisions and tensions over the emotion than could have been predicted just a few decades before. Europeans have shared in some of these innovations but not in all; and they have responded with a more forceful effort to minimize shame even in novel contexts. A comparative challenge continues, but now with new interest in the unexpected contemporary U.S. variant.

CHAPTER 5

The Revival of Shame
Contemporary History

A new period in the history of shame and shaming opened in the United States after the 1960s. Older trends continued: there were many extensions of the previous interest in containing shame, including the more decisive objections to shame that began to dominate psychological and much social science research. But there were vital innovations as well, as the emotion gained new uses in several social venues. Rather separately, shaming efforts also went global, with new effort to deploy the emotion in international relations—though with debatable results.

This chapter focuses particularly on developments in the United States. Some U.S. trends had parallels elsewhere, but again it is reasonable at least to suggest some national peculiarities while urging further comparative analysis. For example, efforts in the European Union to limit shaming potential were not fully matched in the United States, while heightened U.S. references to shame were not precisely reflected in British word use though there was some overlap. East Asian societies continued to rely heavily on shame, though without the new initiatives that emerged in the United States.

U.S. patterns were complicated and in many ways blatantly contradictory. The campaign against shame continued, probably with renewed energy. Various therapists weighed in more vigorously in opposition to the emotion, with new remedies suggested. We have seen already that nonchalance in some venues, such as athletic coaching, was upended after the 1960s, with far more systematic resistance in the name of individual dignity and effectiveness. While ambivalence in the schools persisted, the self-esteem movement ratcheted up, with measurable results in terms of students' assumptions about their own importance and competence. Also, these trends contributed to the opposition to shaming, or at least in generating heightened sensitivity.

Against this, however, a new legal current openly revived shaming as a component in penology—another development that went further in the United States than in Western Europe. Several factors converged in encouraging some judges, mainly on the conservative side of the spectrum, to utilize public shaming as an alternative to other punishments. Here was a change in fact, and a new source of considerable debate.

Shame and shaming also played a new role in the partisan and cultural divides that opened in the United States after the 1960s, and here liberals and conservatives were both active (without much mutual recognition of shared emotional tactics). Liberals delighted in shaming politically incorrect references, often forcing culprits out of jobs, particularly in the entertainment industry but also in politics. Conservatives—some of whom voiced their wish for a revival of the good old days when behaviors like adultery could be publicly shamed—stepped up efforts to use shame, for example against real or imagined abuses of the welfare system. Shaming was also altered by important steps on behalf of previously marginal groups—gays most obviously but also people with disabilities—to shuck off any hints of a shameful status. This provided another component to the complex public discourse about shame and its applicability or inappropriateness.

Less surprisingly—for this maintained a theme that had been clear in the previous period—various groups also seized on shame as a weapon against new social problems. Shame was widely deployed in efforts against obesity—along with resistance to this emotional tactic. Shame might also be directed against environmental offenders, with varying degrees of effectiveness.

Finally, particularly in the early twenty-first century, changes in technology and media communication opened vast new possibilities for shaming. Anonymous, often vicious, shaming efforts took advantage of new channels such as Twitter and Facebook.

Tracing these various paths—the continued campaign, the uses in law, the political currents and clashes; the new disciplinary efforts, and the communications framework—identifies both complementarities and contradictions. We must consider as well the actual emotional experience: as shame revived, did sensitivity to it abate somewhat, or was the emotion still, as so many had argued in the previous period, a largely destructive force? And the social results require assessment as well (including a separate comment on the global efforts):

did shame regain greater social utility? Should there in fact, as some argued, be even more extensive shaming efforts, against the various sins and abuses that beset modern U.S. society?

There is also the question of causation, given the measurable movement away from the shaming trends that had taken shape—amid admitted complexities—during the nineteenth and earlier twentieth centuries in Western society. New technologies and political divisions played a key role: social media made public shaming easier than ever before, while partisan battles freely employed the emotion as a weapon. Was there also a new effort to try, in a fractured society, to build new kinds of communities, and to use shame to help define and bolster identity? As the numbers rise of Americans living in an increasingly privatized suburbia, where conventional audiences for shame were hard to identify, there may have been a real effort to invent new forms of shame in hopes of creating new social linkages.[1] To what extent, finally, did revived shame respond to manifest failures of prior patterns of emotional discipline? Elements here would include the growing disillusionment with the once-touted (and still massively utilized) prison system, or more broadly a sense that guilt—shame's putative replacement in areas like child rearing—was no longer up to the job.

Did shame also respond to a broader shift in predominant U.S. character? Already in the 1950s, social scientists thought they perceived a decline in the kind of individualism and individual self-referencing that had surfaced in the nineteenth century, and over time this might well affect approaches to shame. In a corporate management culture, Americans became more sensitive to the opinions of others, recurrently checking to make sure that what they were doing was not perceived as out of line by their relevant colleagues. As a result many Americans became, in David Riesman's phrase, more "other-directed."[2] In the process, many also became less private, eager to reveal personal details on television talk shows or, later, Facebook; but they also, according to some comparative studies, were increasingly interested in concealing some emotional reactions that might not pass muster with the wider community. For example, one analysis showed Americans (compared to the Dutch or French) particularly eager to conceal sexual jealousy, anxiously inquiring among their friends whether they had let this unseemly emotion show.[3] None of this was a direct invitation to shaming. Indeed, reputational concerns might enhance sensitivities and resentments when the emotion was deployed. But the new atmosphere arguably invited more reliance on shaming in fact, more temptation to use to the emotion to spoil projected personal images, more willingness to accept shaming (of others) as part of the new reliance on community signals.

The transformation of privacy—whatever the larger merits of the character change argument—was measurable, and not just in the United States. Deborah

Cohen has charted a sea change in British family life, developing between the 1930s and the 1950s. Previously, concerns about shame and respectability had driven families to keep all sorts of secrets: homosexuality, illegitimate birth, disability, adoption. Increasingly, however, these barriers began to fall. Newspapers in the 1930s offered money for "confessions"—for example, the *Daily Mirror*'s "What Is the Skeleton in Your Cupboard?" column elicited admissions under such banner headlines as "I Smashed a Good Woman's Life." Marriage counseling invited people to become comfortable sharing secrets with strangers, while popularized psychotherapy encouraged a belief that openness would bring mental comfort. A 1950s poll showed a stark British generation gap: people in their fifties clung to the idea that family should be private, but for young adults privacy now meant being able to lead one's life as one wished—and not necessarily keeping the results a secret. One result, visible on both sides of the Atlantic, was an increasingly intrusive press—the paparazzi, for the rich and famous—and new kinds of television shows rooted in open confessions. A new genre of book, the "misery memoir," reached best-seller status by the early twenty-first century.[4] Shaming was finding new ways to serve as public entertainment.

This huge shift, at least in segments of Western society, had an ambivalent relationship to shame. On the one hand, it linked with growing efforts to reduce the emotion, to support more flexible standards in areas such as sexuality, while attacking any sense of shamefulness for groups like homosexuals. It supported, in other words, the intensification of older trends attacking shame: it was all right to be more open about subjects that should now no longer be shameful. On the other hand, shame did not vanish, and open confessions could generate new opportunities to seize on unguarded statements and turn them into unprecedented shame bombardments—particularly when new media could be drawn into action.[5] And without question, not only a new capacity but a new eagerness to pry into other people's thoughts—encouraged by often heedless candor—could translate into zealous shaming. We see both sides—the relaxation of shame, but also the exploitation of the sometimes overwhelming impulse to tell all—in the sections that follow.

The overall result was not at all a return to a traditional pattern of shame, though commentators delighted in historical potshots of varying degrees of accuracy. Discussing a shaming incident as "medieval" (actually, "early modern" would be more accurate) or lamenting the good old days when adultery was castigated in public was part of the new emotions debate. The fact was, however, that it was a debate, not a tidy restoration of agreed-upon community standards, and this alone made the new climate distinctive and, possibly, particularly vexed. Not only were values in dispute—was environmental degradation

CHAPTER 5

shameful or not? when was it appropriate to turn a personal revelation into a social media tirade?—but the very use of shame roused discordant views depending on the individual and, sometimes, on the issue in question.

It is possible to say, without exaggerating the significance of the move toward greater use of shame in contemporary U.S. history, that the new trends both reflected and enhanced significant larger changes in emotional expectations and interactions. They certainly promoted dispute and no small amount of confusion. Different groups, different settings now called forth impressively contradictory impulses where shame was concerned.

The Signs of Change

At one level, the data are absolutely clear. *Shame* began to gain ground once again in U.S. word use among other things, beginning to catch up with *guilt*, where usage frequency stabilized and then declined a bit in the later twentieth century. Seen in figures 6 and 7, both Google Ngram and the *New York Times* Chronicle show a striking and consistent increase from the 1960s (*Times*) or the 1980s (Google) onward—the *Times* data may be particularly revealing, since they clearly do not reflect any particular southern regional upsurge.[6]

British trends contrasted somewhat, with shame reviving a bit in the later twentieth century but then flattening more clearly (fig. 8)—again, a partial U.S. twist is suggestive.[7] Frequency of reference, of course, points in no particular

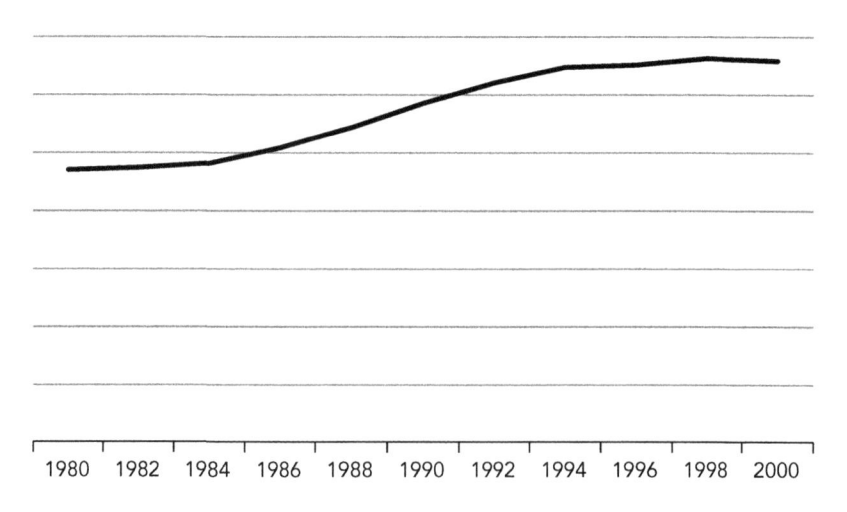

FIGURE 6. The frequency of the word *shame* in U.S. English, 1980–2000, according to Google Books Ngram Viewer.

The Revival of Shame

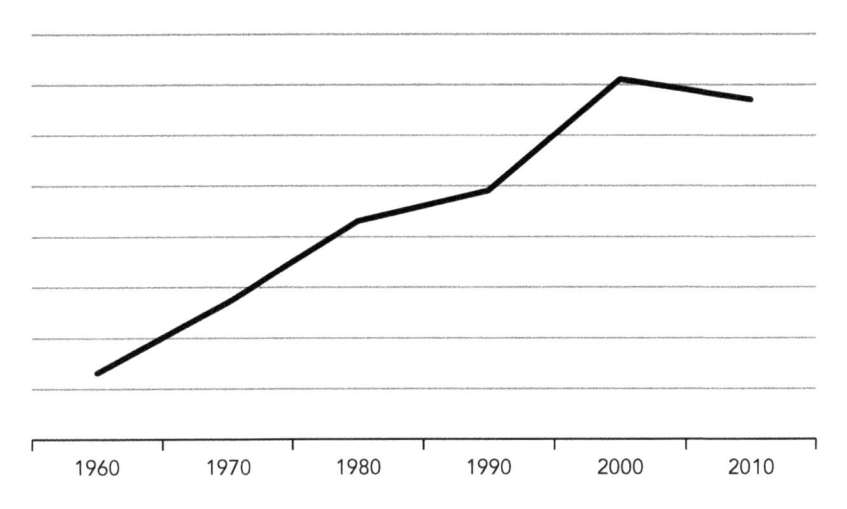

FIGURE 7. The frequency of the word *shame* in U.S. English, 1960–2010, according to the *New York Times* Chronicle.

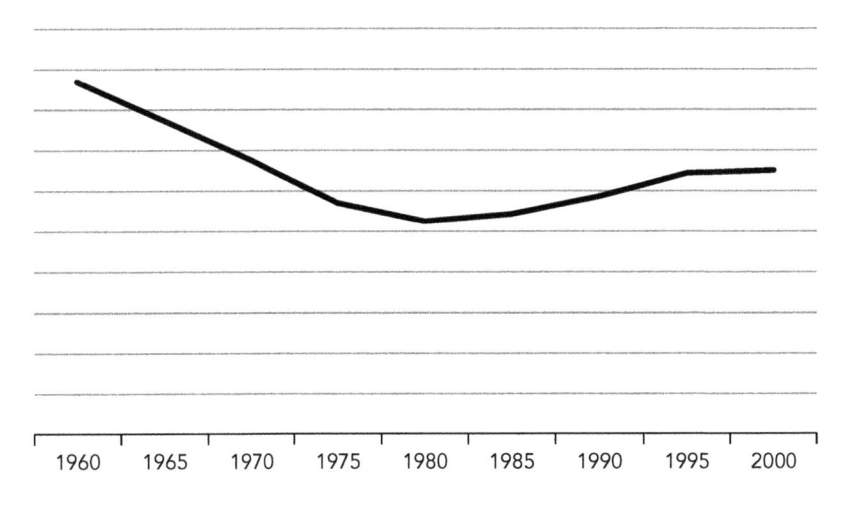

FIGURE 8. The frequency of the word *shame* in British English, 1960–2000. Source: Google Books Ngram Viewer.

direction—though it does contradict the earnest social scientists who continue to insist that the term has become taboo. The pattern is, however, at the least, an invitation for further analysis. Ironically, shame gained new attention both because of more vigorous efforts to quell the emotion and because of the variety of attempts, whether explicit or not, to extend it.

CHAPTER 5

THE ONGOING CAMPAIGN AGAINST SHAME

Many factors helped to maintain, indeed to intensify, the efforts against shame that had begun in the early nineteenth century. We have seen that sensitivities to blatant shaming in the schools increased measurably after World War II, even as more moderate shaming pressures persisted. Teachers who singled out students before a classroom risked parental and community sanction and risked their jobs—even anonymous death threats on occasion.

Exposure of offending coaches increased. More and more literature was devoted to the evils of shaming athletes and to the damages to morale and actual performance. Coaches who concentrated on more positive motivations were held up as models. Again, the results were not consistent, and shaming persisted in many venues. But formal opposition was a new element.

The campaign against shame extended into newer territory as well, though with incomplete results. Families were urged not to accept shame or blame when a family member committed suicide or faced problems of addiction; the emotional burden of shame should not spill over into wider groups. But individuals required protection from shame as well. A need for psychological therapy was no longer to be regarded as shameful—an interesting area where changing U.S. standards contrasted with a continued sense, in East Asia, that seeking therapy reflected badly on the family as well as on the person directly involved.[8] In Western Europe and the United States, great effort also went into reducing any shame associated with HIV diagnoses. Here was another case where the general campaign against shame combined with specific needs to encourage victims to seek help (and in this case to limit opportunities for additional infection as well).[9]

Efforts against shaming were aided by the further loosening of some traditional standards, again a process that had been launched before. Adultery and premarital sex, even for women, drew far less comment than had been the case even in the 1930s, and this meant fewer occasions to call upon shame. Even illegitimate births might increasingly pass without comment—when for example they resulted from the aspirations of single, middle-class women to experience the joys of parenthood. Of course change had some limits: welfare mothers with many children still drew shaming comments, of which they were often quite aware. Slut shaming reflected the hold of older value systems and gender distinctions, a point to be taken up below. And new elements did enter in. Sexual offenders, though not usually publicly shamed, were now required to register with the police for the rest of their lives, even after serving prison time; this was a latter-day branding that some found excessive, particularly given the wide boundaries of sexual offense under the law. Concerns about harassment in the workplace gained far greater attention, though discipline did not usually highlight public shaming. Overall, however, despite the new cautions, shame and sex were probably further separated in the United States than ever before.

Shame and shamefulness were in fact directly attacked in one other sexual domain, as part of the feminist surge from the 1960s onward, though with rising intensity from the 1990s to the present: rape victims were widely urged to rise above any sense of shame and recognize that they had been physically attacked and bore no responsibility for the crime. Shame should not hold them back from seeking justice and should not distort their lives. Obviously, recommendations did not transform emotional reality for many victims, some of whom continued to attempt to conceal. But the consistency with the larger effort to control shame was both vigorous and clear-cut.[10]

Shame was also undermined, at least potentially, by a steady increase in efforts to promote self-esteem, another theme that had earlier origins but now received more systematic attention from the 1960s onward. School programs welcomed the chance to highlight this positive motivation, providing students with an array of activities in which they might at least modestly excel and inflating grades to produce more favorable results. Parents responded as well, picking up more enthusiastically on the longstanding efforts of the child-rearing manuals to rely on positive incentives for good behavior. No small amount of the fabled helicopter parenting that emerged in the final decade of the twentieth-century involved parents seeking opportunities for their offspring to win success, while defending them vigorously against school or other authorities who did not give them due credit.

And the efforts paid off, for better or worse. A 2013 report argued that U.S. collegians valued opportunities to enhance self-esteem more than any other pleasure—including sex; the authors found the focus amounting to a virtual obsession. Polls showed that up to 80 percent of all U.S. young people believed they were important in the world. In international examinations, U.S. students routinely scored well above peers from other countries in believing that they had done better on the tests than they actually had. For all the uncertainties of U.S. youth, self-esteem was a valued commodity.[11]

There is no need to detour into a more elaborate examination of this aspect of U.S. culture; the implications for shame are obvious. Promotion of self-esteem heightened hostility to shaming efforts, logically reducing their frequency and certainly promoting resentment, even defiance, rather than acquiescence should they occur. To be sure, some children responded to overpraise with heightened personal expectations, which could create pressures of their own—even vulnerabilities to personal shame, particularly in later stages of schooling, when it turned out that all sorts of other people were exceptional also. Even here, however, the promotion of self-esteem at the least complicated reactions to shame. The current also measurably spurred many parents to protect their offspring against any implication of shame. All this formed another component of a climate in which shame should have continued a downward spiral.[12]

Three other innovations concentrated even more specifically on the reduction of shame, contributing important ingredients to the contest around the emotion by the end of the twentieth century.

EXPERT INITIATIVES

Armed with increased scholarly confidence in the drawbacks of shame, including the increasingly widespread acceptance of distinctions between shame and guilt, a variety of experts began not only to study the impact of shame on self-image, but to encourage programs that would concentrate on alternatives.

U.S. prisons, launched boldly as an alternative to shaming, had long since become places of shame and humiliation. Practices varied, of course. In many instances simple lack of attention left mental-health issues, broadly construed, untreated. But often prison guards delighted in explicit shaming. Strip searches intended to degrade and humiliate prisoners were frequently deployed and continue to be used. For more shaming before their peers, inmates might be required to lie face down on the mess hall floor prior to being allowed to eat their meal.

Into this setting, at least occasionally, came psychological or psychiatric experts, armed with a deep belief that shame and lack of dignity were at the root of violence and that other emotional approaches were both possible and desirable. Thus James Gilligan worked to change the framework of a Massachusetts prison, beginning in the 1980s, where rates of violence and suicide were exceptionally high. He approached with respect even criminals guilty of the most hideous crimes, conscious of their need to maintain or regain a sense of dignity: "it is not my job to humiliate them." For in his view it was shame, and its destruction of self-respect, that was responsible for violent acts in the first place. Replacing the emotion was a vital first step toward rehabilitation. And indeed, prisoner behavior responded strikingly, with rapid reductions of in-house offenses, significant gains in post-sentence behavior.[13]

Other psychologists worked in similar ways. June Tangney was not content to chart the different results of shame and guilt in a prison population. She and her colleagues worked with courts and jail officials to recast the approach to prisoners, and to provide more active therapeutic services aimed at targeting the prior impact of shame above all. Similar work occurred in parts of Western Europe, where findings about the destructive effects of shame paralleled those in the United States.[14]

Reforms moves were, admittedly, modest, and many prisons and prisoners remained untouched, even as the U.S. inmate population continued to swell. Still, the effort to find new ways to combat shame was a significant step beyond the previous reliance on advice alone.

WIDER THERAPIES

Extending beyond penal expertise, but capturing many of the same basic ideas, was a growing popular movement to help people attack shame in new ways. During the years after 2000, social worker Brené Brown was a leading popularizer here, with many books to her credit and appearances in venues such as the *Oprah Winfrey Show*; a Brown TEDx talk on shame and vulnerability generated over 7 million views to date, impressive by any standard.[15]

Brown's belief that shame must be tackled explicitly, and head-on, went beyond previous advice bent on avoiding or sidestepping the emotion. The approach surely helps explain why *shame* as a word began to gain in usage after decades of decline. Most obviously, Brown and kindred experts and popularizers not only added to research on the devastating effects of shame but sought to develop both advice and (when possible) therapy directed at remediation.

Brown found shame literally the predominant emotion among her subjects—what she called a "silent epidemic." Regardless of whether the issue was being a good parent, having the right body type, or doing well in school, shame was omnipresent. If her findings were accurate—they derived mainly from interviews—her work may serve as a powerful reminder that, however important the earlier efforts against shame, they had only scratched the surface. Had the efforts won any impact at all, or had they been counteracted by other developments that increased U.S. sensitivity, for example, in the growing focus on body imagery? Brown's participants (initially mainly women) reported experiences of shame in terms such as "devastating," "excruciating," "rejected," and "diminished" or "small." They seemed acutely able to distinguish shame from guilt, seeing guilt as a response to a bad behavior in contrast to shame's focus on a bad self. (The apparent sophistication was striking; Brown's correspondents may have learned little about how to deal with shame, despite over a century of advice, but they seemed impressively versed in psychological nuance.)[16]

Small wonder that Brown joined other contemporary observers, among them Karen Horney and Paul Trout, in seeing shame, in Trout's words, as "the preeminent cause of emotional distress in our time."[17] Shame lies behind our failure to eat right, even though we know what to do. It makes people pretend that things are all right when they definitely are not. It lurks in money troubles, addiction, sex, aging, religion—the list of venues became virtually limitless. "Shame is that warm feeling that washes over us, making us feel small, flawed, and never good enough." It's one of the most primitive emotions we have. It's the flip side of desirable qualities like empathy—for only people who lack the capacity for warm human contact can avoid shame.[18]

But the emotion is not only damaging but insidious. For people fail to talk about shame. Brown claimed that her interviewees initially, and unanimously, insisted they did not want to discuss shame, even as they proceeded to report daily bouts with the emotion. Precisely because shame takes root in a fear that others will turn away from us and find us wanting, we keep our shame to ourselves—we fear that revelation will actualize the very rejection we worry about. "We don't have to experience shame to be paralyzed by it—the fear of being perceived as unworthy is enough to force us to silence our stories."[19]

There is, however, a remedy, in what Brown calls shame resilience theory, or "speaking shame." Drown shame in openness. Talk about it, publicly, to friends and colleagues, whenever it occurs. When Brown feels shamed by a colleague at work, and feels "small and stupid," she rushes home and posts the incident on Facebook. And sure enough, she will get twenty comments from strangers that echo her frustration: "hate when that happens, it's happened to me, you're not alone brother." (The results of this process on the offending colleague are not specified—perhaps he or she will feel ashamed by the same public airing? Here too, the shame equation may be extremely complex.)[20]

The approach should spill over into child rearing, though recommendations here were somewhat more vague. Parents, obviously, should not use shame with their children. They should prevent the kids from watching television shows that shame. But they cannot fully control school or sports situations where shame may intrude. So teaching shame resilience—the capacity to label shame and to reach out to others for *supportive* connections—becomes vital, an interesting expansion of older child-rearing advice.

Shame resilience thus involves a heightened critical awareness, so that a person is alert to any experience of shame and willing to label it clearly. But then it must be aired, widely discussed. "The first thing we need to understand about shame resilience is that the less we talk about shame, the more we have it." Shame thrives on the impulse to conceal, which the emotion unquestionably promotes: "when something shaming happens, and we keep it locked up, it festers and grows." People need friends and confidants to whom they can tell their story. "They reach out and share their stories with people they trust. They speak shame, they use the word shame, they talk about how they're feeling, and they ask for what they need." In the process they will not only rise above shame but develop new levels of capacity and compassion as well.[21]

By the early twenty-first century, Brown and several colleagues moved beyond writing and speaking about their approach, which earned them a substantial audience, to offering online courses and consulting widely. Brown's organization, the Daring Way, offered training and certification for businesses and professionals who sought to reduce their vulnerabilities, build their emotional courage. The idea of direct attacks *on* shame was clearly winning wide resonance.

This extension of the effort against shame highlighted one other striking feature, fairly explicitly: The person who has been shamed has been wronged. Shaming is "cruel"; it never leads to permanent improvements, for it scars all parties involved. There is no need to pay attention to actions that prompted a shaming incident, for their review would not address the key problem. The damaging emotional experience of shame, and the need to rally support, transcends any misdeed. Classic shame is in this sense stood on its head, and shame to the shamers.[22]

REJECTING SHAMEFULNESS

Traditional societies, as they valued and utilized shame, characteristically also identified certain groups as inherently somewhat shameful. The results could play an important emotional role, for example in preparing some people for the experience of shame and even, at least in moderate doses, for its acceptability.

This approach had been questioned even in the nineteenth century, though largely indirectly. Groups that fought for women's rights, even equality, were obviously casting doubt on any idea that women should bear any burden of collective shame. The target was not specifically identified amid the larger issues involved. More general redefinitions of femininity, and particularly the growing idea that women had superior domestic virtues, even superior morality, also undermined classic patriarchal assumptions about shamefulness. This does not mean of course that women did not continue to bear some special burdens. Even the contemporary inquiries of people like Brown raise questions about disproportionate gender experience of shame. But in principle, with the twin advances of women's virtue and feminism, earlier assumptions about shamefulness were at least diluted.[23]

The same applied to race and ethnicity, at least by the later twentieth century. Black Pride campaigns, as part of the civil rights movement, took on shame somewhat more directly than feminism had, but here too the focus was multifaceted. The challenge to the idea that certain groups should be shame prone, or seen as shame prone by white society, was present, but diffuse.

Shame was taken on far more directly in the gay liberation movement that opened in the United States with the Stonewall riots of 1969. "Gay pride" became the rallying cry in the effort to achieve sexual freedom and equal rights. Gay leaders worked against both individual shame—the daunting, often dangerous sense of inferiority that self-identification could bring—and group shame from the wider society. Combatting the emotion served as a central, unifying theme in the campaign as it blossomed and expanded over the ensuing half-century.

Homosexuality had long been shameful, at least in the Christian tradition. Homosexual activities, in the larger cities, were typically shrouded in secrecy, though group cohesion may have helped individuals counter shame to some extent. Public pressure against homosexuality increased in the United States in the early twentieth century, spurred among other things by the growing belief that one was either heterosexual or homosexual, with no gray areas between. Patterns of emotionally and sometimes physically intense same-sex friendships, that had flourished in the nineteenth century, were now challenged, and many college-age individuals spent no small amount of time scrutinizing their own impulses to make sure that shameful tendencies were absent.[24]

In this context, the larger arguments of the civil rights movement, and perhaps more broadly the global human rights movement, as they unfolded in the postwar decades and particularly the 1960s, raised new hopes and opportunities. Shame could now be a target. Gay Pride parades were meant to counter individual shame and simultaneously to challenge the wider community to reexamine its own tendency to impose shame on others. In the opening article in the first issue of *GLQ: A Journal of Lesbian and Gay Studies*, Eve Kosofsky argued that queer identity and resistance were both rooted in the experiences of shame. Questioning shame, but acknowledging its power, could be central to the wider exploration of what it means to be gay.[25]

The concept remained tricky. Many gay leaders worried about too much exploration of shame, lest it revive the bad old days of gay invisibility and social scorn: maintaining the positive emphasis on pride seemed more important. A wider concern developed—and remains—that the effort to counter shame imposed constraints on gays both individually and collectively. Aspects of gay behavior that might seem to feed older stereotypes now needed to be downplayed, in the interests of the new, non-shameful public persona. But some gay leaders were even interested in using shame to tease out hypocrisies within the gay community. Thus two consecutive Gay Shame rallies in San Francisco urged gays to take on leaders who were exploiting the movement for their own

The Revival of Shame

benefit, for example as politicians or real estate moguls. Gay Shame rallies also, more broadly, encouraged some gays to bring out particular themes and issues that had been buried in the initial public relations campaigns. Arguably, growing attention to transgender concerns was one result of this renewed exploration.

Gay shame continued to be both complex and disputed. Particularly for many adolescents and college-age individuals, the tensions about recognizing identity, and deciding whether or how to reveal it, continued to present agonizing encounters with shame. For a time, widely publicized problems with AIDS provided new fodder for those who would maintain a shaming posture. Gay shaming, in turn, though it undoubtedly declined, maintained potent force—enough to drive some individuals, still, to suicide, as in the Rutgers student who took his life in 2012 after a roommate placed on social media a video of his homosexual encounter.[26]

But there was no question that shame had been newly and widely challenged, in a cultural shift that gained surprising strength and success in most of the Western world. Gays themselves reported that "the shame of being gay has subsided," "many have begun to rethink shame," and "we can kiss gay shame goodbye."[27] Here was a key setback to any wider idea that groups can and should be identified in terms of a particular burden of shame.

Somewhat more quietly, but as part of the same current, classic associations of disability with shamefulness were also disputed. Here was one of the oldest traditions of group shaming: the sense that the disabled were shameful in themselves and that their existence brought shame to the families that bore them. Both in the United States and Europe, disability spokespeople began to drop apologetic arguments for more equal treatment—for appropriate access, for example, to education and jobs—in favor of assertions of positive identity. The shift applied to physical and mental disabilities alike.

Thus in the 1940s and 1950s, new groups formed over the issue of what was then referred to as mental retardation. Parents combined with experts in the field, bent on helping each other overcome shame and despair but also, in the same breath, seeking to convince a wider audience that retardation was a societal issue and not just a private problem. In the United States the National Association for Retarded Children launched in 1950. "Retarded" people, in the new view, were normal, not shameful objects to be hidden away. They had rights to training and appropriate types of work. Public responsibility, not emotional attack, was the suitable response.[28]

Movements to attack group shamefulness obviously built on many of the same motives that were disputing shame in other venues. The emotion was damaging; it was unacceptable; traditional standards must be thoroughly reviewed.

. . .

The expansions of the efforts to root out shame were impressive and significant. They added knowledge, tactics, and range to the trends that had been taking shape for over a century. Indeed, they were in most respects a logical outgrowth of earlier efforts, benefiting from additional changes, such as the push for human rights. Of course they fell short of full success. Indeed, it is quite possible that here, as in other historical experiences, the new push to name a problem called forth more symptoms than had previously been identified. It was hard to bury shame, at least in Western culture, and that could make it seem more ominous.

The overall directions, however, seemed clear enough. Shame was under persistent, critical review. But as already indicated, this was not the whole story of the past half century, at least in the United States. The harmony between new vigor and older impulses made it all the more startling that, in a number of pathways, efforts to revive and utilize shame emerged with new potency as well.

Expanding Shame: New Targets and Old

The first complication to the efforts to circumscribe shame is the least surprising, for it constituted an updated version of the patterns we earlier explored for the later nineteenth century. Even as shame was under attack in many settings, Americans (and others) began to find new issues that seemed to cry out for a shaming response. In some cases the people involved were remote from the campaigns against the emotion, but in other instances they had feet in both camps, deploring shame in some situations while piling it on in others; inconsistency concerning shame is both obvious and, in terms of clear historical experience, unsurprising.

Many observers have noted that moderate forms of shame continued to apply in many areas, both old and new. Men are more likely to wash their hands in public restrooms if other people are present. Seatbelt use goes up when there are other people in the car. The anxiety about shame here is mild—not Brené Brown–level devastation; but the examples remind of ongoing—and arguably constructive—sensitivities. Other uses may be found, extending the emotion into unexpected daily domains. Thus an exercise facility, aware that workout fanatics might intimidate people with more modest capacities, installs a "lunk alarm" system to shame individuals who are trying too hard.[29]

More serious extensions include academic administrators, seeking an effective way to discipline and warn faculty about scientific misconduct without going to the extreme of dismissals. The remedy? Require plagiarists, in mild cases, to recant publicly, typically in the journal where the offense first appeared. (Interestingly, however, a shaming approach has not been applied to student plagiarists.) Or, in another expanding orbit, after the financial crisis of 2008, the Securities and Exchange Commission pressed steadily for open corporate reports on salary ratios. The idea was that wide recognition would curb the growing gap between executive remuneration and other pay grades, as no other policy seemed able to do. As one consumer think tank put it, the results "will be a public shaming, just as all adverse financial results are public shaming. . . . [out of balance salaries] are shameful," adding somewhat obscurely, "welcome to capitalism."[30]

In some cases, of course, vivid shame reflected more a persistence of earlier patterns, than a real policy extension. Thus some groups have maintained a proclivity for shame over issues that other segments of U.S. society had reevaluated. Centers for Disease Control and Prevention studies, for example, highlighted the continued sense of shame in several minority populations, particularly among young people, over seeking treatment for mental health issues. For U.S. society generally this was another stigma that was unquestionably changing, but several subcultures continued to resist.

But deliberate policy was frequently in play as well. The later twentieth century brought several new issues to the fore where shame or shaming could play a role. Campaigns against smoking on the whole focused on health issues and potential guilt for individuals who lacked the necessary self-control to quit. But shame could enter in as well. Social practices such as isolating smokers in outdoor locations—based on outrage at the disputed effects of secondhand smoke—arguably involved a definite shaming element. Here was a new group that could and should be persuaded of its shamefulness.

Environmental concerns opened another frontier. Prompted by school campaigns, many children delighted in shaming their parents into more fervent recycling efforts or other forms of compliance. The preface notes the invocation of social shaming to identify excessive water users amid the environmental crisis in California.

Obesity shaming, however, highlighted the most striking emotional target, with origins earlier in the twentieth century but with the full emotional outpouring awaiting the turn-of-the-century decades. Here was an arguably legitimate concern, with both social and individual implications. Here also was a new way to identify groups that should be sensitive to their shamefulness: if women in general were emerging from this category, for example, overweight women might be a convenient substitute. Obesity shaming, in other words, may have combined new problem identification with larger social needs for acceptable emotional disdain.

Extremely obese people had been teased before, but concerns about weight began to gain new importance from the late nineteenth century onward. Both medical and actuarial data pointed to the health risks of excessive weight. Fashion standards began to emphasize slenderness—for example, in turn-of-the-century debates over whether women should continue to wear corsets or should manage slenderness on their own. Modern industrial societies were facing a new problem: most segments of the population now had access to overabundant food, just as many aspects of life were becoming more sedentary. Various groups mobilized to try to come to terms with the issue.

Scattered examples of fat shaming dot the early decades of the twentieth century. Postcards depicted fat women overwhelming their hapless husbands. Immigrant groups were ridiculed for excessive weight—thus combining an old and a new shaming target in one swoop. Feminists might be targeted—Elizabeth Cady Stanton's unfashionable body image was often noted.[31] At the same time, the growing popularity of slender film stars and fashion models presented an increasingly vivid alternative standard, against which a host of groups and individuals might be measured. Even doctors, gradually becoming concerned about weight as a health issue, reported their frequent aversion at having to deal with patients who did not seem able to control their eating: they might offer demanding advice and some shaming in the same encounter.[32]

Pressures mounted from the 1950s onward, which is when fat shaming turned from an occasional incident into a larger social obsession. The facts were that data about the adverse health effects of being overweight became increasingly clear, while obesity rates (both adult and child) continued to mount. Translating the dilemma, the new beauty standards, emphasizing slenderness, turned fatness into ugliness to a greater extent than ever before—only a century earlier, plumpness had been valued as a sign of health and prosperity. In the United States particularly, fat was also increasingly connected to moral weakness, a failure in impulse control—and possibly even some psychological flaw. Links with residual shamefulness for certain racial minorities where obesity was a particularly visible problem, or for women more generally, could compound the emotional targeting.[33]

The result went well beyond jokes or accusing images. Overweight people were regularly turned away from job interviews (though this was technically illegal after the 1970s): "come back when you've lost some weight"; "it won't kill you to go hungry." Diners reported hostile looks from others in the restaurant, when they had the temerity to eat in public: "I am constantly underestimated. My intelligence, my strength, my talents, my tenacity, my humanity." A sorority at one university, in 2006, abruptly expelled twenty-one members because their weight might discourage new, and more desirably slender, applicants. In the same vein, some overweight people were advised against pursuing higher education: "fat people are not disciplined enough to get an advanced degree." Or as an NYU professor put it in a 2013 tweet: "Dear obese PhD applicants: if you didn't have the willpower to stop eating carbs, you won't have the willpower to do a dissertation." Total strangers might feel empowered to approach a parent in a playground, whose offspring is chubby, urging them to take remedial steps. Overweight people often felt, as one put it, that they were supposed to "apologize" for their appearance on a daily basis. "It's intolerable to be surrounded by people who believe I have a major character flaw, based on my waistline."[34] While the United States probably excelled in linking fat to moral failure, French obsession with appearance could stigmatize the overweight even more brutally.[35]

And of course shaming entered the policy arena as well, as health officials cast about for measures that might address a growing problem. Schools in several U.S. states and in Australia began to identify students whose body mass index suggested a problem, not only notifying the parents involved but exposing them to the notice of their classmates as well.

The campaign drew clear resistance as well: no major new shaming effort escaped the anti-shame advocates. In the United States, the civil rights movement helped spawn opposition in this new shaming category. The National Association to Aid Fat Americans, for example, formed in 1969. The goal: to encourage the overweight to gain "enough self-confidence to fight for size acceptance." Some groups stressed legal rights. Others argued that the whole anti-fat campaign was based on medical myth, that there was no real health problem, only an effort to target women, or welfare recipients, or some other segment. A crucial argument, clearly important, stressed the ineffectiveness, indeed the counterproductive quality of fat shaming: the crushing emotional burden that resulted simply made targeted individuals eat even more, in search of comfort and reassurance.[36]

Fat shaming became something of a battleground. The stigma continued in daily life, a clear example of shame's advance in response to new problems and standards. But there was no overall evidence that the emotional tactic worked: obesity still advanced, in the United States and elsewhere. For some, the dilemma provided yet one more example of shame's destructive power, not only its unfairness in supporting latter-day shamefulness for groups and individuals, but its actual spur to defiant behavior: people might eat more to compensate for the agony of shame.

Fat shaming also, however, had its own additional capabilities. As corporations worked to increase discipline and cut health expenses, after 2000, there were reports that shaming was widely used to press employees to participate in a range of wellness or well-being programs, with peer reactions meant to add to job advancement incentives.

SHAMING AND THE COURTS

Shame's continued availability to address new areas played an important role in the tensions and outright contradictions surrounding the emotion by the later twentieth century. The specifics here were new, but in many ways the tension between novel usage and the larger hostility to shame replicated the kind of complexity that had already been apparent by the end of the nineteenth century. Far more striking was a return to public shaming as a legal recourse in the United States. The move flew in the face of the resistance trends, compounding confusions over the emotion's role. And of course it provoked extensive debate and disagreement.

Several components combined. For many conservatives, including evangelical Protestants, the ferment of the 1960s had demonstrated a tragic national moral decline. Shame might need to be mobilized to defend basic standards of decency. Beyond this, it seemed to many increasingly clear that guilt or other forms of emotional discipline short of shame were not doing their job in preventing more and more individuals to go off the rails. More pointedly still, the legal alternative to shaming—the prison system—was expanding beyond reasonable measure, and its results, in terms of preventing crime or recidivism, were at least open to serious question. Many advocates of the revival of judicial shaming pointed directly to the massive and rising costs of the prison system and the vital need for an effective alternative—reviving some of the arguments that had swirled around the stocks in the early nineteenth century, but now with new evidence. All of these factors, operating in an increasingly polarized U.S. political context, supported the idea of bringing back an approach that had been one of the first victims of the modern movement against shame. And the revival, as one other result, was distinctively U.S.

Intriguing examples emerged as the pattern took shape from the 1970s onward. In 1989 the Rhode Island Superior Court ordered a convicted child molester, as a condition of probation, to place an ad in the Providence newspaper, stating his name and his crime and including this sentence: "If you are a child molester, get professional help immediately, or you may find your picture and name in the paper, and your life under control of the state." Similarly, a judge in Oregon, also in the 1980s, began to require a number of offenders to buy newspaper ads to apologize for their misdeeds. Kansas City posted the names and pictures of men caught soliciting prostitutes on the community access television channel, in a show that quickly became known as "John TV." Other miscreants have had to wear signs in public confessing to their crimes. Nevada allowed convicted drunk drivers a choice between a jail term and doing community service while wearing clothing that identified them as DUI offenders. A Tennessee judge required a car thief to confess before his church congregation, a particularly interesting echo of former times.[37]

A Florida judge further explained the role of shaming in dealing with drunk drivers. Many have substantial social standing and decent jobs, and are more responsive to shaming—in this case, the obligation to put glow-in-the-dark stickers on their cars—than to heavier fines. "The DUI sticker... capitalized on their fear of public notice" by bringing "shame, disgrace, and a ruined reputation." Other new penalties that harbored shame potential included required apologies to victims and meetings with victims and their families.[38]

Shaming punishments have been particularly applied to driving and some sexual offenses, but other extensions have been tempting as well. A mother convicted of completing a drug purchase in front of her children was thus ordered to apologize publicly. A Georgia judge offered a man convicted of eight counts of theft (but who was also the source of support for a large family) a choice between six months in jail or a few weekends in jail plus standing for thirty hours in front of the courthouse bearing a sign that read "I am a convicted thief." The man chose the latter. A juvenile who threw a brick that blinded a man in one eye was required to wear an eye patch, taking it off only for sleep. A convicted slum landlord in New York must put a sign in front of his property giving his name and phone number. A thief (who stole steaks) had to give a public shaming speech in Wisconsin. The range of offenses, and the geography of shaming punishments, both became impressively extensive over three decades.[39] Indeed one authority, probably prematurely, contended as early as 1996 that the "political acceptability of shaming penalties... is nearly an established fact."[40] The judges involved, further, have been quite aware of the emotional ammunition they are dealing with, at points even taking on the shame critics directly. Thus Texas judge Ted Poe, an ardent advocate of shaming, notes: "A little shame goes a long way. Some folks say everyone should have high self-esteem, but that's not the real world. Sometimes people *should* feel bad."[41]

The revival of shaming as a legal instrument differed in important ways from its traditional antecedent. It was not accompanied by supportive violence—nothing as uncomfortable or torturous as stocks and pillories are involved, and so far at least U.S. publics have not responded with stonings or other abuses. The target is shame, pure and simple. Nor in most instances did contemporary shaming occur within the confines of a clearly established community. People were to expose their wrongdoing in a shopping mall or a more general space, or in the case of automobile stickers to address an even more random public. But the core emotional experience, for the offender, and the resultant warning to others unquestionably and quite deliberately recalled earlier patterns, with shame front and center.

And this served, predictably, to set off a firestorm of debate among legal scholars, as older rationales that had attacked shaming were combined with newer arguments deriving from the more recent stages of the anti-shaming movement. While shaming's revival continued, in itself forming a vital part of the emotion's complex contemporary history, the controversies won their own importance in further highlighting the apparent inability of Americans today to agree, even in broad outline, on an overall approach to shame.

Attacks on penal shaming have taken several forms, though of course these can be variously combined. Many scholars dismiss shaming as ineffective, at least in the U.S. urban context. They point to the lack of relevant communities. Shaming, they contend, must involve a fear of exclusion—but standing with a sign in a shopping mall does not necessarily involve this connection at all. They worry that many criminals operate in groups that simply do not share the community's standards that might prompt shame. These miscreants distrust police and the courts and do not recognize their authority. Hence they will feel no particular emotion in performing whatever rituals these officials require: they will not be deterred from repeat offenses, and their example will not warn off others in their group. Adding to this line of argument is the rehearsal of the strong psychological attacks on shame itself. If shame simply leads to demoralization or defiance, punishments that push in this direction, rather than concentrating either on guilt or on more positive motivations, will be worse than useless.[42]

This kind of pragmatic objection may be quite compatible with an admission that in another culture—for example, Japan—public shaming might work quite well, and measurably limit crime. But in the U.S. context there is no evidence that it either rehabilitates or deters.

A second, more strident line of attack involves basic principle, of the sort that much earlier provoked the movement against the emotion in the first place:

shaming is essentially a cruel and unusual punishment, which has no role in a modern society. It is incompatible the standards of dignity that Americans should vow to maintain. Thus a civil liberties spokesperson: "I'm very skeptical when criminologists and sociologists say that the best way to rehabilitate someone is to isolate him and put some sort of scarlet letter on him. We need to integrate criminals back into our community." Or again: "gratuitous humiliation of the individual serves no societal purpose at all," adding the pragmatic point that "there's been no research to suggest it's been effective in reducing crime." Martha Nussbaum writes in the same vein: it is a threat to liberty and an "assault on our humanity" deliberately to seek to induce shame. "State-enforced shaming authorizes public officials to search for and destroy or damage an offender's dignity."[43]

Horrible social examples can be adduced in this countercampaign. A New Jersey judge reminds of the branding of Jews in Nazi Germany, before the outright Holocaust. "This Court must determine" whether requiring public notifications amounts to a "branding" of miscreants, "thus rendering them subject to perpetual public animus." Or more simply, "It's not civilized to tell somebody 'you're going to sit in the stocks and we're going to throw stones at you.'" Shaming here may be directly linked to other reproved punishments, like whippings or beheadings; none has any place in a civilized society.[44]

And—again in keeping with the larger campaigns against shame—there is the recurrent hope that positive measures, including more enlightened education, might do the job of limiting crime. "Instead of thinking about ways in which we can shame people, let's think about ways in which we can honor or hold up examples of the many heroes that we read about every week . . . teaching by positive example that this kind of behavior is rewarded and respected and admired."[45]

One final, particularly imaginative component to the objection in principle turns to a quite different facet of the arguments that, two centuries ago, began to wean authorities from shaming: the impact not on the offender, but on the public itself. Law professor James Whitman worries about giving free rein to crowd psychology, to encouraging the public to indulge in its instincts for anger and cruelty in responding to open displays of shame. Public opinion is unstable and potentially harsh, which is incompatible with prudent standards. In opening to shaming, the government is turning its authority over "to a fickle and uncontrolled general populace."[46]

These arguments are not abstractions. They have complicated judicial rulings on shaming, and they are often reflected in objections raised by ordinary defendants. Thus in an Illinois case, a person convicted of assault was ordered to put a sign in front of his house identifying himself as a "violent felon" with the warning to "enter at your own risk." He argued that this subjected him unfairly to ridicule, and as such departed from normal sentencing guidelines; and ultimately the Illinois Supreme Court agreed that the sign might be "inconsistent with the rehabilitative purposes of probation." A Florida man, required to place his photo in the local paper along with details of his offense (drunken driving) objected to being subjected to "ridicule and humiliation." The court in this case found the requirement consistent with "penal ends" in serving potentially rehabilitative purposes. A lower New York court upheld a similar verdict, in this case a sign in the car identifying the driver as having driven drunk, stipulating only that it should be removable so that other family members would not be shamed while they were driving; the sign would presumably protect potential innocent victims by alerting them that there was a problem, and hopefully the driver himself would be motivated to seek further treatment in response to shame. But an appeals court sided with the accused, agreeing that this kind of obligation constituted "cruel and unusual" punishment and so was banned by the Eighth Amendment. And back and forth it has gone. The Tennessee Supreme Court voided a requirement that a sex offender put a sign in his front yard reading "Warning all children. Wayne Burdin is an admitted and convicted child molester. Parents Beware"; it based its decision on the grounds that legally it was a "breathtaking departure," well beyond the normal scope of probation.[47]

Overall, higher courts have tended to rule against shaming, with lower courts displaying more openness to this type of discipline. Some jurists have argued against shaming as a direct punishment while accepting it as part of probation where standards are tighter. Miscreants themselves disagree. Some welcome shaming as vastly preferable to jail time; others, clearly, are deeply offended and even defiant—as many contemporary psychologists would anticipate. The opportunity to offer options—with miscreants given the chance to choose between shame and more conventional punishments—clearly helps square the circle in some instances.

There are, finally, important efforts to advance additional compromise positions, by defining appropriate shame more clearly. Some arguments urge a link between shame and guilt—against the currently fashionable dissociation, seeing in the combination a real possibility of using shame to convince a miscreant to reevaluate his approach and avoid offense in future. Shame must not be taken to the extent of humiliation or stigma—in this sense some of the recent impositions may go too far. But some inducement to question not just a specific act, but one's own basic worthiness, might be a good thing, promoting the goal of rehabilitation. Shaming must also be accompanied by a clear opportunity for reintegration. Led by John Braithwaite, the Australian criminologist, "reintegrative shaming" projects have developed both in several Australian cities and in U.S. centers like Indianapolis. Offenders are brought together with their victims, who can then explain the impact of the crime; and the offenders are able to apologize. Shame is involved, but with focus on the offense more than the offender and with clear opportunities to make amends and reenter a circle of respectability. The approach often works—perhaps more clearly with violent crimes than with thefts—but its proponents admit that the data remain inconclusive.[48] The possibility of a compromise approach, which would define and delimit shaming more clearly than many recent U.S. courts have done, and attach it more explicitly to specific disciplinary goals that go beyond vague hopes of punitive and deterrent impact, has yet to emerge definitively.

Meanwhile, real beliefs in shame and awareness of the limitations and burdens of alternatives such as imprisonment sustain this option in many courts and for several types of crime. No overall resolution is in sight, in a society that has become deeply divided over this form of emotional discipline. The rise of new reliance on shaming has in turn galvanized the many opponents of the emotion to spirited and multifaceted opposition. The result is an intriguing addition to the most recent phase of shame history, and a vivid reminder about how an emotion's tradition can be revived and diversely interpreted.

RIGHTEOUS SHAME: EMOTION AND COMMUNITY

New efforts to oppose shame, extensions to areas like fat shaming, and even the unexpected renewal of shaming in the courts all offer reasonably clear records and all respond to reasonably precise, if contradictory, motivations. We turn, in this section and the next, to two somewhat related expansions of contemporary shame that are less easy to chart in any systematic way, and to some extent less easy to explain.

U.S. society famously emerged, after the 1960s, with deep political and cultural divisions. At the same time, Americans themselves arguably became more individually isolated, less firmly linked than in the past to definable communities and associations.[49] This was the setting in which new disagreements about shame could emerge—part indeed of the famous culture wars. But this was a setting as well in which shame might be projected as a means of defining some recognizable group identities, to stipulate through the utilization of shame who belonged and who did not. A similar approach might be projected at the international level, where again divisions and cultural disputes loomed large.

The most obvious evidence, in demonstrating important extensions of shame, involve the familiar conservative-liberal political alignments. Both groups—conservatives fairly openly, liberals with more inconsistency—began to use old and new opportunities for shaming as part of their platforms, to expand their identities and to demonstrate deep wells of righteous indignation. In both cases as well, shaming was employed particularly in situations where, for whatever reason, legal recourse was inadequate: shaming should do the job that democratic legislation could not fully accomplish. Shame in this political context highlighted the policy gap between left and right in the United States, but it also played a direct role in the growing personal dislike that members of each group felt toward the "other side," which became a growing factor in the political divide.[50]

Conservatives might hanker directly for the good old days of social shaming, and of course the revival of court-ordered shaming built into this impulse explicitly. Jeb Bush, the former Florida governor, mused in his 1994 memoir that "society needs to relearn the art of public and private disapproval and how to make those who engage in undesirable behavior feel some sense of shame." His sharpest barbs were directed at welfare recipients and their illegitimate children, but he even waxed nostalgic about the long lost past when more general "public condemnation" was aimed at sexual misconduct more generally, and when juvenile delinquents were more effectively humiliated. (Indeed, during his governorship, Florida passed a law requiring single women to publish information about past sexual partners if they sought to put a child up for adoption, though this was repealed before it could be declared unconstitutional. And Bush also pondered a suggestion that male juvenile offenders be required to wear frilly pink jumpsuits in public.)[51]

A great deal of the conservative shaming impulse was directed at classic targets, already visible in the nineteenth century: the poor, certain immigrant groups. Shamefulness circulated through conservative literature, again helping to confirm identity and righteous indignation. But it could also burst forth in public as well, with insults against certain ethnic groups or with outbursts in situations where an immigrant had the effrontery to speak a language other than English.

The most significant extension of shaming from the right, however, focused on abortion. This was a phenomenon that had long been surrounded with shame in U.S. culture (less so in some other countries), even as legal barriers dwindled. One of the many goals of the anti-shame campaign was to assist women in dealing with the shame abortion caused, to support them in emotional resilience. But for anti-abortion crusaders, the clear goal was and is more shame, not less. And the tactics have gone well beyond public outcry or insult.

Thus gatherings frequently assembled around abortion clinics, armed with posters depicting dead fetuses or throwing dismembered doll parts, shouting "murderer" and other epithets, clearly hoping to shame women into reconsidering their decision. In Montana anti-abortionists created a "Hall of Shame," designed to identify abortion seekers by name. Many groups also posted the names and addresses of doctors and staff involved in abortion, seeking to apply shame (and in some cases, also inviting violence) to these people as well. And the efforts could hit home, even with people who persisted in their determination: "It gave me a bad feeling in my stomach and still haunts me.... It embodied all the fears and judgment I felt from society"; "Getting an abortion was already the hardest day of my life. To have these people who don't know the first thing about me or why I was even there apply such impersonal hatred and judgment on me was infuriating." But for the most avid pro-lifers, deployment of every emotional weapon was absolutely justified for the higher goal of saving a baby's life.[52]

New forms of shaming from the liberal side of the equation were sometimes equally strident but not couched in quite such blatant emotional terms. And methods more commonly involved virtual rather than literal crowds—assembled through the press, more recently through Twitter or Facebook. Finally, the most common efforts were frequently designed to promote the larger effort to rescue groups from shamefulness, even though the standard arguments of the anti-shame movement were ignored in the excitement of using the emotion for a righteous cause.

The target, most commonly, was an offense against political correctness—an individual who had let slip a comment or a term that suggested hostility to women, to racial minorities, or to gays. Examples dot recent history. A British scientist, a Nobel Prize winner, tells a conference that women should not work in laboratories with men because they fall in love, or are fallen in love with, and besides they cry when they are criticized. His remarks trigger an internet firestorm, including carefully reasoned rebuttals from women scientists, quickly adopting a larger shaming tone that questioned his reputation more generally. Two days later, after an inadequate effort at apology, the scientist resigns his London university post. Radio commentators who slip into dubious racial references or apparent homophobia are similarly and rapidly tarred with shame, and usually hounded into resignations or dismissals. Even remarks made a few decades earlier, but now rediscovered, can be targets for shaming attacks.[53]

One of the most widely explored cases of shaming in the name of political correctness broke out in 2013. A woman, a publicist for an NGO, tweeted what she thought was a joke as she boarded a flight to South Africa. She expressed the hope that she would not get AIDS on her trip but then foolishly added "Just kidding. I'm white." By the time her flight landed, her unfortunate comment had exploded on social media, leading to widespread condemnations of her racism, insistence that she be fired, and worse. And indeed, in short order, she did lose her job and found it difficult to get other work as the shame storm continued. As one critic noted, "your tweet lives on forever."[54]

Liberal shaming was also recurrently applied to big-game hunters. A journalist who wrote about killing baboons was thus quickly accused of being a bully. Even more famously, in 2015, a U.S. dentist who shot and killed an iconic lion while on safari in Zimbabwe was quickly hauled up for global shaming, forced to go into hiding, his house covered with belligerent graffiti, his dental practice jeopardized. Here, even more than with more conventional political correctness, a host of people had decided that shaming action was essential even where, at least for the moment, the law was silent.

The boundaries of political correctness might themselves expand. As college students and administrators sought to respond to growing sensitivities, early in the twenty-first century, some sought to use shaming, along with regulations and the law, to curb even potentially upsetting speech on campus—the kind of speech that became known as microaggressions. Certain kinds of references to gender or race might unintentionally upset some members of the community, and so such terms should be proscribed, with people who used them made to apologize. Thus one faculty member who noted on a student paper that the word *indigenous*, used mid-sentence, should not be capitalized, was publicly singled out for potentially disturbing the author's sense of identity. A student who satirized this new campus climate was himself shamed, not only on social media but with smashed eggs and critical signs on the door of his dorm room in a latter-day chiravari.[55]

There is no need to supply more examples. On both sides of the bitter U.S. political divide, though on very different specific issues, a wide range of individuals and groups were spurred by a deep sense of righteousness to deploy massive public shame on offenders of various sorts.

The result both resembled and differed from classic shaming strategies. It did help draw together community spirit, even in the new virtual assemblies made possible by the internet. It helped define standards—as in the interesting recasting of hunting as a shameful sport. It could be accompanied by hints or acts of violence, though this was more common on the conservative than on the liberal side. Families, as well as individuals, were frequently drawn into the shaming experience—as in the AIDS joke case, where the offender's family felt publicly attacked—again, an involvement that had a familiar ring. But contemporary righteous shaming also and quite clearly trampled on individual rights, that category that had helped spur attacks on shame two centuries before. And, surprisingly often, it had economic consequences: victims, particularly of liberal shaming, were often fired from their jobs. The most vulnerable worked in politics, entertainment, or communications, but academics and others might not be spared. Here, shaming now spilled over to employers, who characteristically beat an immediate retreat regardless of how trivial, or atypical, or distant in time the offense might have been, eager to limit the damage contemporary shame could call forth.

Shaming strategies were also now be applied in the international arena, becoming part of global political disputes as well. From the days of the anti-slavery campaigns onward, reformers had recurrently tried to mobilize public opinion against unacceptable behaviors elsewhere, hoping that shame could spur remediation. Identification of Germany as responsible for World War I imprudently applied shaming to a whole nation. But the blossoming of international shaming awaited the Cold War and the ability to use contemporary media to try to organize world opinion. Thus Amnesty International, founded in 1961, urged the use of emotional pressure on human rights offenders: reports of torture and imprisonment were sickening, "yet if these feelings of disgust all over the world could be united into common action, something effective could be done." The group sought various remedies, including direct diplomatic pressure and in some instances economic boycott, but mobilizing petitions and, soon, internet campaigns designed to shame wrongdoers became fundamental to Amnesty's strategy. A woman is about to be stoned to death for adultery in northern Nigeria? Send such a mass of petitions to the government that it will be shamed into intervention. A U.S. state is about to condemn yet another prisoner to execution? Again, letters and petitions, combined sometimes with special voices such as that of the papacy. Similar strategies applied to reports of labor abuses, particularly where global corporations were involved: shaming in this case might have added weight since it came from potential consumers. Companies like Nike, and public-figure investors like Kathy Lee Gifford, were effectively shamed into promises of better treatment for their workers in places like Indonesia and Vietnam. Finally, individual governments got into the act. The U.S. government issued annual reports on human rights abuses, initially as part of the Cold War, hoping that the list would apply both political and emotional pressure to some of the worst offenders. Shame attacks on reported human rights violations became part of the regular diplomatic interaction between the United States and China. As Human Rights Watch puts it, "Our goal is to make governments pay a heavy price in reputation and legitimacy if they violate the rights of their people.... Often our best tool is to publicize our information on abuses in order to embarrass a government before its own citizens and in the eyes of the international community." Shaming, in a nutshell.[56]

Wider diplomatic considerations aside, global shaming resulted from many of the same impulses as liberal shaming domestically. Passionate attachment to moral standards confronted a situation where, despite in-principle acceptance of human rights charters, international law made little headway. Shaming might galvanize internal discontent, or it might simply employ the nebulous "international community" as an audience of its own, before which an abusive nation or corporation could be brought to task.

Righteous shaming is by definition difficult to assess, because many analysts are likely to agree with some of the causes involved. Who, among liberal academics, wants to dispute the importance of careful speech on racial or gender issues, or the need to press for greater international human rights compliance? But shaming is shaming, and the partisan and international expansion risks neglect of some of the findings that, simultaneously, were spurring the ongoing campaign against the emotion. If shaming criminals is unjust or counterproductive, why is its application to politically incorrect speech a different category? Consistency has proved difficult, and in fact it is losing ground in practice. Indeed, the 2015–16 U.S. presidential primary campaign revealed the huge gaps that now existed in shaming standards, including the anger that had built up against efforts to enforce political correctness: various groups in the United States sought greater license to express high emotion through shame, and in the process to shame one another.

One other expansion of shaming spilled over from some of the political applications, where social media came to play a vital role in public campaigns. But random attacks on individuals, another result of the new technology, deserve attention in their own right. As with other contemporary manifestations of shame, these attacks revived several older themes while introducing new, and often troubling, elements as well.

MEDIA SHAMING: USES AND ABUSES OF THE NEW TECHNOLOGY

Many reality television shows, as they expanded from the 1990s onward, depended on public shaming. On the *Jerry Springer Show*, which launched in 1991, individuals sought to use public statements to shame spouses into sexual fidelity or renunciation of other troubling habits. Quest for higher ratings led to a growing number of guests who openly discussed various kinds of deviant behavior, while insults against various groups became more explicit as well. Shaming here fused with the eagerness to win public attention as well as the declining attachment to privacy, and it was not always clear what motive predominated.

Another contributor to a more open shaming atmosphere was what was called, by the 1990s, slut shaming. While the range of shaming situations involving sexuality had narrowed with more tolerant standards, a connection persisted. The focus was on girls or women whose dress or behavior seemed to suggest a busy sex life—men might be slut shamed as well, but a double standard largely prevailed. Attacks might come from public figures—a conservative commentator branded a student a slut because she advocated more available birth control devices. But the most common setting was within a school, the perpetrators most often girls targeting other girls. And while slut shaming could be by word of mouth, it was increasingly common to use social media to get the message out more quickly and more rapidly.[57]

And here was the biggest innovation: a new technology that could allow even one individual to reach an unprecedentedly broad audience—people with no other community ties—unprecedentedly quickly. A pair of young women take a mocking photo at Arlington National Cemetery; posted on Facebook, where it is detached from the women's "running joke about disobeying signs," the photo eventually spurs a mass shaming public to insist—successfully— that the principal perpetrator be fired from her job. A man makes a poor-taste gesture at a movie, and an offended audience member takes his picture, puts it on Facebook, and we are all off to the races. Another man—himself a social media shamer—posts an ironic reference, "bring back bullying," and quickly becomes a victim of what one author aptly calls the "internet shame machine."[58] Shaming becomes one of several components that increasingly make social media a channel for interpersonal viciousness.

Motives of the new class of shamers were varied. Some used the opportunity to get back at a professional rival—in one case a big-game hunter whose real mistake was to write bad reviews of the work of an ardent tweet shamer. Some were undoubtedly sincerely outraged, and simply used new means to replace face-to-face community disapproval. Some simply enjoyed creating a stir. Some were involved with internet companies that depended on juicy news for their livelihood. One observer contended that the clearest common denominator was a new kind of crowd psychology, a group mania that built on the heady capacity to cause pain. But it was also possible to see in the new frenzy not only the impact of new technology, but an extension of what many would regard as useful, politically correct applications of shame in the 1960s

CHAPTER 5

and 1970s—the kind of shame directed against objectionable racial or gender references. The pattern was not easy to evaluate.[59]

Results varied as well, but they were almost always bad. Loss of job—especially rapid loss of job—was a common outcome, though not invariable. Many of the shamed had to move, had to abandon family and social connections. Many fell ill or entered a deep depression. Once in a while retaliation was possible: the man shamed by the movie joke tweeted about his loss of job, and attention turned to the woman who had posted the accusing video, shaming her in turn. The new shaming atmosphere left many people deeply fearful of a past indiscretion being publicized.

Even clear offenses were often punished beyond reasonable limits. Around the turn of the millennium, several journalists were correctly accused of plagiarism. They not only lost their jobs—arguably a proper outcome—but found themselves beleaguered wherever they went: "shame was following him."[60] And forgiveness seemed impossible to achieve, both because of the permanence of the social media record and because some persecutors delighted in maintaining pressure.

By the early twenty-first century, media shaming was spread to parents of young teenagers who, apparently, could find no other means of effective discipline. A thirteen-year-old girl posts a flirty picture on Twitter against her father's orders; he retaliates by posting a film of his response on Facebook. Despite subsequent counseling, the girl is shattered and commits suicide soon thereafter. Another father, infuriated by his son's skinny jeans, puts a video on YouTube. Less imaginatively, another father forces an eleven-year-old to stand on the street with a sign detailing her disobedience—clearly taking a page from the new approaches in criminology. A number of parents began to punish children, mainly girls, by cutting their hair—an old approach—but now videotaping the process and posting it publicly, for offenses ranging from bad grades to losing a cell phone.[61]

Experts of course quickly pointed out the folly of this approach. They repeated the standard wisdom about how a shamed child simply loses all self-respect while gaining little incentive to improve his or her behavior. They correctly insisted that using social media to shame a child established a durable record that could haunt the person for decades to come, in school or job applications. But in some quarters, the new opportunity, and the anger or righteous zeal attached, continued to be too tempting to resist.[62] The contemporary ascent of shame persisted.

A few voices, finally, were heard not only opposing the intensification of shame, but also warily suggesting opportunities for resistance. Several victims of public humiliation noted that, with a bit of time and perspective, public shaming episodes were not quite as bad as they first seemed—though most retained deep anger against the arbitrary behavior of the shamers and against the loss of privacy. A law professor whose mistake in sending pornographic materials to her class caused deep pain—though not, thanks to academic protections, loss of job—realized after a while that life went on. It was possible to regain a sense of dignity: "there are worse things than humiliation. If the speed and intensity of the new forms of shaming could be resisted, damage might in some cases be limited."[63] And for their part, an increasing number of teenagers resorted to websites that preserved complete anonymity—like YikYak or Snapchat—in order to reduce at least this opportunity to incite shaming.

Assessing the Contemporary Period

Sorting out the recent history of shame in the United States is no easy task—far more difficult, obviously, then untangling the complexities of the previous period in which shame, on balance, had been in decline.

New levels of division form the most obvious theme. Liberals and conservatives disagree about shame. So, often, do those subjected to shame compared to those doing the shaming. Partisan divide is not the only factor involved, and many disputes depend on specific issues and circumstances.

Older trends and patterns leave their mark. Despite some recommendations to the contrary, Americans are still not in the main explicitly socialized to shame, which may make it a more difficult emotion to deal with even as its usage revives. Sensitivities show in the defiant responses to shame, but also in what are frequently quick capitulations to humiliation and misery.

The innovative aspects of contemporary shame are at least as striking, even aside from the technology involved. The nature of community changes with more anonymous exchanges, and arguably this has enhanced opportunities for distortion and cruelty. Shame has always risked unfairness and overexcitement on the part of the shamers, but these qualities seem to have intensified with nebulous or virtual communities rather than in-person contacts. In many cases, shaming has become part of the nasty side of contemporary U.S. life and culture.

Particularly troubling is the decline of any clear channels for apology or reintegration. Patience, simply waiting for social media to turn to some other victim or social evil, seems the best recourse. But many contemporary shamers are far more focused on victory than on remediation, and the results can be painful. Many of the recent expansions of shaming highlight pure punishment, or a chance to crush a victim, with no particular interest in remediation.

CHAPTER 5

Not surprisingly, in these circumstances, important new movements have developed not simply to reassert the common wisdom about shame's ill effects, but to curb some of the recent abuses. The moment reminds of the earlier and successful campaign to abolish the stocks, with much the same rationale in terms of protecting human dignity. But the targets are more flexible and elusive than the stocks were, so results are uncertain.

Thus an Illinois legislator proposes punishments for parents who publicly humiliate their children, whether through signs or through use of the internet. The European Union, ahead of the United States on this general issue, allows individuals to delete internet references from services like Google—under the heading of a "right to be forgotten." The European courts, building on a 1995 Data Protection Law, ruled in 2010 that a Spanish citizen had the right to require deletion of a public reference to a previous property foreclosure, on grounds that this was needlessly shameful because the incident had been resolved and was in any event lodged in the past. The new "right" is hedged with restrictions, notably toward assuring freedom of expression for third parties, and operates on a case-by-case basis. Its longer-term effects are unclear. But over seventy thousand people applied for internet deletions within the first three months of the new ruling. Several U.S. states have moved in a similar direction, though specifically for minors whose youthful indiscretions should not haunt them into adulthood. Thus California has enacted a controversial "eraser button" rule, applicable to all websites that allow minors to register, permitting them to destroy prior posts once they attain their majority. Similar legislation is under consideration elsewhere, both in other states and at the federal level. Some advocates reach for more: not only erasure of one's own childish remarks, but capacity to erase postings that others have re-shared and even third-party submissions—of offensive photographs, for example—where the depicted individual was not involved in the posting at all. Extensions of this sort, of course, run up against freedom of expression criteria, and an acceptable policy has not yet emerged. What is clear, however, is that the campaign against shame has been renewed, under dramatically different circumstances.[64]

Finally, amid all the flux of the contemporary period, what of the effectiveness of shame? Predictably, opinions and data vary. Many jurists and some parents report that public shaming has generated remediation—some drunk drivers learn the error of their ways, some disobedient children shape up. Though surprisingly slowly and unevenly, most public figures learn to hew to political correctness—making the lapses into racist or other offensive references that do still materialize all the more striking. Claims that shame uniformly leads to self-destructive despair, rather than remediation or deterrence, may not consistently hold up. On the other hand, shame can unquestionably overshoot. It can lead to unwarranted misery, even to suicide—and even some partisans of contemporary shaming are admitting that some current shaming practices have gone too far.

Some cases are simply difficult to call. Shaming on behalf of human rights has clearly helped prevent some executions and led to the release of some political prisoners. But some governments, as in China, have largely rebutted the shame approach, arguing that Western criticism is a form of neocolonialism and that Chinese conditions are improving by relevant standards. Nation shaming can have limited impact, and it can even backfire.[65]

Contemporary shaming seems to have little impact in financial circles. International financiers may be self-selected for personalities that resist shame. Certainly, their criteria for success—steadily advancing profits—clearly trump any impact of shame, which is why they rebound so quickly from blatant financial mismanagement or chicanery save in the rare instances when they actually serve jail time. Notoriously, U.S. efforts to use shaming publicity to curb bloated executive salaries have failed outright to date. The executives use information about salaries in other corporations to demand even more for themselves—shame be damned.

Yet shame advocates, even when receptive to some contemporary curbs, persist. They point to current philanthropists initially shamed into public awareness by a shaming critique of their corporate practices (e.g., for antitrust violations), or to tax delinquents who pay up as a result of exposure on public websites (a procedure used in California). They note the deficiencies of other methods of discipline, including guilt. They point to growing problems, like environmental degradation, that may only respond to public critique—"we are going to need a lot of help from shame."[66] The debate continues, spurred by the variety of experiences and perspectives that has opened up over the past half-century.

Afterword

Shame is a problem emotion. This remains a fair statement historically: even in societies that successfully use shame in many ways, the emotion can generate undue conformity or it can inhibit recognition of problems such as mental illness. And always, in any context, shaming can go too far, causing levels of emotional pain out of proportion to offending behaviors. Particularly in individualistic societies, shame not only generates great distress but can cause resentment and counterproductive behaviors as well. Some societies, finally, have disagreed vigorously about aspects of shame, and this certainly applies to the contemporary United States, where the emotion joins a number of topics where consensus has clearly collapsed.

Shame also has a complex and revealing history, despite the desirability of additional, particularly comparative, research. Understanding changes and continuities over time helps connect patterns of shame and shaming to other topics, not only penology and child rearing but also education and cultural context. The historical record is virtually inescapable in sorting through the current national disputes and inconsistencies where shame is concerned. Most important, historical understanding contributes actively to interdisciplinary analysis, even linking past trends to contemporary dilemmas.

For the history of shame offers more than a confirmation of the emotion's complicated qualities. It certainly shatters any remnants of the old distinction between shame-based and guilt-based societies that might feed a Western sense of superiority. What we know about shame-based societies and their history demonstrates more constructive opportunities for the emotion than some of the most dismissive critiques allow for. Equally important, the West's own long commitment to reliance on shame, and its continued if disputed uses of the emotion, qualify any facile dichotomies. Distinctions do exist—whether the contrast is Southern California and an Indonesian fishing village, or the more complex juxtaposition of contemporary East Asian and Western data—but they are more nuanced than a simple shame-guilt divide allows for.

The history of shame and shaming also raises questions about some of the dominant psychological views of the emotion, quite apart from the thorny shame-guilt dichotomy, which simply does not entirely apply historically or even, often, linguistically. Historical work clearly benefits from many current formulations, offering confirmation of how shattering the emotion can be and also on how many communities in the past relied on shame's devastation both to enforce desired standards and to express real cruelty. At the same time, complementing work on the sociology of shame, a historical assessment highlights the variety of shame experiences and the possibilities for constructive management of the emotion.[1] Practices of the past cannot be revived in modern contexts, but awareness of precedent may nevertheless provide some useful guidelines. Thus those societies that develop clear warnings about shame's dangers, even to the point of providing specific cautionary words like *shamefast*, suggest options that might be adapted to more contemporary settings. Shame's social role, historically, has gone beyond enforcement of community standards and support for community cohesion, though these functions can be vital and clearly help explain the continued survival of shaming amid massive objections to the emotion. The importance of shame *anticipation*, in supporting the relationship between individuals and larger social bonds, proves central to the historical record and, again, persists in the contemporary context as well. Overall, a sensitive approach to past uses of shame, and not anachronistic dismissal based on contemporary attacks on the emotion, reveals qualities that can usefully be considered even in current situations. The validity of past precedent very definitely applies to the importance of combining shame's disciplinary role with opportunities for recovery, for rejoining a relevant community after shame's impact has been assimilated. It is perfectly valid to argue, with Andrew Morrison, author of *The Culture of Shame*, that overcoming shame should require hard work and discipline—but it should be possible, as a curb on the emotion's destructive potential.[2]

This study has emphasized the importance of a new Western approach toward shame, emerging from novel ideas about the individual and the nature of dignity initially developed during the Enlightenment. It has of course cautioned against any simplistic invocation of a "modern" movement away from shame. And it has not sought to demonstrate the kind of radical decline suggested by the notion of shame as emotional taboo—though it certainly provides some evidence for the somewhat more subtle approach of scholars like Gersten Kaufman, with his 1989 contention that "American society is a shame-based culture, but shame remains hidden. . . . There is a shame about shame."[3]

Change has been quite real, and important in social relationships and individual experience alike. The decline of the many traditional forms of public shaming significantly altered both social and personal life. In this vital sense, the history of shame confirms one of the main functions of emotions history more generally, to chart and explain significant shifts and to place contemporary formulations in the context of past trends. Public practices have been transformed, advice against shame has proliferated, individual reactions to shame have shifted—and of course formal scholarship itself has responded to the larger adjustment in standards, to provide additional evidence about shame's harmful effects.

Change has been immensely complicated, however, and here too historical analysis adds to our understanding of an emotion in practice. Disagreements about shame's role have surfaced at various points, if sometimes only implicitly. The U.S. South long held out for a greater retention of shaming, as did elements of the European aristocracy. Schoolteachers, less systematically, continued to depend on shaming for a number of reasons, while more recently public health advisors have turned to the emotion from their primary concern with combatting obesity. And disagreement over shame's validity flared quite openly from the 1960s onward, particularly in the United States, as the emotion's revival clashed with explicit resistance.

Disagreement was only part of the story. The modern U.S. record, over the past two centuries, shows how difficult it is to reduce shame levels in complex societies, because of the hold of custom but also a variety of social needs, both old and new. This is not necessarily surprising, but it adds to the difficulties of finding agreed-upon guidelines for the uses of shame in a modern Western context. Historians work on continuity as well as change, and the trajectory of shame over the past two centuries abundantly illustrates the combination. And the unexpected resurgence of shame more recently, and perhaps particularly the eagerness with which many people now seize on new technologies to express an apparent delight in shaming, add an important challenge in interpretation and emotion management alike.

Modern patterns, including the contemporary disputes over the emotion, raise questions about basic approach that are not easy to answer. The "decline of shame" theme proves misleading to a degree, and this has serious implications for experts and the wider public alike. The challenge to shame and shaming, particularly in Western culture, has produced important results, but its success has been incomplete, and the effort may well have reduced our capacity to discuss appropriate standards for the shame that persists. Experts have become more comfortable attacking shame than exploring how it can best be used and managed: scholarship on shame might usefully seek a more careful balance between reproving the emotion and discussing the social needs it seems to serve. Parents who are working to shield their children from shaming while boosting their self-esteem may not be fully preparing their offspring for the real world of shame that still exists and in some venues is expanding. Shame reduction remains a valid goal in many areas, but shame management may be equally important, and a grasp of the emotion's complex modern history is essential to achieve both.

Notes

Preface

1. Ruth Benedict, *The Chrysanthemum and the Sword: Patterns of Japanese Culture* (Boston: Houghton Mifflin, 1989), 22–27; note how Benedict specifically cites the Japanese lack of the kind of moral compass that only guilt can provide; David Weir, "Honour and Shame," *Islam Watch*, last modified September 17, 2007, www.islam-watch.org, accessed January 12, 2016; Pauline Kent, "Ruth Benedict's Original Wartime Study of the Japanese," *International Journal of Japanese Sociology* 3, no. 1 (1994): 81–97. See also Edward Said's trenchant comments on distortions of Islam through the culture of shame approach: *Orientalism* (New York: Vintage, 1979), 48.

2. Richard Shweder, "Toward a Deep Cultural Psychology of Shame," *Social Research* 70, no. 4 (2003): 1109–30; on the importance of words, see Anna Wierzbicka, *Emotions across Languages and Cultures: Diversity and Universals* (Cambridge: Cambridge University Press, 1999); Cliff Goodard and Anna Wierzbicka, eds., *Words and Meanings: Lexical Semantics across Domains, Languages, and Cultures* (New York: Oxford University Press: 1991); Catherine Lutz, *Unnatural Emotions: Everyday Sentiments on a Micronesian Atoll and Their Challenge to Western Theory* (Chicago: University of Chicago Press, 1988).

3. Thomas J. Scheff, "Shame and the Social Bond: A Sociological Theory," *Sociological Theory* 18, no. 1 (2000): 84–99.

4. Janine Wedel, *Unaccountable: How Elite Power Brokers Corrupt our Finances, Freedom, and Security* (San Jose, Calif.: Pegasus, 2014), 211.

5. Ute Frevert, "Shame and Humiliation," *History of Emotions—Insights into Research* (October 2015), doi:10.14280/08241.47; Willard Gaylin, quoted in Linda Wolfe, "A Sub-

jective Subject," *New York Times*, February 11, 1979, 3, www.nytimes.com, accessed February 2, 2017.

6. Monica Lewinsky, "Shame and Survival," *Vanity Fair*, June 2014, www.vanityfair.com, accessed June 15, 2015.

7. David Nash and Anne-Marie Kilday, *Cultures of Shame: Exploring Crime and Morality in Britain 1600–1900* (London: Palgrave, 2010); John Demos, "Shame and Guilt in Early New England," in *Emotions and Social Change: Toward a New Psychohistory*, ed. C. Z. Stearns and P. N. Stearns (New York: Holmes and Meier, 1988), 69–86.

8. Olwen A. Bedford, "The Individual Experience of Guilt and Shame in Chinese Culture," *Culture and Psychology* 10, no. 1 (2004): 29–52; see also Jin Li, Lianqin Wang, and Kurt Fischer, "The Organization of Chinese Shame Concepts," *Cognition and Emotion* 18, no. 6 (2004): 767–97. I am deeply grateful for Norman Kutcher's take on the Chinese historical literature, again largely confirming the gap between attention to Confucian culture and studies on the contemporary role of shame.

9. Susan J. Matt and Peter N. Stearns, eds., *Doing Emotions History* (Urbana: University of Illinois Press, 2014); Ute Frevert, *Emotions in History Lost and Found* (New York: Central European University, 2011); William M. Reddy, *The Navigation of Feeling: A Framework for the History of Emotions* (New York: Cambridge University Press, 2001); Barbara H. Rosenwein, "Worrying about Emotions in History," *American Historical Review* 107 (June 2002): 821.

Chapter 1. Exploring Shame: The Interdisciplinary Context

1. Jessica L. Tracy, Richard W. Robins, and June Price Tangney, eds., *The Self-Conscious Emotions: Theory and Research* (New York: Guildford Press, 2007).

2. On Freud and generally on shame's devastating impact, see Andrew P. Morrison, *The Culture of Shame* (New York: Ballantine Books, 1996), 17; see also Erik Erikson, *Childhood and Society* (New York: W. W. Norton, 1963).

3. My thanks to June Tangney for news of this meeting.

4. Michael Lewis, "Self-Conscious Emotions: Embarrassment, Pride, Shame, and Guilt," in *Handbook of Emotions*, edited by Michael Lewis and Jeannette M. Haviland-Jones (New York: Guilford Press, 2000), 623–36.

5. The basic emotions issue continues to be debated: Paul Ekman's idea of six emotions, for example, has recently been challenged by researchers who claim there are only four. The controversy relates only tangentially to shame, which links to the "basics" presumably through sadness—though sham*ing* clearly calls on anger, disgust, and possibly fear. The question however of whether shame, though not basic, is inevitable and must come up in our analysis. See James A. Russell, "Is There Universal Recognition of Emotion through Facial Expression? A Review of the Cross-Cultural Studies," *Psychological Bulletin* 115 (1994): 102–41.

6. Erikson, *Childhood and Society*.

7. Another interesting tangent—which ultimately reminds us again of how difficult the definition of shame may be—involves the exploration of blushing. This was a phe-

nomenon that fascinated nineteenth-century scientists who dealt with emotion, including Charles Darwin, mainly because it is one of the few human emotional signals that cannot be found in other animals. Blushing suggests, on the one hand, a spontaneous reaction to an audience of others—it might imply that self-conscious emotions are basic to the human condition after all. But several complexities cast doubt on clear conclusions. First, not everyone blushes, even among Caucasians. Second, blushing may occur when a person feels shamed, but it can also occur on the basis of guilt, or probably even more commonly embarrassment; and in fact blushing can even be produced by good news, such as flattery. Blushing seems to be a response, for those individuals who experience it, to the gaze of others, rather than a definition of any particular emotion, self-conscious or not. It may have a role: while blushing can suggest some vulnerability, it may also generate mild social sympathy and take some of the sting out of a situation that causes shame or embarrassment. This may prove significant given the difficulty many people face in escaping discomfort from self-conscious emotions, and shame above all. The redemptive potential for blushing, in helping an individual overcome group reactions to shame or embarrassment, has been explored in Japanese culture. But again, overall, blushing does not really advance the basic effort at definition, and its extreme variability reduces its relevance still further. See Ray W. Crozier, "Differentiating Shame from Embarrassment," *Emotion Review* 6, no. 30 (2014): 269–76; R. J. Edelman, *The Psychology of Embarrassment* (Chichester, U.K.: Wiley, 1987); C. R. Darwin, *The Expression of the Emotions in Man and Animals* (Chicago: University of Chicago Press, 1965); Gerhart Piers and Milton B. Singer, *Shame and Guilt: A Psychoanalytic and Cultural Study* (New York: Norton, 1971). Mary Ann O'Farrell, *Telling Complexions: The Nineteenth-Century English Novel and the Blush* (Durham, N.C.: Duke University Press, 1997); Katsuaki Suzuki, Nori Takei, Masayoshi Kawai, Yoshio Minabe, and Norio Mori, "Is Taijin Kyofusho a Culture-Bound Syndrome?," *American Journal of Psychiatry* 160, no. 7 (July 2003): 1358.

8. Lewis, "Self-Conscious Emotions," 623–36.

9. Ibid.

10. Brené Brown, "The Power of Vulnerability," filmed June 2010, TEDxKC video, 2010, 20:19, www.ted.com, accessed June 15, 2015.

11. K. V. Korostelina, *Political Insults: How Offenses Escalate Conflict* (Oxford: Oxford University Press, 2014).

12. Some contrarian views are worth noting. On internal shame, see Gabriele Taylor, *Pride, Shame, and Guilt: Emotions of Self-Assessment* (Oxford, U.K.: Clarendon Press, 1985); also Gerhard Piers and Milton B. Singer, *Shame and Guilt: A Psychoanalytic and a Cultural Study* (Springfield, Ill.: Charles C. Thomas, 1953), which actually argues not only that shame can be internal, but that it is actually more useful than guilt which mainly involves the sometimes disconcerting recollection of past disciplinary actions; Carl Schneider, *Shame, Exposure, and Privacy* (Boston: Beacon Press, 1977), also offers a more optimistic view, contending that if one can maintain a positive attitude amid the disorienting aspects of shame, useful adjustments can result; finally, see Bernard Arthur Owen Williams, *Shame and Necessity* (Berkeley: University of California Press, 1993).

13. Todd Kashdan, *The Upside of Your Dark Side: Why Being Your Whole Self—Not Just Your "Good" Self—Derives Success and Fulfillment* (New York: Hudson Street Press, 2014).

14. June Tangney, et al., "Assessing Jail Inmates' Proneness to Shame and Guilt: Feeling Bad about the Behavior or the Self?," *Criminal Justice and Behavior* 38, no. 7 (2011): 710–74.

15. D. Stearns and G. W. Parrott, "When Feeling Bad Makes You Look Good: Guilt, Shame, and Person Perception," *Cognition and Emotion* 26 (2012): 407–30.

16. M. W. Sullivan, "The Emotions of Maltreated Children in Response to Success and Failure," presented at the biennial meeting of the Society for Research in Child Development, Albuquerque, N.M.; N. J. Kaslow, L. P. Rehm, S. L. Pollack, and A. W. Siegel, "Attributional Style and Self-Control Behavior in Depressed and Non-depressed Children and Their Parents," *Journal of Abnormal Child Psychology* 16 (no date): 163–75; K. A. Kendall-Tackett, L. M. Williams, and D. Finkelhor, "Impact of Sexual Abuse on Children: A Review and Synthesis of Recent Empirical Studies," *Psychological Bulletin* 113 (no date): 164–80.

17. J. Tangney, J. Jeffrey Stuewig, and A. Martinez, "Two Faces of Shame: The Roles of Shame and Guilt in Predicting Recidivism," *Psychological Science* 25 (no date): 799–805.

18. James Gilligan, *Violence: Reflections on a National Epidemic* (New York: Vintage Books, 1997); Marcia Webb et al., "Shame, Guilt, Symptoms of Depression, and Reported History of Psychological Maltreatment," *Child Abuse and Neglect* 31, no. 11 (2007): 1143–53.

19. S. Pattison, *Shame: Theory, Therapy, Theology* (Cambridge: Cambridge University Press, 2000).

20. Lewis, "Self-Conscious Emotions," 623–36. Psychologists would recognize of course that societies may vary in the standards they enforce through shame—some for example very concerned about adultery, others worried about some other behavior; but this would not alter the basic individual shame experience.

21. Norbert Elias, *The Civilizing Process* (New York: Pantheon Books, 1982); Richard Sennett, *Authority* (New York: W. W. Norton, 1993).

22. "Shame," Merriam-Webster, last modified October 12, 2015, www.merriam-webster.com, accessed January 12, 2016; see also "guilt."

Chapter 2. Shame and Shaming in Premodern Societies

1. David Ho, Wai Fu, and S. Ng, "Guilt, Shame and Embarrassment: Revelations of Self and Face," *Culture and Psychology* 10, no. 1 (March 2004): 64–84, esp. 66–7; Stephanie Trigg, *Shame and Honor: A Vulgar History of the Order of the Garter* (Philadelphia: University of Pennsylvania Press, 2012).

2. Bruce G. Trigger, *Ancient Egypt: A Social History* (New York: Cambridge University Press, 1983), 81.

3. Jennifer L. Goetz and Dacher Keltner, "Shifting Meanings of Self-Conscious Emotions across Cultures: A Social-Functional Approach," in Tracy, Robins, and Tangney, *Self-Conscious Emotions*, 153–73. For the issues in generalizations about the premodern, see Barbara Rosenwein, *Generations of Feeling: A History of Emotions, 600–1700* (Cambridge: Cambridge University Press, 2015).

4. Daniel M. T. Fessler, "From Appeasement to Conformity: Evolutionary and Cultural Perspectives on Shame, Competition, and Cooperation," in Tracy, Robins, and

Tangney, *Self-Conscious Emotions*, 174–94; Jason P. Martens, Jessica L. Tracy, and Azim F. Shariff, "Status Signals: Adaptive Benefits of Displaying and Observing the Nonverbal Expressions of Pride and Shame," *Cognition and Emotion* 36, no. 3 (2012): 390–406; Paul D. MacLean, "Brain Evolution Relating to Family, Play and the Separation Call," *Archives of General Psychiatry* 42, no. 4 (1985): 405–17.

5. Michelle Z. Rosaldo, "The Shame of Headhunters and the Autonomy of Self," *Ethos* 11, no. 3 (1 October 1983): 135–51; Robert Knox Dentan, *The Semai: A Nonviolent People of Malaya* (New York: Holt, Rinehart, and Winston, 1968), 68–70; Jean L. Briggs, *Never in Anger* (Cambridge, Mass.: Harvard University Press, 1970), 350; Harry Blagg, "A Just Measure of Shame? Aboriginal Youth and Conferencing in Australia," *British Journal of Criminology* 37 (1997): 481–501.

6. For a vital discussion of the social uses of shame, with emphasis on its positive functions as opposed to glib generalizations about the superiority of guilt cultures, see Piers and Singer, *Shame and Guilt*.

7. Naomi Kipury, *Oral Literature of the Masai* (Nairobi: Heinemann Educational Books, 1982), 43, accessed at HathiTrust Digital Library, www.hathitrust.org.

8. D. M. T. Fessler, "Shame in Two Cultures: Implications for Evolutionary Approaches," *Journal of Cognition and Culture* 4 (2004): 207–62.

9. Robert I. Levy, *Tahitians: Mind and Experience in the Society Islands* (Chicago: University of Chicago Press, 1975).

10. Thomas Gregor, *The Mehinaku: The Dream of Daily Life in a Brazilian Indian Village* (Chicago: University of Chicago Press, 2009), 220–22. There are of course other cases; see, for example, Catherine A. Lutz, *Unnatural Emotions: Everyday Sentiments on a Micronesian Atoll and Their Challenge to Western Theory* (Chicago: University of Chicago Press, 1988).

11. Fessler, "From Appeasement to Conformity," 174–94.

12. M. E. J. Richardson, trans., *Hammurabi's Laws* (London: T&T Clark International, 2000), 27.

13. Trigger, *Ancient Egypt*, 81.

14. Christina Tarnopolsky, "Prudes, Perverts, and Tyrants: Plato and the Contemporary Politics of Shame," *Political Theory* 32, no. 4 (August 2004): 468–94.

15. Cynthia Patterson, *The Family in Greek History* (Cambridge, Mass.: Harvard University Press, 1998), 178–79.

16. Williams, *Shame and Necessity*.

17. Aristotle quoted in Jennifer Welchman, "Virtue Ethics and Human Development: A Pragmatic Approach," in Stephen Mark Gardiner, ed., *Value Ethics, Old and New* (Ithaca, N.Y.: Cornell University Press, 2005), 149.

18. David Konstan, *The Emotions of the Ancient Greeks: Studies in Aristotle and Classical Literature* (Toronto: University of Toronto Press, 2007), 91–110; Konstan, "Shame in Ancient Greece," *Social Research* 70, no. 4 (2003): 1031–60, esp. 1040.

19. Goetz and Keltner, "Shifting Meanings of Self-Conscious Emotions"; Trigg, *Shame and Honor*: Ho, Fu, and Ng, "Guilt, Shame and Embarrassment."

20. Jane Geaney, "Guarding Moral Boundaries: Shame in Early Confucianism," *Philosophy East and West* 54, no. 2 (April 2004): 113–142.

21. Bryan W. Van Norden, "The Emotion of Shame and the Virtue of Righteousness in Mencius," *Dao* 2, no. 1 (2002): 45–77, esp. 63; Geaney, "Guarding Moral Boundaries"; Antonio S. Cua, "The Ethical Significance of Shame: Insights of Aristotle and Xunzi," *Philosophy East and West* (2003): 147–202; Bongrae Seok, "Moral Psychology of Shame in Early Confucian Philosophy," *Frontiers of Philosophy in China* 10, no. 1 (2015): 21–57.

22. Anne Behnke Kinney, *Chinese Views of Childhood* (Honolulu: University of Hawaii Press, 1995), 83. Unfortunately, the best book on the history of Chinese childhood, focused in any event on a later period, does not deal directly with shame, though it remains well worth exploring for wider familial contexts; Ping-Chen Hsiung, *A Tender Voyage: Children and Childhood in Late Imperial China* (Stanford, Calif.: Stanford University Press, 2005).

23. Anne Behnke Kinney, *Representations of Childhood and Youth in Early China* (Stanford, Calif.: Stanford University Press, 2004).

24. Beryl Rawson, *Marriage, Divorce, and Children in Ancient Rome* (Canberra: Humanities Research Centre, 1991), 153.

25. David Hunt, *Parents and Children in History: The Psychology of Family Life in Early Modern France* (New York: Basic Books, 1970).

26. Hugh D. R. Baker, *Chinese Family and Kinship* (New York: Columbia University Press, 1979), 124.

27. Hsien Chin Hu, "The Chinese Concepts of 'Face,'" *American Anthropologist* 46, no. 1 (1944): 45–64.

28. Cited in Sara Forsdyke, *Slaves Tell Tales: And Other Episodes in the Politics of Popular Culture in Ancient Greece* (Princeton, N.J.: Princeton University Press, 2012), 11.

29. Patterson, *Family in Greek History*.

30. Christian Lange, "Legal and Cultural Aspects of Ignominious Parading (Tashhīr) in Islam," *Islamic Law and Society* 14, no. 1 (2007): 97.

31. Peter Burke, *Popular Culture in Early Modern Europe* (Surrey: Ashgate, 2009); E. P. Thompson, *Customs in Common* (New York: New Press, 1991).

32. Kate Rousmaniere, *The Principal's Office: A Social History of the American School Principal* (Albany: State University of New York, 2013), 30.

33. Robert Muchembled, *Popular Culture and Elite Culture in France, 1400–1750*, trans. Lydia Cochrane (Baltimore, Md.: Johns Hopkins University Press, 1985); Nash and Kilday, *Cultures of Shame*.

34. Michel Foucault, *Discipline and Punish: The Birth of the Prison* (New York: Vintage Books, 1995); Joel F. Harrington, *The Faithful Executioner: Life and Death, Honor and Shame in the Turbulent Sixteenth Century* (New York: Picador, 2013).

35. Lisa Ann Raphals, *Sharing the Light Representations of Women and Virtue in Early China* (Albany: State University of New York Press, 1998), 236.

36. Usha Menon and Richard A. Shweder, "Kali's Tongue: Cultural Psychology and the Power of Shame in Orissa, India," in *Emotion and Culture: Empirical Studies of Mutual Influence*, ed. Shinobu Kitayama and Hazel Rose Markus (Washington, D.C.: American Psychological Association, 1995), 241–85, esp. 247, 252.

37. Jean G. Peristiany, ed., *Honour and Shame: The Values of Mediterranean Society* (Chicago: University of Chicago Press, 1966).

38. Anne Cheng, "Filial Piety with a Vengeance: The Tension between Rites and Law in the Han," *Filial Piety in Chinese Thought and History*, ed. Alan Kam-leung Chan and Sor-hoon Tan (London: RoutledgeCurzon, 2004), 32.

39. Eiko Ikegami, "Shame and the Samurai: Institutions, Trustworthiness, and Autonomy in the Elite Honor Culture," in "Shame," special issue, *Social Research* 70, no. 4 (winter 2003): 1353–54; Ivan Morris, *Nobility of Failure: Tragic Heroes in the History of Japan* (Fukuoka, Japan: Kurodahan Press, 2013), 244; Peter N. Stearns, *Jealousy: The Evolution of an Emotion in American History* (New York: New York University Press, 1989), 15.

40. Dov Cohen, Joseph Vandello, and Adrian K. Rantilla, "The Sacred and the Social: Cultures of Honor and Violence," *Shame: Interpersonal Behavior, Psychopathology, and Culture*, ed. Paul Gilbert and Bernice Andrews (New York: Oxford University Press, 1998), 261–82.

41. Ikegami, "Shame and the Samurai"; Morris, *Nobility of Failure*, 244.

42. Lama Abu Odeh, "Honor Killings and the Construction of Gender in Arab Societies," in "Critical Directions in Comparative Family Law," special issue, *American Journal of Comparative Law* 58, no. 4 (fall 2010): 911–52.

43. Sarah B. Pomeroy, *Families in Classical and Hellenistic Greece: Representations and Realities* (Oxford, U.K.: Clarendon Press, 1997), 83.

44. Takie Sugiyama Lebra, "The Social Mechanism of Guilt and Shame: The Japanese Case," *Anthropological Quarterly* 44, no. 4 (October 1971): 241–55; Benedict, *Chrysanthemum and the Sword*; Helen Merrell Lynd, *On Shame and the Search for Identity* (London: Routledge, 1999).

45. Consider also an interesting claim that Athens, by the sixth century, had developed a sense of guilt rather than relying on fear of public opinion in Emiel Eyben, *Restless Youth in Ancient Rome* (London: Routledge, 1993).

46. David Lester, "The Role of Shame in Suicide," *Suicide and Life-Threatening Behavior* 27, no. 4 (winter 1997): 352–60.

47. John Braithwaite, "Shame and Modernity," *British Journal of Criminology* 33, no. 1 (winter 1993): 1–18.

48. For an example of boundaries for concealment, see Marc J. Swartz, "Shame, Culture, and Status among the Swahili of Mombasa," *Ethos* 16, no. 1 (March 1988): 21–51.

49. John Demos, *Past, Present, and Personal: The Family and the Life Course in American History* (New York: Oxford University Press, 1986).

50. Anne McTaggart, *Shame and Guilt in Chaucer* (New York: Palgrave Macmillan, 2012); Robert Kolb, *Martin Luther as Prophet, Teacher, Hero: Images of the Reformer, 1520–1620* (Grand Rapids, Mich.: Baker Books, 1999); Barbara H. Rosenwein, *Emotional Communities in the Early Middle Ages* (Ithaca, N.Y.: Cornell University Press, 2006); Leon Wurmser, *The Mask of Shame* (Baltimore, Md.: Johns Hopkins University Press, 1981), 17; Virginia Burrus, *Saving Shame: Martyrs, Saints, and Other Abject Subjects* (Philadelphia: University of Pennsylvania Press, 2011), 54, on Tartullian.

51. Damien Boquet and Piroska Nagy, *Sensible Moyen Âge. Une histoire des émotions dans l'Occident medieval* (Paris: Seuil, 2015), 4, 135.

52. Burrus, *Saving Shame*, 7.

53. Mary C. Flannery, "The Concept of Shame in Late-Medieval English Literature," *Literature Compass* 9, no. 2 (2012): 166–82, esp. 166, 167; see also Burrus, *Saving Shame*; Brian Cummings, "Animal Passions and Human Sciences: Shame, Blushing, and Nakedness in Early Modern Europe and the New World," in *At the Borders of the Human: Beasts, Bodies and Natural Philosophy in the Early Modern Period*, ed. Erica Fudge, Ruth Gilbert, and Susan Wiseman (London: Macmillan Press, 1999), 26–50; E. R. Dodds, *The Greeks and the Irrational* (Berkeley: University of California Press, 1951); Ewan Fernie, *Shame in Shakespeare* (London: Routledge, 2002); Gail Kern Paster, *The Body Embarrassed: Drama and the Disciplines of Shame in Early Modern England* (New York: Cornell University Press, 1993); Stephanie Trigg, "'Shamed Be . . .': Historicizing Shame in Medieval and Early Modern Courtly Ritual," *Exemplaria* 19 (2007): 67–89; Trigg, *Shame and Honor*; Barbara Hanawalt, *Of Good and Ill Repute: Gender and Social Control in Medieval England* (New York: Oxford University Press, 1998).

54. An additional approach to emotion in premodern history involves tracing patterns in specific emotional communities. Barbara Rosenwein has advanced this approach in stressing the variety of premodern Western experience. In her most recent formulation, shame appears as a major emotional factor in some communities, spurring virtue and devotion to Christ through the suffering it entails or, alternatively, providing an experience worse than death where the family's honor is involved; but it looms less large in other cases. Rosenwein, *Generations of Feeling*, 201–5.

55. Stanley W. Jackson, *Melancholia and Depression: From Hippocratic Times to Modern Times* (New Haven, Conn.: Yale University Press, 1990).

56. Another related facet worth exploring, also in relation to the rise of honor, is the Christian effort to restrain any extreme of shame that might lead to suicide. A study from 2000 suggests that shame-based suicides were rare in Western Europe, in contrast to earlier Rome or contemporary East Asia, until the eighteenth century, when they began to surface again. Marzio Barbagli, *Farewell to the World: A History of Suicide* (New York: Macmillan Reference, 2000), 304–5.

57. Trigg, *Shame and Honor*, 67–89.

58. Fernie, *Shame in Shakespeare*.

59. Trigg, *Shame and Honor*, 85.

60. Cited in Paster, *Body Embarrassed*, 38; Cummings, "Animal Passions and Human Sciences"; Erica Fudge, Ruth Gilbert, and S. J. Wiseman, *At the Borders of the Human: Beasts, Bodies and Natural Philosophy in the Early Modern Period* (New York: St. Martin's Press, 1999), 26–50.

61. Boquet and Nagy, *Sensible Moyen Âge*; Bénédicte Sère and Jörg Wettlaufer eds., *Shame between Punishment and Penance: The Social Usages of Shame in the Middle Ages and Early Modern Times* (Florence: Micrologus Library, 2013).

62. Jacques Le Goff and Jean-Claude Schmitt, eds., *Le Charivari* (Paris: Editions de l'EHESS, 1981); Muchembled, *Popular Culture and Elite Culture*.

63. Norbert Elias, *The Civilizing Process* (New York: Pantheon Books, 1982); see also Paster, *Body Embarrassed*.

64. Elias, *Civilizing Process*, 130, 139.

65. Kathryn Preyer, "Penal Measures in the American Colonies: An Overview," *American Journal of Legal History* 26, no. 4 (October 1982): 326–53, 333.

66. Demos, "Shame and Guilt," 72–74.

67. Gregory LeFever, "Shame on You!," *Early American Life* (August 2009): 63; Marquis Eaton, "Punitive Pain and Humiliation," *Journal of Criminal Law and Criminology* 6, no. 6 (May 1915–March 1916): 894–907.

68. Preyer, "Penal Measures in the American Colonies."

69. Demos, "Shame and Guilt," 72–74.

70. Amitai Etzioni, "Back to the Pillory?," *American Scholar* 68, no. 3 (summer 1999): 43–50; Norval Morris and David J. Rothman, *The Oxford History of the Prison: The Practice of Punishment in Western Society* (New York: Oxford University Press, 1995); Lawrence Meir Friedman, *Crime and Punishment in American History* (New York: Basic Books, 1993); Thomas G. Blomberg and Karol Lucken, *American Penology: A History of Control* (New Brunswick, N.J.: Transaction Publishers, 2010); Thomas G. Blomberg and Stanley Cohen, *Punishment and Social Control* (New York: Aldine de Gruyter, 2003).

71. Cited in Demos, "Shame and Guilt," 72.

72. Ibid.

73. John D'Emilio and Estelle B. Freedman, *Intimate Matters: A History of Sexuality in America* (New York: Harper and Row, 1988), 21.

74. Thomas Shepard, *God's Plot: the Paradoxes of Puritan Piety* (Amherst: University of Massachusetts Press, 1972), 26; Isaac Pennington quoted in Philip J. Greven, *The Protestant Temperament: Patterns of Child-Rearing, Religious Experience, and the Self in Early America* (Chicago: University of Chicago Press, 1988), 125; the Rev. Michael Wigglesworth quoted in Rom Harre and W. Gerrod Parrott, eds., *The Emotions: Social, Cultural, and Biological Dimensions* (London: Sage, 1996), 80; Demos, "Shame and Guilt," 72.

75. Michael Stephen Hindus, *Prison and Plantation: Crime, Justice, and Authority in Massachusetts and South Carolina, 1767–1878* (Chapel Hill: University of North Carolina Press, 1980), 45–8.

76. Demos, *Past, Present, and Personal*; John Demos, *A Little Commonwealth: Family Life in Plymouth Colony*, 2nd ed. (New York: Oxford University Press, 2000); Greven, *Protestant Temperament*.

77. Mather quoted in Greven, *Protestant Temperament*, 54–56; Demos, *Little Commonwealth*.

Chapter 3. The Impact of Modernity: Some Possibilities

1. For a recent summary, see Jan Plamper, "The History of Emotions: An Interview with William Reddy, Barbara Rosenwein and Peter Stearns," *History and Theory* 49 (May 2010): 237–65; see also Rosenwein, "Worrying about Emotions in History."

2. Peter N. Stearns, "Modern Patterns in Emotions History," in Matt and Stearns, *Doing Emotions History*, 17–40; Susan J. Matt, *Homesickness: An American History* (New York:

Oxford University Press, 2011); Susan J. Matt, *Keeping Up with the Joneses: Envy in American Consumer Society, 1890–1930* (Philadelphia: University of Pennsylvania Press, 2013).

3. Fessler, "From Appeasement to Conformity."

4. Adam J. Hirsch, "From Pillory to Penitentiary: The Rise of Criminal Incarceration in Early Massachusetts," *Michigan Law Review* 80, no. 6 (1982): 1179–269.

5. Albert O. Hirschman, *The Passions and the Interests Political Arguments for Capitalism before Its Triumph* (Princeton, N.J.: Princeton University Press, 1997).

6. William M. Reddy, *The Invisible Code Honor and Sentiment in Postrevolutionary France, 1814–1848* (Berkeley: University of California Press, 1997).

7. Peter N. Stearns, *Schools and Students in Industrial Society: Japan and the West, 1870–1940* (Boston: Bedford Books, 1998), 119–24.

8. Ying Wong and Jeanne Tsai, "Cultural Models of Shame and Guilt," in *Handbook of Self-Conscious Emotions*, ed. J. Tracy, R. Robins, and J. Tangney (New York: Guilford Press, 2007), 210–23; Sungeun Yang and Paul C. Rosenblatt, "Shame in Korean Families," *Journal of Comparative Family Studies* 32, no. 3 (summer 2001): 361–75; Bedford, "Individual Experience"; Zhimin Zou and Dengfeng Wang, "Guilt Versus Shame: Distinguishing the Two Emotions from a Chinese Perspective," *Social Behavior and Personality* 37, no. 5 (2009): 601–4; Ji Li, Wang, and Fischer, "Organization of Chinese Shame Concepts."

9. Heidi Fung, "Becoming a Moral Child: The Socialization of Shame among Young Chinese Children," *Ethos* 27, no. 2 (1999): 180–209.

10. Wong and Tsai, "Cultural Models"; Fung, "Becoming a Moral Child."

11. Michael Bond, "Emotions and Their Expression in Chinese Culture," *Journal of Nonverbal Behavior* 17, no. 4 (1993): 245–62; Daniel Bahk, "Excommunication and Shunning: The Effect on Korean Churches in America as a Social Networking Structure," *Rutgers Journal of Law and Religion* 3 (2002), http://lawandreligion.com (accessed January 19, 2016); Sam Louie, "Asian Shame and Honor," Minority Report, *Psychology Today*, June 29, 2014, www.psychologytoday.com (accessed January 19, 2016); Young Gweon You, "Shame and Guilt Mechanisms in East Asian Culture," *Journal of Pastoral Care* 51, no. 1 (spring 1997), accessed at http://jafriedrich.de (January 19, 2016).

12. Ute Frevert, "Shame and Humiliation," *History of Emotions—Insights into Research* (October 2015), doi: 10.14280/08241.47.

13. Yang and Rosenblatt, "Shame in Korean Families."

14. Fessler, "From Appeasement to Conformity."

15. Murong Xuecun, "China's Tradition of Public Shaming Thrives," Opinion Pages, *New York Times*, March 20, 2015, www.nytimes.com (accessed August 12, 2015). Other important reinventions can be studied as part of a contemporary history of shame. As traditional public shaming declined in India, as a means of disciplining women's behavior, a new approach was introduced: acid attacks on women who rejected suitors or other men seek to brand as a result of jealousy or dowry disputes. The tactic is new and dreadful, but the idea of permanent marks of shame to reinforce social standards was deeply rooted in community custom. Interestingly, the groups that protest this kind of defilement

themselves seek to rouse public outrage under the slogan "Spot of Shame." See Frevert, "Shame and Humiliation."

Chapter 4. Reconsidering Shame in Western Society: The Nineteenth and Twentieth Centuries

1. Nathaniel Hawthorne, *The Scarlet Letter* (Project Gutenberg EBook, 1992). I am grateful to Roger Lathbury for expert guidance on Hawthorne's work.

2. Demos, "Shame and Guilt."

3. This analysis is based on inspection of the Google Ngram Viewer and the *New York Times* Chronicle databases. Patterns for relative frequency use for guilt and embarrassment were different. Guilt actually declined more rapidly than shame for a time—which probably warrants further analysis, but then bounced above shame from the 1920s onward, which is what Demos's analysis would predict. Embarrassment, in contrast to the other two, rose a bit early in the nineteenth century and then stabilized—which means as we will see that it has not, in recent decades, actually replaced shame, where a recent increase in usage contrast to embarrassment's level trajectory.

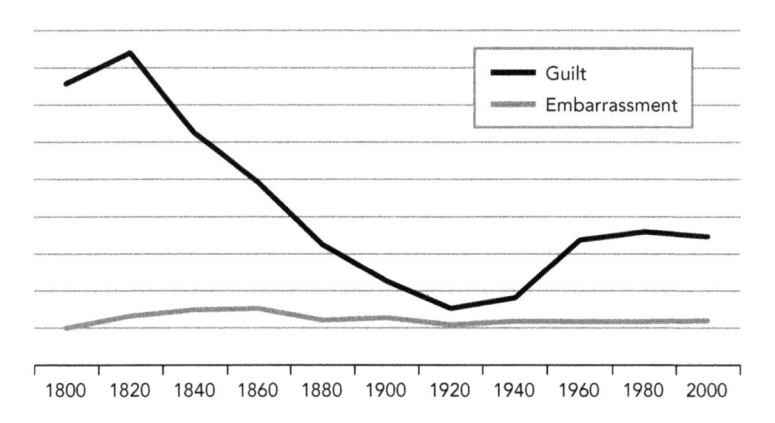

FIGURE 9. The frequency of the words *guilt* and *embarrassment* in U.S. and British English, 1800–2000, according to Google Books Ngram Viewer.

4. Demos, "Shame and Guilt."

5. Benjamin Rush, "An Enquiry into the Effects of Public Punishments Upon Criminals, and Upon Society, read in the Society for Promoting Political Enquiries, convened at the House of His Excellency Benjamin Franklin, Esquire in Philadelphia, March 9th 1787, (Philadelphia: Printed by Joseph James in Chestnut Street, 1787)," accessed September 28, 2016, at Readex, a Division of NewsBank database.

6. Nash and Kilday, *Cultures of Shame*, ch. 5.

7. Robert Graham Caldwell, *Red Hannah: Delaware's Whipping Post* (Philadelphia: University of Pennsylvania Press, 1947).

Notes to Chapter 4

8. David J. Rothman, *The Discovery of the Asylum: Social Order and Disorder in the New Republic* (Boston: Little, Brown, 1990).

9. Thomas J. Blomberg, *Juvenile Court and Community Corrections* (Lanham, Md.: University Press of America, 1984).

10. Friedman, *Crime and Punishment*, 75.

11. Adam Jay Hirsch, *The Rise of the Penitentiary: Prisons and Punishment in Early America* (New Haven, Conn.: Yale University Press, 1992), 242.

12. Hirsch, "From Pillory to Penitentiary."

13. Caldwell, *Red Hannah*, 19, 72.

14. E. Bruce Thompson, "Reforms in the Penal System of Tennessee, 1820–1850," *Tennessee Historical Quarterly* 1, no. 4 (1942): 291–308.

15. Jacob Abbott, *The Mother at Home and the Principles of Maternal Duty* (Boston: N.p., 1834), 86.

16. Catherine Sedgwick, *Home* (Boston: N.p., 1834); Demos, *Past, Present, and Personal*.

17. Demos, *Past, Present, and Personal*.

18. Catharine Beecher, *Treatise on Domestic Economy* (Boston: T. H. Webb, 1842), 220–33, accessed September 28, 2016, at the Institute for Advanced Technology in the Humanities, the University of Virginia.

19. Lydia Child, *The Mother's Book* (Boston: Carter, Hendee and Babcock, 1831), 6–10, accessed September 28, 2016, at HathiTrust Digital Library, www.hathitrust.org.

20. Felix Adler, *The Moral Instruction of Children* (New York: D. Appleton, 1892), accessed September 28, 2016, at HathiTrust; Alice Birney, *Childhood* (New York: F. A. Stokes, 1905), 57, accessed September 28, 2016, at HathiTrust; Edwin Kirkpatrick, *Fundamentals of Child Study* (New York: MacMillan, 1929), 128–29, accessed September 28, 2016, at HathiTrust.

21. J. Sidonie Gruenberg, *Guide to Everyday Problems of Boys and Girls* (New York: Random House, 1958), 64–67.

22. Benjamin Spock, *Baby and Child Care* (New York: Pocket Books, 1976), 322, 464–66; Benjamin Spock and Steven J. Parker, *Baby and Child Care* (New York, 1998), 464–66; see also Benjamin Spock, *Dr. Spock Talks with Mothers: Growth and Guidance* (Boston: Houghton Mifflin, 1961).

23. Benedict, *Chrysanthemum and the Sword*.

24. Kenneth A. Lockridge, *A New England Town: The First Hundred Years, Dedham, Massachusetts, 1636–1736* (New York: Norton, 1970); John Braithwaite, *Crime, Shame, and Reintegration* (Cambridge: Cambridge University Press, 1989).

25. Hirsch, "From Pillory to Penitentiary."

26. Lynn Avery Hunt, *Inventing Human Rights: A History* (New York: W. W. Norton, 2008).

27. Nicole Eustace, *Passion Is the Gale: Emotion, Power, and the Coming of the American Revolution* (Chapel Hill: University of North Carolina Press, 2008), 353. Colin Campbell, *The Romantic Ethic and the Spirit of Modern Consumerism* (Oxford, U.K.: Basil Blackwell, 1987); Dror Wahrman, *The Making of the Modern Self Identity and Culture in Eighteenth-Century England* (New Haven, Conn.: Yale University Press, 2004).

28. Frederick S. Lane, *American Privacy: The 400-Year History of Our Most Contested Right* (Boston: Beacon Press, 2009); Sarah Knott, *Sensibility and the American Revolution* (Chapel Hill: University of North Carolina Press, 2009).

29. Lane, *American Privacy*; Greven, *Protestant Temperament*.

30. Steven Mintz, *Huck's Raft: A History of American Childhood* (Ann Arbor: University of Michigan, 2009), ch. 4.

31. Peter N. Stearns, "Obedience and Emotion: A Challenge in the Emotional History of Childhood," *Journal of Social History* 47, no. 3 (2014): 593–611.

32. Ibid.

33. Mintz, *Huck's Raft*, ch. 4; Stearns, "Obedience and Emotion."

34. Bertram Wyatt-Brown, *Southern Honor Ethics and Behavior in the Old South* (New York: Oxford University Press, 2007).

35. Ibid., 353.

36. Friedman, *Crime and Punishment*.

37. D'Emilio and Freedman, *Intimate Matters*, 77.

38. John F. Kasson, *Rudeness and Civility: Manners in Nineteenth-Century Urban America* (New York: Hill and Wang, 1990), 168.

39. D'Emilio and Freedman, *Intimate Matters*; Cas Wouters, *Sex and Manners: Female Emancipation in the West, 1890–2000* (Thousand Oaks, Calif.: Sage, 2004).

40. Carl F. Kaestle, "Social Change, Discipline, and the Common School in Early Nineteenth-Century America," *The Journal of Interdisciplinary History* 9, no. 1 (1978): 1–17. This section was developed in collaboration with Clio Stearns, to whom I owe my thanks.

41. Heather A. Weaver, "Object Lessons: A Cultural Genealogy of the Dunce Cap and the Apple as Visual Tropes of American Education," *Paedagogica Historica* 48, no. 2 (2012): 215–41.

42. William Holmes McGuffey, *McGuffey's Third Eclectic Reader* (New York: American Book, 1920).

43. Laura Ingalls Wilder, *Farmer Boy* (New York: HarperCollins, 1981), 9–10.

44. Kaestle, "Social Change, Discipline."

45. Jacob Middleton, "The Experience of Corporal Punishment in Schools, 1890–1940," *History of Education* 37, no. 2 (2008): 253–75.

46. Sandra Rollings-Magnusson, "Slates, Tarpaper Blackboards, and Dunce Caps: One-Room Schoolhouse Experiences of Pioneer Children in Saskatchewan, 1878–1914," *Prairie Forum* 35, no. 1 (2010): 21–52.

47. Laura Ingalls Wilder, *Little House on the Prairie* (New York: HarperCollins, 1981).

48. Carol Ryrie Brink, *Caddie Woodlawn* (New York: Aladdin Books; London: Collier Macmillan, 1990).

49. Sophia Wyatt, *The Autobiography of a Landlady of the Old School: with personal sketches of eminent characters, places, and miscellaneous items* (Boston: Wright and Hasty Printers, 1854), accessed September 28, 2016, at HathiTrust.

50. William Hawley Smith, "Weergo, Weergeeneese," *Missouri School Journal* (August 1898): 499–501.

51. Franklin C. Brownell, "Ends and Means in Teaching," *Connecticut Common School Journal and Annals of Education* 9 (Case, Tiffany and Burnham, 1854), 388.

52. John R. Shook, *Dewey's Social Philosophy: Democracy as Education* (New York: Palgrave Macmillan, 2014).

53. Alistair McCartney, *The End of the World Book: A Novel* (Madison: University of Wisconsin Press, 2008).

54. Keastle, "Social Change, Discipline."

55. Vincent Vinikas, "Lustrum of the Cleanliness Institute, 1927–1932," *Journal of Social History* 22, no. 4 (1989): 613–30.

56. Erikson, *Childhood and Society*.

57. "Maintaining Classroom Discipline," Teacher Education Series, McGraw-Hill, 1947, YouTube video, 13:43, posted by "rosaryfilms," June 16, 2007, www.youtube.com/watch?v=gHzTUYAOkPM, accessed September 28, 2016.

58. Kate Rousmaniere, *The Principal's Office: A Social History of the American School Principal* (Albany: SUNY Press, 2014).

59. Peter N. Stearns, *Anxious Parents: A History of Modern Childrearing in America* (New York: New York University Press, 2003).

60. Maureen Stout, *The Feel-Good Curriculum: The Dumbing-Down of America's Kids in the Name of Self-Esteem* (Cambridge, Mass.: Perseus Books, 2000).

61. Barry Leibowitz, "Punishment by Idaho Teacher Gets Poor Marks from Parents; School District, Teachers Investigate," *CBS News*, November 21, 2012, www.cbsnews.com, accessed August 12, 2015; Joel Landau, "Ohio Teacher Fired after Confronting Elementary School Bully," *New York Daily News*, May 17, 2015, www.nydailynews.com, accessed August 12, 2015.

62. On the persistence of shaming in teacher practice, and the deleterious psychological effects, see R. Leitch, "The Shaming Game: The Role of Shame and Shaming Rituals in Education and Development," paper presented at the American Educational Research Association, Montreal, 1999; J. Luby et al., "Shame and Guilt in Preschool Depression: Evidence for Elevations in Self-Conscious Emotions in Depression as Early as Age 3," *Journal of Child Psychology and Psychiatry* 50, no. 9: 1156–66; A. Monroe, "Shame Solutions: How Shame Impacts School-Aged Children and What Teachers Can Do to Help," *Education Forum* 73, no. 1 (2009): 58–66.

63. Dave Foley, "6 Classroom Management Tips Every Teacher Can Use," National Educations Association, undated, www.nea.org/tools/51721.htm, accessed August 12, 2015. On the "data wall" movement, see Launa Hall, "This Tool Meant to Motivate Students Shames Them Instead," Outlook, *Washington Post*, May 22, 2016.

64. Peter N. Stearns, *American Cool: Constructing a Twentieth-Century Emotional Style* (New York: New York University Press, 1994); Anthony E. Rotundo, *American Manhood Transformations in Masculinity from the Revolution to the Modern Era* (New York: Basic Books, 1993).

65. George Chauncey, *Gay New York: Gender, Urban Culture, and the Makings of the Gay Male World, 1890–1940* (New York: Basic Books, 1994).

66. I appreciate advice from scholars Ron Smith, Michael Oriard, and Richard Crepau on the surprisingly difficult task of identifying the origins of sports shaming, particularly by coaches. See also Michael Oriard, *King Football: Sport and Spectacle in the Golden Age of Radio and Newsreels, Movies and Magazines, the Weekly and the Daily Press* (Chapel Hill: University of North Carolina Press, 2001), esp. 146–61, and Ron Smith, ed., *Big-Time Football at Harvard, 1905: The Diary of Coach Bill Reid* (Urbana: University of Illinois Press, 1994), 85–6, 301.

67. Todd M. Kays and Jack Schlabig, "Stop the Shame in Youth Sports: The Problem with 'Shaming' and Youth Sports," blog, *Athletic Mind Institute: Sport and Performance Psychology*, www.athleticmindinstitute.com, accessed August 12, 2015. The role of shame in music and dance instruction beyond beginner levels, also deserves attention.

68. Scott A. Sandage, *Born Losers: A History of Failure in America* (Cambridge, Mass.: Harvard University Press, 2005), 16.

69. Richard Sennett, *Authority* (New York: W. W. Norton, 1993), 47; Richard Sennett, *The Hidden Injuries of Class* (New York: Norton, 1993), 96.

70. Helen Merrell Lynd, *On Shame and the Search for Identity* (London: Routledge, 1999).

71. Sandage, *Born Losers*.

72. Sennett, *Authority*.

73. Jennifer D. Keene, *Doughboys, the Great War, and the Remaking of America* (Baltimore, Md.: Johns Hopkins University Press, 2003), 11 and passim; Chris Walsh, *Cowardice: A Brief History* (Princeton, N.J.: Princeton University Press, 2014).

74. Ute Frevert, "Piggy's Shame," in *Learning How to Feel: Children's Literature and Emotional Socialization, 1870–1970* (Oxford: Oxford University Press, 2014), 134–54.

75. Nash and Kilday, *Cultures of Shame*. British references to humiliation also declined, as in the United States.

76. Wahrman, *Making of the Modern Self*.

77. "A Bill to Abolish the Punishment of the Pillory," *House of Commons Parliamentary Papers: 19th Century, 1801–1900*, vol. 2, ProQuest.

78. Emma Griffin, "The 'Urban Renaissance' and the Mob: Rethinking Civic Improvement over the Long Eighteenth Century," in *Structures and Transformations in Modern British History*, ed. David Feldman and Jon Lawrence (New York: Cambridge University Press, 2011), 54–73.

79. François Billacois, *The Duel: Its Rise and Fall in Early Modern France* (New Haven, Conn.: Yale University Press, 1990), 206; Ute Frevert, *Men of Honour: A Social and Cultural History of the Duel* (Cambridge, Mass.: Blackwell Publishers, 1995).

80. William M. Reddy, *The Invisible Code: Honor and Sentiment in Postrevolutionary France, 1814–1848* (Berkeley: University of California Press, 1997), 135–37.

81. Erika Vause, "'The Business of Reputations': Secrecy, Shame, and Social Standing in Nineteenth-Century Debtors' and Creditors' Newspapers," *Journal of Social History* 48, no. 1 (2014): 47.

82. Fabrice Virgili, *Shorn Women: Gender and Punishment in Liberation France* (Oxford, U.K.: Berg, 2002).

Chapter 5. The Revival of Shame: Contemporary History

1. Robert D. Putnam, *Bowling Alone: The Collapse and Revival of American Community* (New York: Simon and Schuster, 2000).

2. David Riesman, *The Lonely Crowd: A Study of the Changing American Character* (Garden City, N.Y.: Doubleday, 1953).

3. Peter Salovey, *The Psychology of Jealousy and Envy* (New York: Guilford Press, 1991); Shula Somers, "Adults Evaluating Their Emotions: A Cross-Cultural Perspective," *Emotion in Adult Development*, ed. Carol Z. Malatesta and Carroll Elliz Izard (Beverly Hills, Calif.: Sage Publications, 1984).

4. Deborah Cohen, *Family Secrets: Shame and Privacy in Modern Britain* (New York: Oxford University Press, 2013), 2, 206, 252.

5. Martha Nussbaum, for example, has written about the growing number of public appeals to shame and disgust as a way to stigmatize others while concealing one's own frailty, Martha Craven Nussbaum, *Hiding from Humanity: Disgust, Shame and the Law* (Princeton, N.J.: Princeton University Press, 2004), 17.

6. This analysis is based on inspection of Google Ngram Viewer and the *New York Times* Chronicle.

7. Google Ngram Viewer chart of the frequency of the word *shame* in British English, 1960–2000. It is also interesting to note that both in the United States and the United Kingdom, references to *humiliation* do not follow the *shame* pattern in recent decades, with only a modest recent uptick.

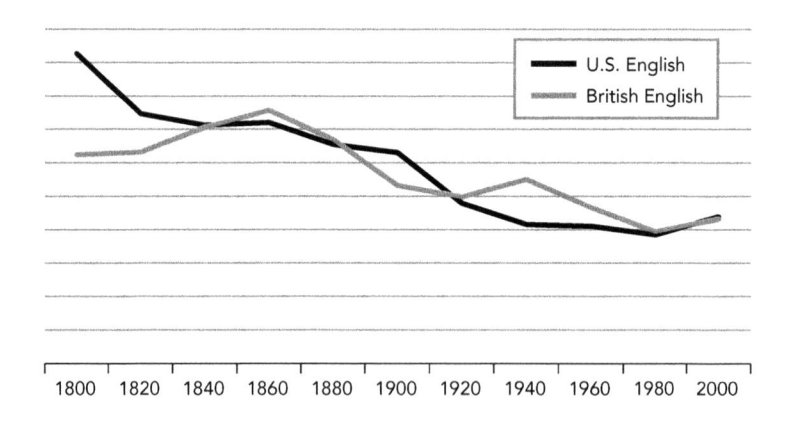

FIGURE 10. The frequency of the word *humiliation* in U.S. and British English, 1800–2000, according to Google Books Ngram Viewer.

8. See Melissa Platt and Jennifer J. Freyd, "Betray My Trust, Shame on Me: Shame, Dissociation, Fear, and Betrayal Trauma," *Psychological Trauma: Theory, Research, Practice, and Policy* 7, no. 4 (July 2015): 398–404; R. P. Bagozzi, W. Verbeke, and F. Belschak,

"Self-Conscious Emotions as Emotional Systems: the Role of Culture in Shame and Pride Systems," in *Understanding Culture: Theory, Research, and Application* (New York: Psychology Press, 2009), 393–409; S. Dickerson, T. Gruenewald, and M. E. Kemeny, "When the Social Self Is Threatened: Shame, Physiology, and Health," *Journal of Personality* 72, no. 6 (December 2004): 1191–216.

9. Stephanie Paterik, "How AIDS Advertising Has Evolved from Shock and Shame to Hope and Humor," *AdWeek*, modified December 1, 2015, www.adweek.com, accessed January 20, 2016.

10. Sharon Lamb, *The Trouble with Blame: Victims, Perpetrators, and Responsibility* (Cambridge, Mass.: Harvard University Press, 1996).

11. Stearns, *Anxious Parents*; "Adolescent Self-Esteem," *Research Facts and Findings*, ACT Youth Center of Excellence (June 2013).

12. Jeffrey Kluger, "In Praise of the Ordinary Child," *Time*, August 3, (2015).

13. James Gilligan, *Violence: Our Deadly Epidemic and Its Causes* (New York: G. P. Putnam, 1996), 33.

14. June P. Tangney, Jeffrey Stuewig, and Andres G. Martinez, "Two Faces of Shame: The Roles of Shame and Guilt in Predicting Recidivism," *Psychological Science* 23, no. 3 (2014): 799–805; James Gilligan, *Violence: Reflections on a National Epidemic* (New York: Vintage Books, 1997).

15. Brené Brown, "Listening to Shame," filmed March 2012, TED video, 2012, 20:38, www.ted.com, accessed September 28, 2016.

16. Brené Brown, *I Thought It Was Just Me: Women Reclaiming Power and Courage in a Culture of Shame* (New York: Gotham, 2007), 2; Brené Brown, "Shame Perfectionism and Embracing Wholehearted Living," *Iris* 61 (fall 2011): 12–16.

17. Paul Trout, "Shame," *National Forum* 80, no. 4 (fall 2000): 3–7.

18. Brené Brown, *The Gifts of Imperfection: Let Go of Who You Think You're Supposed to Be and Embrace Who You Are* (Center City, Minn.: Hazelden Publishing, 2010), 45–46. Steve Safigan, "Shame Resilience Theory," *Positive Psychology Quarterly*, May 16, 2012, positivepsychologynews.com, accessed January 25, 2016.

19. Brené Brown, "Shame Resilience Theory: A Grounded Theory Study on Women and Shame," *Iris* 61 (fall 2011): 12–16.

20. Safigan, "Shame Resilience Theory." Brown, "Shame Resilience Theory."

21. Brown, *Gifts of Imperfection*, 40.

22. Brown, *I Thought It Was Just Me*, 2, 272.

23. Nancy F. Cott, *No Small Courage: A History of Women in the United States* (New York: Oxford University Press, 2000).

24. Martin B. Duberman, Martha Vicinus, and George Chauncey, *Hidden from History: Reclaiming the Gay and Lesbian Past* (New York: New American Library, 1989).

25. Eve Kosofsky Sedgwick, "Queer Performativity: Henry James's *The Art of the Novel*," *GLQ: A Journal of Lesbian and Gay Studies* 1, no. 1 (1993): 1–16.

26. Ian Parker, "The Story of a Suicide: Two College Roommates, a Webcam, and a Tragedy," *New Yorker*, February 6, 2012, www.newyorker.com, accessed September 28, 2016.

27. Scott McCarney, *Saints and Sinners: Gay Pride and Straight Shame* (Rochester, N.Y.: Scott McCarney / Visual Books, 2005), 246–47; Greshen Kaufman, *Coming Out of Shame: Transforming Gay and Lesbian Lives* (New York: Doubleday, 1996).

28. Despo Kritsotaki, "Turning Private Concern into Public Issue: Mental Retardation and Parents' Movements in Post-War Greece," *Journal of Social History* 49, no. 4 (2015): 982–98; James W. Trent Jr., *Inventing the Feeble Mind: A History of Mental Retardation in the United States* (Berkeley: University of California Press, 1994).

29. Anahad O'Connor, "No Grunting, They Said, and He Was at the Gym," *New York Times*, November 18, 2006, www.nytimes.com, accessed January 20, 2016.

30. Drew Harwell and Jena McGregor, "This New Rule Could Reveal the Huge Gap between CEO Pay and Worker Pay," *Washington Post*, August 4 2015, www.washingtonpost.com, accessed January 15, 2016.

31. Amy Farrell, *Fat Shame: Stigma and the Fat Body in American Culture* (New York: New York University Press, 2011).

32. Emily Post, *Etiquette* (New York: Funk and Wagnalls, 1940), 208; Lulu C. Graves, "Coping with Overweight by means of Diet Therapy," *Modern Hospital* 32 (1929): 62, citing comments by a doctor; James McLester, "The Principles Involved in the Treatment of Obesity," *Journal of the American Medical Association* 82 (1924): 2103.

33. "Psychiatrists have exposed the fat person for what he really is—miserable, self-indulgent and lacking in control"; "Girls get fat because they're emotionally disturbed." From "Dieting When You're Unhappy," *Ladies Home Journal* (1969): 62; Hilde Bruch, "Psychological Aspects of Reducing," *Psychosomatic Medicine* 62 (1952): 338.

34. Rachel Fox, "Too Fat to Be a Scientist?," *Chronicle of Higher Education*, July 17, 2014, http://chronicle.com, accessed August 1, 2015; Tara Parker-Pope, "The Fat Trap," *New York Times Magazine*, December 28, 2011, www.nytimes.com, accessed August 1, 2015.

35. Peter N. Stearns, *Fat History: Bodies and Beauty in the Modern West* (New York: New York University Press, 1997).

36. Farrell, *Fat Shame*; Stearns, *Fat History*.

37. Toni M. Massaro, "Shame, Culture, and American Criminal Law," *Michigan Law Review* 89, no. 7 (June 1991): 1880–944.

38. Massaro, "Shame, Culture," 1925. Shaming punishments are sometimes conflated with other judicial innovations, and this can be slightly distracting. A thief for example was ordered to allow his victim to enter his house and steal one item. Another miscreant was required to make a charitable contribution relevant to his offense. Experiments of this sort may be interesting and imaginative, but they have little or nothing to do with shaming. The only connection is the felt need to find some alternatives to the conventional patterns of the past two centuries.

39. Stephen P. Garvey, "Can Shaming Punishments Educate?," *University of Chicago Law Review* 65, no. 3 (summer 1998): 733–94.

40. See Dan Kahan, "What Do Alternative Sanctions Mean?" *The University of Chicago Law Review* 63 (1996): 630–53.

Notes to Chapter 5

41. Amitai Etzioni, "Back to the Pillory?," *American Scholar* 68, no. 3 (summer 1999): 43–50.

42. Massaro, "Shame, Culture."

43. Etzioni, "Back to the Pillory?"; Nussbaum, *Hiding from Humanity*.

44. Massaro, "Shame, Culture."

45. Etzioni, "Back to the Pillory?"

46. James Q. Whitman, "What Is Wrong with Inflicting Shame Sanctions?," *Yale Law Journal* 107, no. 4 (January 1998): 1055–92.

47. Aaron S. Book, "Shame on You: An Analysis of Modern Shame Punishment as an Alternative to Incarceration," *William and Mary Law Review* 40, no. 2 (February 1999): 653.

48. Braithwaite, "Shame and Modernity."

49. Putnam, *Bowling Alone*.

50. Danielle Kurtzleben, "Americans Don't Disagree on Politics as Much as You Might Think," *National Public Radio*, November 27, 2015, www.npr.org, accessed January 20, 2016.

51. Jeb Bush and Brian Yablonski, "Restoration of Shame," in *Profiles in Character* (Tallahassee: Foundation for Florida's Future, 1995).

52. Liz Welch, "Six Women on Their Terrifying, Infuriating Encounters with Abortion Clinic Protesters," *Cosmopolitan*, February 21, 2014, www.cosmopolitan.com, accessed August 15, 2015.

53. Marc V. Calderaro, "Social Shaming: The Right to Be a Giant, Self-Righteous Asshole," *Medium*, May 13, 2015, https://medium.com, accessed September 28, 2016.

54. Jon Ronson, "How One Stupid Tweet Blew Up Justine Sacco's Life," *New York Times Magazine*, February 12, 2015, www.nytimes.com, accessed February 9, 2017. See also *So You've Been Publicly Shamed* (New York: Riverhead Books, 2015).

55. Greg Lukianoff and Jonathan Haidt, "The Coddling of the American Mind," *Atlantic*, September 2015, www.theatlantic.com, accessed July 25, 2015.

56. Cited in Alan M. Wachman, "Does Diplomacy of Shame Promote Human Rights in China?," *Third World Quarterly* 22, no. 2 (April 2001): 257–81. See also Peter N. Stearns ed., *Global Outrage: The Impact of World Opinion on Contemporary History* (Oxford, U.K.: Oneworld, 2005).

57. Leora Tanenbaum, *I Am Not a Slut: Slut-Shaming in the Age of the Internet* (New York: Harper Perennial, 2015), and *Slut! Growing Up Female with a Bad Reputation* (New York: Perennial, 2000).

58. Ronson, *So You've Been Publicly Shamed*; Jon Ronson, "How One Stupid Tweet Blew Up Justine Sacco's Life," *New York Times Magazine*, February 12, 2015, www.nytimes.com, accessed July 15, 2015.

59. Ronson, *So You've Been Publicly Shamed*; Jennifer Jacquet, *Is Shame Necessary? New Uses for an Old Tool* (New York: Pantheon Books, 2015), 103.

60. Ronson, *So You've Been Publicly Shamed*.

61. Susanna Schrobsdorff, "Why Parents Should Not Punish Kids with Public Shaming," *Time* 186, nos. 1–2 (July 2015): 31–32.

62. Jacquet, *Is Shame Necessary?*

63. Lisa T. McElroy, "After a Public Shaming, Reclaiming My Dignity," *Washington Post*, April 24, 2015, www.washingtonpost.com, accessed July 25, 2015.

64. Caitlin Dewey, "How the 'Right to Be Forgotten' Could Take over the American Internet, Too," *Washington Post*, August 4, 2015, www.washingtonpost.com, accessed February 9, 2017; Ronson, *So You've Been Publicly Shamed*.

65. Wachman, "Does Diplomacy of Shame?"

66. Jacquet, *Is Shame Necessary?*; Shelby Steele, *Shame: How America's Past Sins Have Polarized Our Country* (New York: Basic Books, 2015).

Afterword

1. Thomas J. Scheff, "Shame and the Social Bond: A Sociological Theory," *Sociological Theory* 18, no. 1 (2000): 84–99.

2. Morrison, *Culture of Shame*, 107.

3. Gershen Kaufman, *The Psychology of Shame: Theory and Treatment of Shame-Based Syndromes* (New York: Springer, 2004).

Further Reading

Literature directly on the history of shame is slender, but what there is helps a great deal.

Introduction to Social Psychological and Anthropological Work on Shame

Benedict, Ruth. *The Chrysanthemum and the Sword: Patterns of Japanese Culture.* Boston: Houghton Mifflin, 1989. A classic in the field.

Fessler, Daniel M. T. "From Appeasement to Conformity: Evolutionary and Cultural Perspectives on Shame, Competition, and Cooperation." In Tracy, Robins, and Tangney, *Self-Conscious Emotions,* 174–94.

———. "Shame in Two Cultures: Implications for Evolutionary Approaches." *Journal of Cognition and Culture* 4 (2004): 207–62.

Lewis, Michael. "Self-Conscious Emotions: Embarrassment, Pride, Shame, and Guilt." In *Handbook of Emotions,* edited by Michael Lewis and Jeannette M. Haviland-Jones, 623–36. New York: Guilford Press, 2000.

Menon, Usha, and Richard A. Shweder. "Kali's Tongue: Cultural Psychology and the Power of Shame in Orissa, India." In *Emotion and Culture: Empirical Studies of Mutual Influence,* edited by Shinobu Kitayama and Hazel Rose Markus, 241–85. Washington, D.C.: American Psychological Association, 1995.

Sennett, Richard. *Authority.* New York: W. W. Norton, 1993.

———, and Jonathan Cobb. *The Hidden Injuries of Class.* New York: Norton, 1993.

Tracy, Jessica L., Richard W. Robins, and June Price Tangney, eds. *The Self-Conscious Emotions: Theory and Research.* New York: Guildford Press, 2007. A particularly important and wide-ranging collection. Both this book and the Michael Lewis article have wide-ranging psychological and social science references.

Shame and Classical Philosophy

Cua, Antonio S. "The Ethical Significance of Shame: Insights of Aristotle and Xunzi." *Philosophy East and West* (2003): 147–202.

Geaney, Jane. "Guarding Moral Boundaries: Shame in Early Confucianism." *Philosophy East and West* 54, no. 2 (April 2004): 113–42. Covers an important aspect of intellectual history.

Konstan, David. *The Emotions of the Ancient Greeks: Studies in Aristotle and Classical Literature.* Toronto: University of Toronto Press, 2007.

Seok, Bongrae. "Moral Psychology of Shame in Early Confucian Philosophy." *Frontiers of Philosophy in China* 10, no. 1 (2015): 21–57.

Van Norden, Bryan W. "The Emotion of Shame and the Virtue of Righteousness in Mencius." *Dao* 2, no. 1 (2002): 45–77, esp. 63.

On Shame in Punishment

Friedman, Lawrence Meir. *Crime and Punishment in American History.* New York: Basic Books, 1993.

Hirsch, Adam J. "From Pillory to Penitentiary: The Rise of Criminal Incarceration in Early Massachusetts." *Michigan Law Review* 80, no. 6 (1982): 1179–269.

Lange, Christian. "Legal and Cultural Aspects of Ignominious Parading (Tashhir) in Islam." *Islamic Law and Society* 14, no. 1 (2007): 81–108.

Le Goff, Jacques, and Jean-Claude Schmitt, eds. *Le Charivari.* Paris: Editions de l'EHESS, 1981.

On Honor

Reddy, William M. *The Navigation of a Feeling: A Framework for the History of Emotions.* New York: Cambridge University Press, 2001.

Frevert, Ute. *Men of Honour: A Social and Cultural History of the Duel.* Cambridge, U.K.: Polity Press; Cambridge, Mass.: Blackwell Publishers, 1995.

Ikegami, Eiko. "Shame and the Samurai: Institutions, Trustworthiness, and Autonomy in the Elite Honor Culture." In "Shame," special issue, *Social Research* 70, no. 4 (winter 2003): 1353–78.

On Relevant Family and Cultural History

Demos, John. *A Little Commonwealth: Family Life in Plymouth Colony.* New York: Oxford University Press, 2000.

Eustace, Nicole. *Passion Is the Gale: Emotion, Power, and the Coming of the American Revolution*. Chapel Hill: University of North Carolina Press, 2008.

Greven, Philip J. *The Protestant Temperament: Patterns of Child-Rearing, Religious Experience, and the Self in Early America*. Chicago: University of Chicago Press, 1988.

Kinney, Anne Behnke. *Representations of Childhood and Youth in Early China*. Stanford, Calif.: Stanford University Press, 2004.

Wahrman, Dror. *The Making of the Modern Self Identity and Culture in Eighteenth-Century England*. New Haven, Conn.: Yale University Press, 2004.

On Premodern Western Patterns

Boquet, Damien, and Piroska Nagy. *Sensible Moyen Âge. Une histoire des émotions dans l'Occident medieval*. Paris: Seuil, 2015.

Burrus, Virginia. *Saving Shame: Martyrs, Saints, and Other Abject Subjects*. Philadelphia: University of Pennsylvania Press, 2011.

McTaggart, Anne. *Shame and Guilt in Chaucer*. New York: Palgrave Macmillan, 2012.

Paster, Gail Kern. *The Body Embarrassed: Drama and the Disciplines of Shame in Early Modern England*. Ithaca, N.Y.: Cornell University Press, 1993.

On More Recent Developments through the Twentieth Century

Cohen, Deborah. *Family Secrets: Shame and Privacy in Modern Britain*. New York: Oxford University Press, 2013.

Demos, John. "Shame and Guilt in Early New England." In *Emotion and Social Change: Toward a New Psychohistory*, edited by C. Z. Stearns and P. N. Stearns, 69–86. New York: Holmes and Meier, 1988.

Nash, David, and Anne-Marie Kilday. *Cultures of Shame: Exploring Crime and Morality in Britain, 1600–1900*. London: Palgrave, 2010.

Ronson, Jon. *So You've Been Publicly Shamed*. New York: Riverhead Books, 2015. Though primarily focused on contemporary shame, the text has brief historical perspectives.

On Contemporary Issues

Farrell, Amy. *Fat Shame: Stigma and the Fat Body in American Culture*. New York: New York University Press, 2011.

Jacquet, Jennifer. *Is Shame Necessary? New Uses for an Old Tool*. New York: Pantheon Books, 2015.

Massaro, Toni M., "Shame, Culture, and American Criminal Law." *Michigan Law Review* 89, no. 7 (June 1991): 1880–944.

McCarney, Scott. *Saints and Sinners: Gay Pride and Straight Shame*. Rochester, N.Y.: Scott McCarney / Visual Books, 2005.

Steele, Shelby. *Shame: How America's Past Sins Have Polarized Our Country*. New York: Basic Books, 2015.

Tanenbaum, Leora. *I Am Not a Slut: Slut-Shaming in the Age of the Internet.* New York: Harper Perennial, 2015.

———. *Slut! Growing Up Female with a Bad Reputation.* New York: Perennial, 2000.

On Contemporary East Asia

Bedford, Olwen A. "The Individual Experience of Guilt and Shame in Chinese Culture." *Culture and Psychology* 10, no. 1 (2004): 29–52.

Benedict, Ruth. *The Chrysanthemum and the Sword: Patterns of Japanese Culture.* Boston: Houghton Mifflin, 1989.

Bond, Michael. "Emotions and Their Expression in Chinese Culture." *Journal of Nonverbal Behavior* 17, no. 4 (1993): 245–62.

Cua, Antonio S. "The Ethical Significance of Shame: Insights of Aristotle and Xunzi." *Philosophy East and West* (2003): 147–202.

Fung, Heidi. "Becoming a Moral Child: The Socialization of Shame among Young Chinese Children." *Ethos* 27, no. 2 (1999): 180–209.

Li, Jin, Lianqin Wang, and Kurt Fischer. "The Organization of Chinese Shame Concepts?" *Cognition and Emotion* 18, no. 6 (2004): 767–97.

Morris, Ivan. *Nobility of Failure.* Kurodahan Press, 2013.

Seok, Bongrae. "Moral Psychology of Shame in Early Confucian Philosophy." *Frontiers of Philosophy in China* 10, no. 1 (2015): 21–57.

Wong, Ying, and Jeanne Tsai. "Cultural Models of Shame and Guilt." In Tracy, Robins, and Tangney, *Self-Conscious Emotions,* 210–23.

Yang, Sungeun, and Paul C. Rosenblatt. "Shame in Korean Families." *Journal of Comparative Family Studies* 32, no. 3 (summer 2001): 361–75.

Zou, Zhimin, and Dengfeng Wang. "Guilt Versus Shame: Distinguishing the Two Emotions from a Chinese Perspective." *Social Behavior and Personality* 37, no. 5 (2009): 601–4.

Wide-Ranging Legal Studies Approach

Braithwaite, John. *Crime, Shame, and Reintegration.* Cambridge: Cambridge University Press, 1989.

Index

Abbott, Jacob, 65
abolitionists, 61
abortion, 120–21
abuse: archaic, 91; child, 36; human rights, 123; labor, 123; physical, 26, 62; sexual, 5; and social media, 10. *See also* violence
Adam and Eve, 14, 37
Adler, Felix, 67
adultery, 26–27, 43, 58, 102
African Americans, 88
alcohol. *See* drunkenness
American Cleanliness Institute, 82
American Revolution, 71, 93
Amnesty International, 123
anger, 2, 5, 28, 33, 136; and children, 66; of crowd, 117, 127; curbing, 31–32; about political correctness, 124
Anglo-Saxons, 38
anthropology, xii, 2, 13–14, 17, 20, 32
Aristotle, 20–21, 23, 28
Augustine, 37
Australia, 93, 113, 119

Beccaria, Cesare, 62
Benedict, Ruth, 68, 91

Bengkulu village, 15
Bentham, Jeremy, 62
Birney, Alice, 67
birth control, 76, 125
Black Pride, 107
blasphemy, 27, 92
blushing, 21, 39, 137
boy culture, 75
Braithwaite, John, 119
Britain, 27, 41, 43, 50, 94
brothels, 76
Brown, Brené, 105, 110,
Bryant, Bear, 88
Bush, Jeb, 120
business failure, 86, 88–89

California, 15, 50, 84, 111, 128, 132
California, University of, 87
Canada, 80
castes, 30–31
chastity, 38
Child, Lydia, 66–67
Child Association of America, 67
child molesters, 114–15, 118
child-rearing. *See* family

Index

China: child-rearing in, 24; Confucianism in, 10, 21, 23; and human rights, 123; modern, 52; philosophers from, 17; and politics, 53, 55, 129; shame in, 21; women in, 31; Zhou dynasty in, 32
chivalry, 38, 39, 40–41
Christianity, 12, 19, 31, 37–38
circumcision, 15
civil rights movement, 88, 107–8, 113
Civil War, 75, 90
coaches, 87–88, 102
Cohen, Deborah, 99
colonial America, 12, 18, 36, 43, 48, 66, 77
communism, 55
Confucianism, xii, 21–22, 23, 31
conservatives, 64, 97, 114, 119, 120, 122, 127
courts (of law), 26, 35, 46, 104, 114, 116, 118–19
credit ratings, 89
crime: in Australia, 119; in Japan, 33; and law, 22; prevention of, 114; and prisoners, 5; punishment for, 27; rates of, 36, 44, 54, 62–63, 64, 69; response to, 72; and responsibility, 103; and shame, 29, 93, 114–15, 116; types of, 19, 44, 63, 93, 119
criminals: character of, 63; convicted, 5, 28; groups of, 116; humiliation of, 75, 104; punishment of, 29, 40, 64; removal of, 63; returned, 62, 117; and shame, 29, 40, 124
crowd psychology, 125

Daily Mirror, 99
dares, 86
Daring Way (organization), 107
"data wall" movement, 85
debt, 25, 94
definitions, 1–3, 5, 7, 18, 136; changes to, over time, 39, 49, 58, 72, 107; contemporary, 34; debates about, 47; emotional, 71, 73; of righteous shaming, 124
Delaware, 62, 64
democracy, 26, 120
demographic transition, 49
Demos, John, 47, 59
depressions (psychological), 5, 126
Dewey, John, 82
Dickens, Charles, 78
disability, 53, 99, 109

divorce, 54, 76
donkeys, 26–27, 40
drought shaming, xi
drugs, 85, 115
drunk driving, 115, 118, 128
drunkenness: public, 44; of seamen and soldier, 63, 90; and stocks, 93
duels, 32, 46, 69, 75, 93–94

East Asia, xii, 6, 34, 52–54; modernity and, 95; suicide in, 142n56; therapy in, 102; urban societies of, 50. *See also* China; Confucianism; Japan
Egypt, 10, 18–19
Eighth Amendment, 118
Elias, Norbert, 42
embarrassment, xi, 3, 7, 15, 35, 137, 145
Enlightenment, 59, 71, 92, 95, 133
environment: degradation of, 99, 111, 129; of home, 83; modern, 50; offenders against, 97; of sports, 86; urban, 69–70
Erikson, Erik, 68, 83
etiquette books, 77
European Union, 96, 128
Eustace, Nicole, 71
executions, 29, 70, 123, 129

family: in agricultural societies, 16; behavior of, 53; British, 99; and child-rearing (*see also* parenting), 66, 72; Chinese, 24, 34; colonial, 46–47; as community, 3, 4, 51; discipline in, xi; and dishonor, 11, 32; emotions in, 18; evangelical, 47, 61; and honor, 34–35, 39, 75; involvement of, 25; modern, 72; and poverty, 53; and privacy, 14, 99; relationships in, 24; reputation of, 39; and shame by association, 102, 118, 122; size of, 72; and violence, 5
fat shaming, 112–14, 119
fear, 1–3, 28, 42, 106; and authority, 81; about being unprotected, 33; children and, 86; about crime, 62, 63; and discipline, 80–81; of exclusion, 116; goal of, 44; levels of, 20; and parenting, 66, 76; Protestant, 45; and public opinion, 22, 57, 115, 126; and punishment, 29, 63; in relationships, 24
football, 87–88

160

forgers, 27
France, 24, 51, 93, 94
Freud, Sigmund, 2

gay liberation movement, 108
Gay Pride, 108
Germany, 5, 94, 117, 123
Gifford, Kathy Lee, 123
Gilligan, James, 104
Google Books, 59, 100
grades: "data wall" movement, 85; inflation of, 84
Greece, 17, 23, 24, 26, 27–28, 34
Gruenberg, Sidonie, 68

Hammurabic code, 18
happiness, 65, 71, 73
Harvard, 87
Hawthorne, Nathaniel, 44, 57, 59
helicopter parenting, 103
hierarchy, 5, 30, 35, 82; awareness of, 22; and child-rearing, 11; and emotion, 85; and identity, 91; premodern, 30; and respectful shame, 20; in school, 77, 81, 83; servants in, 22; social, 15, 17, 22, 29, 32; in traditional societies, 32
Hinduism, 31
HIV, 102
homosexuality, 87, 94, 99, 108
Hong Kong, 54
honor, xiii, 11, 27, 32–34, 46, 75; chivalric, 38–39; codes of, 74, 77; colonial, 46; commercial, 51; and commitments, 17; decline of, 71; familial, 30, 34, 39, 46, 75; in France, 94; in Germany, 94; in Japan, 54; loss of, 93; and obedience, 90; and tradition, 32, 50–51; Western, 42
Horney, Karen, 105
Human Rights Watch, 123
Hume, David, 62
humiliation, 20 26, 39, 118; definition, 70; public, 29, 40, 53, 64, 127; in prisons, 104; as punishment, 29, 118; sexual, 26
hunting (sport), 122
hunting and gathering, 13–14

Illinois, 117–18, 128
immigration, 69, 82

India, 18, 31, 54, 144
individualism, 52, 55, 70, 72–73, 93, 98
Indonesia, 15, 50, 51, 56, 123, 132
"informalization," 77
Islam, 27, 31

Japan: ancient, 18; business in, 50, 54; emotions in, x, 34, 137; exaggeration in, 18; honor in, 33–34; and public shaming, 116; schools in, 54; suicide in, 35; voting in, 54; and Westernization, 52; women in, 26
jealousy, 33, 98, 144
Jews, 82, 117
juvenile delinquents, 120

Kali, 31–32
Kashdan, Todd, 4
Kasson, John, 76
Knight, Bobby, 88
Korea, 18, 52, 53, 54
Ku Klux Klan, 75

language, 3, 7, 8, 15, 81, 82, 120
Lasorda, Tommy, 88
liberals, 97, 119, 121–22, 123–24, 127
lien, 25
littering, 54
love: and discipline, 80–81; familial, 72; of gain, 51; maternal, 47, 65–66; parental, 4, 24, 49, 68; sexism regarding, 121
Luther, Martin, 37–38
lynching, 75

manners, 7, 42, 67, 74–75, 76, 77
Masai, 15
Massachusetts, 43–45, 46, 63, 69, 104
masturbation, 76
Mather, Cotton, family of, 47
Mehinaku tribe, 16
Mencius, 22
mental health issues, 5, 104, 111, 126
mental retardation, 109
merchants, 27
microaggressions, 122
Middletown (conceptual city type), 77
military, 32, 74, 86, 90, 93
modernity, 49–52, 54–55, 58, 69, 95

mothers, 19, 24, 47, 52, 65, 72, 102, 115. *See also* family; parenting
Muslims. *See* Islam

nakedness, 21–22, 26, 38, 42, 45
National Association to Aid Fat Americans, 113
Native Americans, 14, 39
New England, 40, 43, 45, 58
New York Times, 59, 62, 100
Nike, 123

obesity, 97, 111–13, 133
other-directedness, 98

parenting: and fear, 66, 76; helicopter, 103; love and, 66, 76; women and, 102, 120 (*see also* mothers). *See also* family
Parker, F. W., 82
Pattison, Stephen, 6, 8
peer culture, 77
penology, 2, 62, 65, 72, 83–84, 92, 97, 131. *See also* prisons
Philippines, 13
pillory, 63, 93
Plato, 20, 23
police, 76, 102, 116
political correctness, 121–22, 124, 128
posture, 15, 43, 46, 76, 109
poverty, 53, 86, 88–89
prisons: American, 104–5; and emotions, 5–6; and execution, 123; modern, 65; political, 129; private, 84; punishment in, 30, 63, 95; research on, xi, 6 (*see also* penology); system of, 59, 98, 114; torture in, 62, 63, 65
privacy, 14, 27, 45, 71, 98–99, 125, 127
pro-life movement, 121
prostitutes, 27, 30, 115
Protestantism, 38, 45–46, 72, 114
Prussia, 93
psychology, 2, 6–8, 28, 35, 117, 125

rape, 103. *See also* sexual offenses
reality TV, 124
recidivism, 5, 114
red-light districts, 75
Reddy, William, 94

Reid, Bill, 87–88
reintegrative shaming, 8, 36, 119
resilience, 106, 120
respectability, 36, 74–75, 77, 90, 92, 119
Riesman, David, 98
righteous shaming, 124
right to be forgotten, 128
Romanticism, 71
Rush, Benjamin, 62
Russia, 55

salary data, 111
samurai, 33–34, 35, 54
San people, 13
scarlet letter, 44, 57, 61, 117
schools: American, 77–79; beatings and whippings in, 29, 79; boys in, 66, 86–87; Chinese, 24, 53, 55; complaints about, 79, 85; discipline in, 74, 79, 82, 102; of early civilizations, 19; East Asian, 54; health and, 82–83, 113; hierarchies (social) in, 85, 125; honor codes in, 36; immigrants in, 82; Japanese, 52, 54; mocking in, 79; modern, 86; positive motivation in, 103–4; reform of, 52, 55, 82, 85; rural, 80; sports in, 88. *See also* teachers
self: American (colonial) sense of, 66; anger toward, 4; destruction of, 21, 128; failure of, 3; Greek sense of, 20; and honor, 11, 34
self-abasement, 3, 5, 47
self-awareness, 2, 71, 108
self-consciousness, xii, 1–3, 137
self-discipline and motivation, 82
self-esteem, 53, 67, 84–85, 97, 103–4, 115, 134
self-image, 2, 83, 104
self-improvement, 53, 75
self-interest, 50, 94
self-presentation, 11, 15
self-respect, 62, 67–68, 83–86, 88, 104, 126
self-restraint, 42, 46, 76, 111
self-understanding, 20
self-worth, 4, 68, 113
Semai, 14
sexuality, 13, 21, 76, 99, 125. *See also* homosexuality; slut shaming
sexual offenses, 26, 28, 102–3, 115
shamefast (term), 8, 11, 41, 48, 61, 132
shyness, 14, 15, 54

sissy (term), 86
slut shaming, 77, 102, 125
Smiles, Samuel, 89
smoking, 111
social media, xi, 10, 126; anger expressed on, 100; bullying on, 125; gay shaming on, 109; political campaigns on, 124; public shaming on, 98, 122; racism on, 122; and reintegration, 127; slut shaming on, 125
sociology, xii, 2, 132
Socrates, 20
sodomy, 93–94. *See also* sexuality
South (U.S.), 65, 69, 74–75, 100, 133; duels in, 46, 75, 93; honor in, 51, 75
South Africa, 121
Spock, Benjamin, 68
sports, 75, 86–88, 106
Springer, Jerry, 124
stocks, public (device), 10, 18; abolishment of, 64, 117, 128; in America (colonial), 43–44, 63; in Britain, 27, 93; in Egypt, 19; in Greece, 26; premodern, 40; revival of, 114
Stoics, 21
suburbia, 98
suicide, 11, 54; and business failure, 89; and families, 102; honor, 54; in Japan, 35; and out-of-wedlock pregnancy, 15; in prison, 104; ritual, 32; and social media, 109, 126

taboo, 58, 61, 101, 133
Tahiti, 15
Taiwan, 52–53
Tangney, June, 104
tashir (practice), 27
teachers, 5; as authority, 30, 78–79, 81–82; beatings by, 79; in China, 24, 52; discipline by, 81–82, 85; and hierarchy, 77, 81; modern, 89, 102; Plato on, 20; and positivity, 81, 83, 84; principals vs., 84; rural, 80; training of, 83–84; Western, 52; women as, 81. *See also* schools
Tertullian, 37–38
theft, 115, 119
toilet training, 3, 24, 68

torture, 71–72, 123. *See also under* prisons
Trout, Paul, 105

United States, 57; civil rights in, 113; contemporary, 18, 73; continuity in, 75; criminals in, 5; decline of, 74, 95; disability in, 109; duels in, 93; Enlightenment in, 92; fat shaming in, 112–13; gay liberation movement in, 108; geographical mobility in, 69; HIV in, 102; immigration to, 82; influence of, 52; internet laws in, 128; middle-class parenting in, 72; modern, 68; nineteenth-century, 50–51, 58, 68, 75; politics in, 97, 120, 123; privacy in, 98; reform in, 91, 93–94, 96, 105; schools in, 80; sex in, 103; shaming as legal recourse in, 97, 114; social-individual relationship in, 71; suicide in, 89. *See also* American Revolution
University of California, 87
urbanization, 18, 49–51, 59, 69, 71
Utku Inuit group, 14

violence, 33, 46, 104, 116, 122

welfare, 89, 97, 102, 113, 120
whipping, 24, 29, 43–45, 62, 117
Whitman, James, 117
Wilde, Oscar, 94
Wilder, Laura Ingalls, 79–80
women: adultery by, 26–27, 102; chastity of, 38; circumcision of, 15; destruction by, 31; discrimination against, 121; and femininity, 107; as first offenders via Eve, 19; health and, 39, 112; in Japan, 26; and Nazis, 95; and parenthood, 102, 120; as reformers, 76; reputation of, 76, 125; rights of, 51, 94, 107; and sex, 31, 76; in sports, 88; as teachers, 81
world opinion, 123
World War I, 75, 82, 90, 93–94, 123
World War II, 2, 54, 83, 95, 102

163

PETER N. STEARNS is University Professor of World History and the Provost Emeritus of George Mason University. His many books include *Peace in World History* and *World History: The Basics,* and he is coeditor of *Doing Emotions History.*

HISTORY OF EMOTIONS

Doing Emotions History   *Edited by Susan J. Matt and Peter N. Stearns*
Driven by Fear: Epidemics and Isolation in San Francisco's
   House of Pestilence   *Guenter B. Risse*
The Science of Sympathy: Morality, Evolution, and Victorian Civilization
   Rob Boddice
Shame: A Brief History   *Peter N. Stearns*

The University of Illinois Press
is a founding member of the
Association of American University Presses.

_____

Composed in 10.5/13 Arno Pro
with Avenir LT Std display
by Kirsten Dennison
at the University of Illinois Press
Cover illustration: Adapted from a poster encouraging
persons with syphilis to seek proper treatment as soon
as possible, 1936 or 1937. Work Projects Administration
Poster Collection, Library of Congress.

University of Illinois Press
1325 South Oak Street
Champaign, IL 61820-6903
www.press.uillinois.edu